The New Global Economic Order

Edited by Lili Yan Ing and Dani Rodrik

Routledge
Taylor & Francis Group
LONDON AND NEW YORK

Designed cover image: Getty Images via Westend61

First published 2026
by Routledge
4 Park Square, Milton Park, Abingdon, Oxon OX14 4RN

and by Routledge
605 Third Avenue, New York, NY 10158

Routledge is an imprint of the Taylor & Francis Group, an informa business

The Open Access version is brought to with the help of Economic Research Institute for ASEAN and East Asia (ERIA).

British Library Cataloguing-in-Publication Data
A catalogue record for this book is available from the British Library

Library of Congress Cataloging-in-Publication Data
Names: Ing, Lili Yan editor | Rodrik, Dani editor
Title: The new global economic order / edited by Lili Yan Ing and Dani Rodrik.
Description: Abingdon, Oxon ; New York, NY : Routledge, 2026. | Includes bibliographical references and index.
Identifiers: LCCN 2025008851 | ISBN 9781032945569 hbk | ISBN 9781032945538 pbk | ISBN 9781003571384 ebk
Subjects: LCSH: Economics
Classification: LCC HB171 .N493 2026 | DDC 330—dc23/eng/20250515
LC record available at https://lccn.loc.gov/2025008851

ISBN: 978-1-032-94556-9 (hbk)
ISBN: 978-1-032-94553-8 (pbk)
ISBN: 978-1-003-57138-4 (ebk)

DOI: 10.4324/9781003571384

Typeset in Times New Roman
by Apex CoVantage, LLC

The New Global Economic Order

As anti-globalization reshapes the world, the divide between East and West, developed and developing countries, and North and South, deepens, creating new challenges for economic policy and global governance. This book provides a nuanced and balanced analysis of economic transformation over the past century, exploring critical themes such as structural change, resource mobilization, and the future of global growth.

Featuring insights from leading economists, this volume offers expert commentary on economic transformation, development strategies, and the evolving global order. It further examines into pressing governance questions surrounding AI, green technology, and the financing of health crises, future pandemics, and energy transitions.

A vital resource for economists, policymakers, and researchers, this book provides strategic guidance on navigating global shifts and mobilizing resources to drive sustainable development in an emerging new global economic order.

Lili Yan Ing is Lead Advisor (Southeast Asia Region) at Economic Research Institute for ASEAN and East Asia. She also serves the Secretary General of the International Economic Association. Dr Ing was appointed as Lead Advisor to the Minister of Trade of Indonesia from 2017 to 2019 and Senior Advisor at the Executive Office of the President of Indonesia from 2015 to 2017.

Dani Rodrik is Ford Foundation Professor of International Political Economy at Harvard's John F. Kennedy School of Government. He is co-director of the Reimagining the Economy Program at the Kennedy School and of the Economics for Inclusive Prosperity network. He was President of the International Economic Association during 2021–2023.

To all who endure the hardship of poverty
To all who strive for dignity and a better life
To the next generations who navigate an AI-dominated world
To all who are committed to building a more just and equitable global economic order

Contents

Acknowledgments

We are deeply grateful to Mari Pangestu, Chatib Basri, Andrés Velasco, David Daokui Li, Keyu Jin, Fukunari Kimura, Gene Grossman, Elhanan Helpman, Gordon Hanson, Yao Yang, and Yongding Yu for their invaluable insights, constructive feedback, and significant contributions to the high-level policy panels.

We extend our earnest appreciation to David Christian and Ria Fortuna Wijaya for their outstanding research assistance. We also acknowledge the generous management and administrative support provided by Hidetoshi Nishimura, Koji Hachiyama, Catherin Safitri, and Andrea Cavallo. Our gratitude also goes to Pramoth Jaikishan at Apex and Katie Hemmings at Routledge, as well as Wandira Larasati at ERIA, for their dedication in overseeing the book's production.

The financial support of the International Economic Association (IEA) and Economic Research Institute for ASEAN and East Asia (ERIA) is gratefully acknowledged.

Figures

Tables

Contributors

Daron Acemoglu, Massachusetts Institute of Technology

Jayati Ghosh, University of Massachusetts Amherst

Lili Yan Ing, Economic Research Institute for ASEAN and East Asia (ERIA) and International Economic Association (IEA)

Justin Yifu Lin, Peking University

José Antonio Ocampo, Columbia University and Former United Nations Under-Secretary-General for Economic and Social Affairs

Kevin Hjortshøj O'Rourke, Sciences Po

Danny Quah, National University of Singapore

Dani Rodrik, Harvard University and International Economic Association (IEA)

Vera Songwe, Africa Growth Initiative at Brookings Institution

Joseph E. Stiglitz, Columbia University

Alessio Terzi, Cambridge University and Sciences Po

Shujiro Urata, Research Institute of Economy, Trade, and Industry (RIETI)

1 Introduction

Lili Yan Ing and Dani Rodrik

No one could have foreseen the unprecedented pace at which the global economy, technology, and climate change have evolved. Since the First Industrial Revolution, spurred by the invention of the steam engine in 1712 (with its modern patent granted in 1776), the world has experienced transformative shifts in production processes and the broader economic landscape. The steam engine served as a catalyst for a cascade of innovations across various technologies, ranging from mechanised looms for textile manufacturing to steam-powered locomotives, iron smelting, and the engines that drove them. This era marked the advent of modern industry in Europe and North America. The Second Industrial Revolution, spanning approximately from 1870 to 1914, was characterised by advancements in steel production, which enabled the mass manufacturing of locomotives, telegraph systems, industrial machinery, and a wide array of component parts.

The Third Industrial Revolution, commencing in 1969, heralded an era defined by the rise of electronics and transformative advancements in information and communication technologies (ICT). This period saw the advent of computers, the creation of the internet, and the application of nuclear energy, reshaping industries and accelerating global economic progress. These successive waves of industrialisation stimulated an extraordinary expansion of the global economy, with GDP surging from $2.6 trillion in 1870 to $29.3 trillion by 1970,[1] (Bolt and Van Zanden, 2024a), underscoring the immense economic transformation wrought by technological progress over the past few centuries.

The Fourth Industrial Revolution, which began in 2011, is characterised by the development of cyber-physical systems (CPS). By 2023, approximately 67% of the global population, or 5.4 billion people, were connected to information and communication technologies (ICT), representing a 4.7% increase over the previous year (International Telecommunication Union, 2024). Global technology company spending is projected to grow by 5.3% in 2024, reaching an estimated $4.7 trillion, with growth occurring across all regions. Two key factors driving this expansion include increased investment in software and IT services—particularly in areas like generative AI (GenAI), cloud computing, security, and digital services—and continued economic growth in the Asia Pacific region (Forrester, 2024).

DOI: 10.4324/9781003571384-1

As latecomers in technology, emerging economies have been advantaged by the latest developments. Over the past five decades, global output has increased sixfold, rising from $29.3 trillion in 1970 to $174 trillion in 2022 (Bolt and Van Zanden, 2024b). This remarkable growth has been driven largely by the economic advancement of developing countries, supported by robust exports, increased investment, and technological innovation.

Alongside advancements in technology, the process of opening global markets and promoting international trade was initiated at the end of the Second World War. Since then, the global economy has undergone profound transformations. The collapse of the Bretton Woods system further reshaped the world economic order, and the establishment of the World Trade Organization (WTO) and the General Agreement on Tariffs and Trade (GATT) catalysed further shifts in the international economic landscape. During the 1970s, the notion of the new international economic order (NIEO) was proposed to address the economic challenges faced by the least-developed and developing countries. The initiative sought to empower these nations economically and politically, with the aim of enhancing the welfare of large portions of the global population (Gebremariam, 2017). On May 1, 1974, the UN General Assembly formally adopted the NIEO declaration and its corresponding programme of action. Rooted in the principle of "*trade, not aid*," the NIEO called for fundamental changes in global trade, industrialisation, agricultural production, finance, and the transfer of technology. As the global economy advanced toward deeper integration and interconnectedness, international trade and the policies shaping it became central to influencing the trajectory of global economic dynamics (Schwab and Smadja, 1994).

Over the subsequent decades, the global economy became increasingly interconnected, with international trade in goods expanding at an unprecedented pace. This expansion has fostered deeper multilateral engagement and a proliferation of trade agreements—ranging from bilateral to regional and multilateral frameworks. Both theoretical and empirical studies have consistently underscored the pivotal role of international trade as a driver of economic growth, as long as appropriate industrial restructuring policies were in place at home, particularly in emerging East Asian economies (Lucas, 1988; Barro, 1991; Frankel, Romer, Cyrus, 1997; Frankel and Romer, 1999; Yew, 2013; Itō and Rose, 2005; Ing and Yu, 2018). The ascendance of middle-power and emerging economies has further reshaped the contours of the global economic order, reflecting their growing influence in driving economic growth and integration (World Bank, 2007).

However, while globalisation and technological advancement have generated significant benefits, they have also introduced substantial costs, including rising inequality and the exacerbation of climate change.

First, as global integration has progressed, with factors of production increasingly moving freely across sectors and borders, rising inequality has become evident. This trend, particularly noticeable since the 1980s in developed economies (Stiglitz, 2014) and since the late 1990s in developing nations (Zhu and Trefler, 2005; Ing, 2009), has led to significant increases in income and wealth disparities. By 2020, more than 75% of the global population resided in countries where income inequality has worsened since the 1990s (United Nations, 2020; UNDP Bureau for Development Policy, 2013).

The widening inequality has been further exacerbated by recent economic and financial crises, particularly the global financial crisis of 2008–2009 and the sovereign debt crisis of 2010, which significantly impacted the United States, Europe, and Russia. These crises led to widespread job losses and financial struggles, disproportionately affecting unskilled workers and the poor, while the upper class remained largely insulated from their effects. Over the past decade, the wealthiest individuals have seen substantial increases in wealth, while middle- and lower-income groups have faced rising living costs (Christensen et al., 2023). These growing disparities have fueled the rise of anti-globalisation sentiments not only in developed economies but also in other parts of the world.

Second, since the Industrial Revolution, industrialisation and economic development have profoundly shaped global economic trajectories while simultaneously exerting significant and enduring impacts on climate change. Central to this dynamic has been the escalation of greenhouse gas emissions, forced by the extensive reliance on fossil fuels during the industrialisation process. Empirical evidence underscores the magnitude of these trends: global CO_2 emissions across all sectors have risen substantially since 1850, with the combustion of fossil fuels serving as the primary contributor (Myhre, Alterskjær, Lowe, 2009; Andres, Boden, Higdon, 2014).

The environmental repercussions of industrialisation manifest across diverse regions, particularly through the expansion of industrial land use, which has been identified as a critical driver of CO_2 emissions. Such developments illuminate the intricate interplay between industrialisation, economic growth, and environmental sustainability, emphasising the imperative for adopting sustainable practices to mitigate adverse ecological outcomes (Cole, 1999; Beg et al., 2002; Akimoto et al., 2012; Ferraz et al., 2021). The industrial sector remains the most CO_2-intensive among end-use sectors, accounting for nearly half of global final energy consumption and emissions. Recent data highlights the sector's continued contribution to global emissions, with approximately 10 gigatonnes (Gt) of CO_2 emissions recorded in 2023—equivalent to over 40% of total energy-related CO_2 emissions (International Energy Agency, 2024). This persistent linkage between industrial activity and environmental degradation underscores the urgency of integrating sustainability into industrial and economic policy frameworks to address the dual challenges of economic growth and climate mitigation.

As a result of eight decades of globalisation and successive industrial revolutions, the contours of a new economic order was beginning to take shape. The waning dominance of the United States and its allies signals a potential realignment of global power as China's economic ascendancy continues to reshape the balance of influence. This transition reflects a broader geopolitical and economic shift, compounded by the pronounced weaknesses currently facing the major engines of global growth, including the United States, Western economies, and China itself (World Bank, 2023a). At the same time, the emergence of middle-power nations—such as Australia, Brazil, India, Mexico, the Republic of Korea, South Africa, Southeast Asian countries (particularly Indonesia), and Türkiye—is exerting a growing influence on the trajectory of the global economic order. These nations are leveraging their strategic positions, economic dynamism, and regional integration to assert themselves as critical players in the evolving landscape of global governance. This confluence of shifting hegemonies, economic vulnerabilities, and the rise of middle powers underscores the complexity of the global economic transition.

The recent trade war unleashed by U.S. President Donald Trump has thrown the future of the world economy in doubt. The populist backlash against the prevailing global order is largely a result of its distributional consequences—within and across nations. The deepening of economic, social, and political cleavages within nations has been reinforced by the rise of China as an economic and geopolitical rival, and perceived threat to the U.S. and other advanced nations. Trumpism fails to offer a serious remedy to these imbalances while exacerbating their negative impacts. The time is ripe, therefore, to reimagine what a healthier, more inclusive, and more sustainable global economic order might look like. We are at a pivotal moment for multilateral cooperation and reconfiguring the structures that will underpin the next phase of globalisation.

Our book aims to explore the evolving dynamics of the global economic order, highlighting the historical progression from the post-World War II era to the present day. It examines the shifting balance of power, with particular focus on the rise of middle-power nations and the role of international trade, governance, and technological advancement in shaping future economic trajectories. It is structured into three main sections, each addressing a distinct aspect of the global economic order and proposing comprehensive global solutions. It begins with Chapter 2, which provides a concise historical overview of the global economic order, tracing its evolution from the 19th century to the present. The first section, encompassing Chapters 3 to 5, delves into the framework of global rules and governance, examining the principles and institutions that have shaped international economic interactions. The second section, spanning Chapters 6 to 9, explores growth and structural transformation, offering insights into the dynamic processes driving economic development across regions and industries. The last section, comprising Chapters 10 to 12, focuses on global resource mobilisation, recommending mechanisms and strategies for harnessing resources to support sustainable economic growth and resilience.

Chapter 2 by Kevin Hjortshøj O'Rourke provides a brief history of the global economic order. The author invites us to reflect on the metamorphoses undergone by the global economic order since the early modern period, concluding with some brief reflections on what the past might have been to teach us about our current situation. The mercantilist period was essentially anarchic and characterised by constant warfare between the leading powers, as well as activist trade and industrial policies that have to be understood in that context. The 19th century saw the gradual emergence of a generally liberal international order, although independent states protected both industry and agriculture. Elsewhere, imperialism implied low tariffs. A "system" characterised by the gold standard and the MFN principle emerged as a result of individual countries' monetary policy choices and the bilateral trade deals they entered into. The system fell apart between the wars, but not before the gold standard helped spark the Great Depression, and the MFN principle was de facto abandoned as the world splintered into blocks.

The post-1945 settlement attempted to remedy these defects with fixed but adjustable exchange rates and capital controls, on the one hand, and a GATT committed to trade liberalisation with MFN as a key principle on the other. A new economic system emerged that was, for the first time, underpinned by multilateral treaties and institutions, although the trade liberalisation it implied was largely Western. Capital mobility and the move to floating by the major currencies, global trade liberalisation, the end of the Cold War, and intellectual changes led to a transition toward our current system, one marked by less domestic policy flexibility. This is now changing as a result of financial crises, pandemics, war, and domestic inequality. None of this is surprising in the light of history. The international order has always been geopolitical, and when rules become too constraining, they are abandoned.

Section 1: Rules and Governance

Chapter 3 by Joseph E. Stiglitz and Dani Rodrik examines the complexities of global governance in an interconnected world, emphasising the need to focus on areas of international cooperation with maximum potential impact to address global challenges such as pandemics and climate change. There are many demands for global governance, but the reality is that the world has limited global cooperation. The authors highlight that while globalisation has increased economic and political interdependence, existing institutions like the WTO, IMF, and UN have struggled to adapt to changing global dynamics. The chapter critiques the one-size-fits-all approach of current global governance, which often prioritises market liberalisation and globalisation over national contexts and equitable development. They argue for a more pluralistic model of governance that respects national sovereignty while fostering international collaboration to tackle global challenges such as climate change, economic inequality, and pandemics. Taking into account political realities—the presence of nation-states as primary political units and the uneven distribution of power in the global economy—a more circumscribed, less ambitious global agenda may be preferable.

Accordingly, they propose a framework for a minimal global governance architecture. They outline some general principles that should govern the design of global governance and provide their justification. The authors propose a framework for a new global governance model that balances global cooperation with local needs, emphasising flexibility, inclusivity, and fairness. Key findings suggest that successful global governance must be built on mutual respect for diverse economic systems and cultural contexts rather than imposing a rigid, universal set of rules. They advocate for multilateral agreements that address pressing global issues while enabling nations to chart their paths to development. They underline the need for enhanced democratic accountability and transparency in international institutions to regain trust among member states and populations. Their work provides a roadmap for building a more sustainable, equitable, and cooperative global order that aligns with the shifting balance of power in the 21st century. The authors also draw the implications in a variety of areas, such as intellectual property rights, trade, financial flows, monetary policy, investment agreements, and debt management.

Chapter 4 by Shujiro Urata assesses the roles of bilateral, regional, and plurilateral economic cooperation. Economic globalisation through the expansion of trade and investment contributed to rapid economic growth in the world from the 1990s through the mid-2000s. He argues, however, that increased uncertainty, mainly resulting from continuing and escalating geopolitical tensions in the world involving two major powers, the United States and China, has resulted in reduced trade and investment by fragmenting the world economy. Urata argues that there is a possibility that further escalation of geopolitical tensions between the United States and China will result in the division of the world economy.

The troubled global trade and investment environment has been exacerbated by the malfunctioning of the global trade system under the WTO in the areas of rulemaking and dispute settlement. To deal with the situation, a group of WTO members has established new types of trade agreements: enlarged regional trade agreements with comprehensive policy coverage, plurilateral agreements, and an alternative dispute settlement mechanism by the name of Multi-Party Interim Appeal Arbitration Arrangement (MPIA). These developments reflect the view of many WTO members that establishing and managing a rules-based trade system is crucially important for maintaining an open and stable trade and investment environment, avoiding the division of the world economy, and achieving economic growth through the expansion of trade and investment. Faced with fierce competition between the United States and China, which have violated WTO rules, a group of middle-power countries such as Australia, Japan, and Korea, and a group of countries belonging to the European Union, Association of Southeast Asian Nations (ASEAN), and the Global South have to lead these new developments toward the establishment of a rules-based trade system through bilateral, regional, and plurilateral cooperations.

Chapter 5 by Danny Quah explores how the relationship between trade interconnectedness and geopolitical tensions influences the current global order. During the so-called centripetal era (1980–2010), economic integration and geopolitical alignment played a crucial role in bridging the interests of developed and developing nations, contributing to a relatively stable world economy. However, the author notes a significant shift that began in the early 2000s, primarily driven by factors such as China's economic rise (i.e., 'China shock'), the emergence of a multipolar world, and evolving practices in multilateral cooperation. These changes have disrupted the previous alignment of interests and played an instrumental part in ushering in the so-called centrifugal era of world economy, where economic and geopolitical forces work in ways that exacerbate global fragmentation.

To mitigate the growing fragmentation, the author offers three key proposals. First, he suggests fostering inadvertent cooperation, whereby mutual benefits emerge even without deliberate collaboration. Second, he advocates for breaking political gridlocks among the Great Powers to mitigate tensions. Finally, the chapter emphasises the potential of plurilateralism and innovative multilateral frameworks to restore global unity in a fractured world. By implementing these strategies, the author argues, the international community can begin to counteract the divisive impacts of current economic and geopolitical dynamics.

Section 2: Growth and Structural Transformation

Chapter 6 by Lili Yan Ing and Justin Yifu Lin illustrates economic transformation in the last half-century and lessons learned drawn from it. Throughout the 20th century, global economic governance was predominantly shaped by major developed countries. However, over the past five decades, the world has undergone a profound economic transformation. This shift is clearly reflected in the changing global shares of developed and developing nations across four key economic indicators: total output, trade in goods, manufacturing value added, and foreign direct investment.

The central argument of the chapter posits that the substantial transformations in the global economy are not predominantly driven by significant shifts in the growth performance of developed countries, but by the rapid catch-up of select developing nations. Sustainable economic growth is an ongoing process, encompassing technological innovation, improvements in labour productivity, and industrial upgrading. Drawing on growth and structural transformation patterns observed in both developed and developing countries, the chapter argues that achieving sustainable economic growth requires (i) optimising comparative advantage and enhancing infrastructure, (ii) managing gradual economic and political transitions, and (iii) leveraging digital transformation to maximise efficiency.

Chapter 7 by Dani Rodrik and Joseph E. Stiglitz addresses the evolving challenges faced by developing economies in the current global landscape. The authors argue that traditional growth models, which heavily emphasise industrialisation and export-led strategies, are becoming less effective due to factors such as technological advancements, climate change, and shifting global demand patterns. The chapter assesses that the world is currently at a turning point in development strategy. Key findings of the chapter highlight the necessity for developing nations to adapt their economic policies to the changing global environment. Development strategies that worked well in the past are unlikely to do so in the decades ahead. In particular, the manufacturing- and export-based growth strategies that drove East Asia's development miracles are no longer very effective in today's low-income countries. They highlight the importance of investing in sustainable technologies and infrastructure to address environmental challenges while fostering economic growth.

New technologies, the climate challenge, and the reconfiguration of globalisation require a novel approach to development. They also advocate for the development of labour-absorbing service sectors, such as health care and education, to create employment opportunities and enhance human capital and green investments to achieve sustainable and inclusive economic development. Additionally, the authors suggest that strengthening domestic markets can reduce vulnerability to external shocks and promote more resilient economic structures. This comprehensive approach aims to equip developing nations with the tools needed to navigate the complexities of the modern global economy effectively.

Chapter 8 by Daron Acemoglu advocates that there is a critical need for multipolar governance in artificial intelligence. The author examines the potential adverse effects of AI technologies, particularly concerning labour markets and economic inequality. He argues that without appropriate governance, AI could exacerbate existing disparities and lead to significant job displacement. He cautions against the concentration of AI control in the hands of a few large technology companies, which could undermine democratic processes and societal well-being. By promoting a more distributed governance model, he believes that AI can be harnessed to benefit a broader segment of society, ensuring that technological progress contributes to shared prosperity rather than deepening inequality.

Acemoglu argues that to redirect AI research and development in a more socially beneficial direction, a multipolar governance structure is essential. The current direction is shaped by the priorities of the tech industry, which do not coincide with pathways that would lead to beneficial outcomes for workers and democracy, and to a lesser extent, by the regulatory oversight coming from the United States and China, which is either weak or inadequate. It is particularly important to have a voice and influence from workers in the industrialised world and the citizens of developing nations because these are the groups that are most likely to suffer under the current direction, and a broadly beneficial direction for AI research needs to incorporate the priorities, interests, and knowledge of these groups. Acemoglu closes the chapter by advocating for a multipolar approach to AI governance, underscoring the need for inclusive institutions that can effectively regulate AI development and deployment.

Chapter 9 by Alessio Terzi presents the consequences of the Green Industrial Revolution. Achieving climate neutrality demands a complete overhaul of fossil fuel-dependent economic activities, encompassing energy, agriculture, transport, and more. Terzi draws parallels between the current shift toward sustainable practices and past industrial revolutions, stressing that such transitions historically involve significant economic and social upheavals and social structures. He argues that while green technologies hold promises for economic growth and job creation, they also pose challenges, including potential short-term disruptions and increased inequalities. Terzi highlights the inevitability of the green transition, pushed by the unsustainable nature of fossil fuel dependence and the pressing need to address climate change. By learning from historical precedents, Terzi's analysis provides valuable insights for policymakers striving to balance economic growth with environmental sustainability in the context of a green industrial revolution.

Despite the promising prospects of green technologies fostering economic growth and job creation, potential short-term disruptions and growing inequalities will pose significant challenges and inevitably unleash some political and economic forces. Consequently, the new economic order can be expected to be marked by (i) proactive government involvement acknowledging that state intervention has historically played a crucial role in guiding industrial transformations, (ii) trade fragmentation, (iii) limited voluntary transfer of technology, and (iv) limited financial transfers between countries. Within the contours of this emerging economic framework, policy decisions can still have first-order repercussions on the speed of climate action, growth, human lives, and livelihoods within and between countries. He concludes by articulating broad recommendations for policymakers in rich and poor countries, suggesting that a coordinated international approach is essential and should be designed to maximise the advantages of the green transition while mitigating its adverse impacts.

Section 3: Resource Mobilization

Chapter 10 by José Antonio Ocampo discusses international financial and tax reforms. The chapter analyses the international financial and tax reform agenda. It first looks at the need to significantly increase financing by the multilateral development banks (MDBs), including supporting the contribution of developing countries to the provision of global public goods. This would require concessional credits, including to finance the contributions by middle-income countries and the private sector, and therefore, funds to support those concessional elements and the capitalisation of the MDBs. The chapter then deals with international monetary reform, an issue that has not been central to recent debates. It underscores the need to develop more precautionary instruments, continue to support capital account regulations, streamline conditionality, and, particularly, a more active use of IMF's Special Drawing Rights (SDRs).

On developing countries' sovereign debt, he points out the need to develop both a permanent institutional mechanism to negotiate sovereign debt restructuring and an ad hoc instrument to manage the debt crises that several countries are currently facing—such as the ones that have been used in previous crises. On international tax cooperation, he points out the very limited advance made in the OECD Inclusive Framework and, therefore, the need to support the ongoing negotiations of a UN tax convention with a much broader agenda and the transformation of the UN Committee of Experts on International Cooperation in Tax Matters into an intergovernmental organ. Finally, Ocampo foregrounds four critical institutional issues: continuing to enhance the voice and participation of developing countries in the Bretton Woods institutions; creating a representative committee in the UN as the main mechanism of international economic cooperation; developing global institutions in sovereign debt and tax cooperation; and the need to have strong regional institutions in all areas, including in the international monetary system and tax cooperation, reproducing the system that is already in place in the MDBs.

Chapter 11 by Jayati Ghosh assesses global resource mobilisation, specifically highlighting health and economic recovery. She starts by sharing the fact that though health has become a global concern, it is still treated and managed in the national context. The current international economic architecture is an active constraint on required health spending, both in terms of absolute levels of spending and its direction and quality. Low and middle-income countries (LIMCs) are constrained in terms of fiscal space because of debt repayment stress, fear of capital flight, and inability to raise revenues through adequately taxing corporations and rich individuals. Food security and nutrition that directly impact health conditions have been hit by profiteering, speculation, and volatility in primary commodity markets that affect food-importing countries. Important international institutions that could coordinate efforts are significantly underfunded.

International financial institutions must change the way they operate, beginning with a regular but more flexible, generous, and directed issuance of Special Drawing Rights by the IMF, whose distribution is not by quota but according to need. Debt distress has to be overcome through urgent and transparent efforts to reduce the repayment burdens without further pressure on embattled populations. Intellectual property regimes need to be reformed to enable greater access to essential knowledge. Fiscal space has to be enhanced through more appropriate rules on international taxation. The quality of finance also has to change from a siloed and short-term approach in both public and private finance to a more comprehensive, inclusive, and cooperative approach for both national governments and international institutions.

Chapter 12 by Vera Songwe explains the importance of the private sector and market-based mechanism in resource mobilisation. Emerging markets and developing economies need $5.3 trillion between 2023 and 2030 to meet the Sustainable Development Goals. Successive crises have left traditional donors in fiscally difficult positions. These have led to a massive contraction in the resources available to LMICs to respond to the development challenges the COVID-19 pandemic and subsequent crises have brought to the fore. To compound the situation, increases in interest rates by advanced economies have precipitated the flow of capital from LMICs to advanced economies. In the meantime, the climate crisis also requires urgent and scaled-up resources. Against this challenging backdrop, the role of the private sector has become central to resource mobilisation and deployment. Governments must create the right governance environment to attract private-sector funding at affordable and sustainable rates. Undercapitalised MDBs must work with the private sector to leverage their resources for better development outcomes.

Concerted collaboration between the private sector, MDBs, and sovereigns is needed to achieve this objective. But more resources will be needed. Countries must look to the regulatory environment to unlock barriers to resource mobilisation that have historically created asymmetries. Unlocking these and creating a level playing field would help improve resource mobilisation in many LMICs. These include abiding by the IMF articles of agreement that call for the issuance of new Special Drawing Rights in times of crisis, SDRs for climate. Most LMICs are nature rich and can monetise these resources, but the market for carbon credits is lack of transparency and accountability, and countries are not benefiting to their fullest. Prudential regulation meant to build financial sector resilience has also resulted in frictions in capital flows to emerging markets. Finally, remittances and important sources of foreign exchange reserves remain costly to transfer, with G20 countries not meeting their pledge to keep costs below 5%, diverting substantial resources away from LMICs. The chapter highlights the costs of these policies to revenue mobilisation. It concludes by proposing policy changes that could deliver better, more transparent, and enforceable global governance systems for improved revenue mobilisation.

Note

1 Data are expressed in US$ at 2023 prices. GDP Deflator based on World Economic Outlook, accessed on December 19, 2024.

References

Akimoto, Keigo, Fuminori Sano, Ayami Hayashi, Takashi Homma, Junichiro Oda, Kenichi Wada, Miyuki Nagashima, Kohko Tokushige, and Toshimasa Tomoda. 2012. "Consistent Assessments of Pathways Toward Sustainable Development and Climate Stabilization." *Natural Resources Forum* 36 (4): 231–44. https://doi.org/10.1111/j.1477-8947.2012.01460.x.

Andres, Robert J., Thomas A. Boden, and David Higdon. 2014. "A New Evaluation of the Uncertainty Associated with CDIAC Estimates of Fossil Fuel Carbon Dioxide Emission." *Tellus B: Chemical and Physical Meteorology* 66 (1): 23616. https://doi.org/10.3402/tellusb.v66.23616.

Barro, Robert J. 1991. "Economic Growth in a Cross Section of Countries." *The Quarterly Journal of Economics* 106 (2): 407. https://doi.org/10.2307/2937943.

Beg, Noreen, Jan Corfee Morlot, Ogunlade Davidson, Yaw Afrane-Okesse, Lwazikazi Tyani, Fatma Denton, Youba Sokona, et al. 2002. "Linkages Between Climate Change and Sustainable Development." *Climate Policy* 2 (2–3): 129–44. https://doi.org/10.3763/cpol.2002.0216.

Bolt, Jutta, and Jan Luiten Van Zanden. 2024a. "Maddison Project Database 2023." *DataverseNL*. https://doi.org/10.34894/INZBF2.

Bolt, Jutta, and Jan Luiten Van Zanden. 2024b. "Maddison-Style Estimates of the Evolution of the World Economy: A New 2023 Update." *Journal of Economic Surveys*, April. https://doi.org/10.1111/joes.12618.

Christensen, Martin-Brehm, Christian Hallum, Alex Maitland, Quentin Parrinello, Chiara Putaturo, Dana Abed, Carlos Brown, Anthony Kamande, Max Lawson, and Susana Ruiz. 2023. "Survival of the Richest: How We Must Tax the Super-Rich Now to Fight Inequality." *Oxfam*. https://doi.org/10.21201/2023.621477.

Cole, Matthew A. 1999. "Limits to Growth, Sustainable Development and Environmental Kuznets Curves: An Examination of the Environmental Impact of Economic Development." *Sustainable Development* 7 (2): 87–97. https://doi.org/10.1002/(SICI)1099-1719(199905)7:2<87::AID-SD102>3.0.CO;2-5.

Ferraz, Diogo, Fernanda P. S. Falguera, Enzo B. Mariano, and Dominik Hartmann. 2021. "Linking Economic Complexity, Diversification, and Industrial Policy with Sustainable Development: A Structured Literature Review." *Sustainability* 13 (3): 1265. https://doi.org/10.3390/su13031265.

Forrester. 2024. "Global Tech Spend to Grow 5.3% In 2024, Reaching $4.7 Trillion." *Forrester (blog)*, January 18, 2024. https://www.forrester.com/press-newsroom/forrester-global-tech-spend-to-grow-5-3-in-2024-reaching-4-7-trillion/.

Frankel, Jeffrey A., and David Romer. 1999. "Does Trade Cause Growth?" *American Economic Review* 89 (3): 379–99. https://doi.org/10.1257/aer.89.3.379.

Frankel, Jeffrey A., David Romer, and Teresa Cyrus. 1997. "Trade and Growth in East Asian Countries: Cause and Effect?" *National Bureau of Economic Research, NBER Working Paper*, no. w5732, January. https://doi.org/10.3386/w5732.

Gebremariam, Fesseha Mulu. 2017. "New International Economic Order (NIEO): Origin, Elements and Criticisms." *International Journal of Multicultural and Multireligious Understanding* 4 (3): 22. https://doi.org/10.18415/ijmmu.v4i3.81.

Ing, Lili Yan. 2009. "Lower Tariff, Rising Skill Premium in Developing Countries: Is It a Coincidence?" *The World Economy* 32 (7): 1115–33. https://doi.org/10.1111/j.1467-9701.2009.01192.x.

Ing, Lili Yan, and Miaojie Yu. 2018. *World Trade Evolution: Growth, Productivity and Employment*, 1st ed. London: Routledge. https://doi.org/10.4324/9781351061544.

International Energy Agency. 2024. *World Energy Outlook 2024*. Paris: International Energy Agency. https://www.iea.org/reports/world-energy-outlook-2024.

International Telecommunication Union. 2024. "The ITU ICT SDG Indicators." *ITU*. https://www.itu.int:443/en/ITU-D/Statistics/Pages/SDGs-ITU-ICT-indicators.aspx.

Itō, Takatoshi, and Andrew Rose. 2005. *International Trade in East Asia. NBER-East Asia Seminar on Economics*, Vol. 14. Chicago: University of Chicago Press. http://www.nber.org/chapters/c0187.

Lucas, Robert E. 1988. "On the Mechanics of Economic Development." *Journal of Monetary Economics* 22 (1): 3–42. https://doi.org/10.1016/0304-3932(88)90168-7.

Myhre, G., K. Alterskjær, and D. Lowe. 2009. "A Fast Method for Updating Global Fossil Fuel Carbon Dioxide Emissions." *Environmental Research Letters* 4 (3): 034012. https://doi.org/10.1088/1748-9326/4/3/034012.

Schwab, Klaus, and Claude Smadja. 1994. "Power and Policy: The New Economic World Order." *Harvard Business Review*, November 1, 1994. https://hbr.org/1994/11/power-and-policy-the-new-economic-world-order.

Stiglitz, Joseph E. 2014. "The Price of Inequality." *Journal of Social Policy* 43 (1): 216–18. https://doi.org/10.1017/S0047279413000718.

UNDP Bureau for Development Policy. 2013. *Humanity Divided: Confronting Inequality in Developing Countries*. New York: United Nations Development Programme. https://www.undp.org/publications/humanity-divided-confronting-inequality-developing-countries.

United Nations. 2020. "Inequality—Bridging the Divide." *United Nations*. https://www.un.org/en/un75/inequality-bridging-divide.

World Bank. 2007. *Global Economic Prospects: Managing The Next Wave of Globalization. Report Number 38138*. Washington, DC: World Bank. http://documents.worldbank.org/curated/en/732761468779449524/The-World-Bank-annual-report-2007.

World Bank. 2023. *Global Economic Prospects, Vol. 1, Global Economic Prospects 186449*. Washington, DC: World Bank. http://documents.worldbank.org/curated/en/099617212132336233/IDU0a14e8a770bcbb047a608c210abe279bbf38c.

World Bank. n.d. "World Development Indicators." https://datacatalog.worldbank.org/search/dataset/0037712/World-Development-Indicators.

Yew, Lee Kuan. 2013. *One Man's View of the World*, 1st ed. Singapore: Straits Times Press.

Zhu, Susan Chun, and Daniel Trefler. 2005. "Trade and Inequality in Developing Countries: A General Equilibrium Analysis." *Journal of International Economics* 65 (1): 21–48. https://doi.org/10.1016/j.jinteco.2003.11.005.

2 The Global Economic Order

A Brief History

Kevin Hjortshøj O'Rourke

2.1 Introduction

The global economic order has undergone several mutations over the past two centuries. This chapter begins with a brief description of international economic relations during the mercantilist era and then considers the late 19th-century, interwar period—the 'Golden Age' of economic growth (i.e. 1950–1973)—as well as the present. Certain features of the historical record are highlighted that are particularly relevant to the circumstances of the present day.

2.2 Emergence of the Global Economic Order

2.2.1 The Mercantilist Period

The mercantilist era—which occurred during the 17th and 18th centuries—was characterised by almost constant warfare amongst the leading powers in Europe, which acquired increasing global significance as European empires expanded overseas. The economic policy of the time cannot be understood without this context (Wilson, 1978). Trade was seen in zero-sum terms; countries were competing for and were willing to go to war for control over lucrative overseas trade routes. Dominating these brought in revenue, an important consideration in an era of ever more costly warfare. A strong merchant marine was also a source of ships and men that could be mobilised in wartime. Countries engaged in widespread industrial policy, encouraging the growth of economically strategic sectors such as textiles and paying particular attention to certain industries vital in times of war, notably metallurgy and chemicals. Contrary to Whig Party claims that the government's role in sparking the Industrial Revolution was limited to protecting intellectual property rights, activist industrial policies and military procurement played critical roles in promoting growth in textiles, metallurgy, and—in France—chemicals during this period, while patents were essentially ineffective (Kelly and O'Rourke, 2024). Supply chain fears led to both investment in naval capacity and import substitution, with the development of the French artificial alkali, *saltpetre*, and beet sugar industries particularly notable.

DOI: 10.4324/9781003571384-2

At this time, the global system was thus largely anarchic, although occasional bilateral trade treaties emerged such as the Methuen and Eden treaties signed in 1703 and 1786 by England and Portugal, and Britain and France, respectively. Domestically, the capitalism of the age co-existed with more or less undemocratic regimes, which Schumpeter (1943) regarded as logical. Countries adopted a variety of specie standards without this becoming a global exchange rate system; they often attempted to restrict emigration, especially for skilled artisans embodying technological knowledge. In addition, capital was surprisingly mobile. East India Company conquests in India foreshadowed the vast late 19th-century overseas empires, but the end of the mercantilist era also saw the United States, Haiti, and most countries in Latin America gaining independence.

2.2.2 The Late 19th Century

The conflicts of the mercantilist era culminated in devasting wars between Britain and France that lasted almost a quarter of a century, dragged many other countries into the conflict, involved fighting on several continents, and significantly disrupted global trade (O'Rourke, 2006). One consequence was the post-war settlement agreed at the Congress of Vienna of 1814–1815, which largely kept peace within Europe for several decades. Another was the rise of Britain to a position of political and naval dominance that it retained for the rest of the century. This would have systemic global consequences when Britain, then the world's leading economy, unilaterally adopted free trade in the mid-19th century—as did Britain's dependent colonies. Imperialism was generally a force for free trade during the late 19th century, and those remaining outside of European empires—such as China, Japan, the Ottoman Empire, Persia, and Siam—were obliged to sign treaties restricting their ability to raise tariffs. Free trade, falling transport costs, and rising commodity demand in industrialised countries contributed to a terms-of-trade boom in the periphery, accompanied by de-industrialisation (Williamson, 2011).[1] This period of globalisation coincided with the Great Divergence as well as the Great Specialisation, which established north-south patterns of trade that would only begin to unravel in the 1960s (Robertson, 1938).

As empires promoted free trade in Africa and Asia during the late 19th century, independent states in Europe and the Americas pursued independent trade policies. In Europe and North America, these generally involved import-substituting industrialisation; in Europe, tariffs were used in many countries to cushion the losses of landowners exposed to falling transport costs (O'Rourke and Williamson, 1999). Agricultural protection has been a notable feature of European trade policy ever since. Towards the end of the century, this anarchic non-system was tempered by a wave of bilateral trade treaties, beginning with the 1860 British-French Cobden-Chevalier Treaty, which lowered tariffs and included unconditional most-favoured nation (MFN) clauses. With some exceptions (e.g. Canada after 1898), European colonies also adopted non-discriminatory trade. As a result of bilateral treaties reflecting individual country calculations, an international trade 'system' spontaneously emerged that combined non-discrimination with fairly high—especially from the 1880s onwards—levels of protection in the industrialised core. The major exception was the United States, whose commitment to non-discrimination was conditional rather than unconditional. These treaties were generally signed for fixed periods of time and had to be periodically renegotiated. Countries were thus not locked in forever.

Another feature of the late 19th century was the gradually expansion of franchises in wealthy countries as well as the adoption of various labour market regulations and social insurance schemes that were the precursors of the welfare states that would emerge after World War II (Huberman, 2012). Several trade treaties included clauses that levelled up these welfare standards in trade partners, which presumably enhanced their political acceptability (Huberman and Meissner, 2010). Nevertheless, trade policy remained a contentious political issue, especially when treaties had to be renewed.

The late 19th century also witnessed the emergence of a global fixed exchange rate system, not as a result of multilateral negotiation but of individual countries' decisions to peg to gold. The lack of exchange controls during the period meant that countries forewent the benefits of independent monetary policies, but this was generally not seen as a problem by politicians or economists, even during the quarter-century-long deflation of 1873–1896. That episode eventually gave rise to a powerful democratic protest movement in the United States, which demanded an end to the gold standard, stronger anti-trust policies, a nationalised rail service, and a graduated income tax. While the Populist Party in the United States faded in part because new gold discoveries led to a recovery of prices, many of its reform proposals were adopted by mainstream political parties.

In Europe, adjustment to the constraints of the gold standard was facilitated by mass emigration, which helped restore internal and external balance, as emigrants sent remittances home (Esteves and Khoudour-Castéras, 2009). Poorer economies, tempted by gold in the hopes that this would make it easier to attract capital inflows, sometimes adjusted through the simple expedient of abandoning the peg altogether (Catão and Solomou, 2005).

Mass migration at this time was also relatively liberal, especially for Europeans who moved in large numbers to the frontier economies of the United States and Oceania. This helped the continents adjust during their phases of rapid population growth associated with a demographic transition (Hatton and Williamson, 1998). Towards the end of the period, however, New World immigration restrictions tightened, a trend that would continue during and after World War I until borders were effectively closed. These restrictions were motivated by labour market competition as well as racism and bigotry. Other regions of the world saw large outflows as well, but these occurred within a racially segmented international labour market famously analysed by Lewis (1978). Capital was extremely mobile, with very large outflows from capital-abundant Europe to the resources-abundant globe, in particular the Americas. By helping cultivate land, these flows were economically productive, but they were primarily directed towards richer countries rather than poorer ones. Extensive capital flows were also associated with periodic financial crises, foreshadowing the experience of the 20th and 21st centuries (Bordo, Meissner, Stuckler, 2010).

2.2.3 The Interwar Period

World War I saw unprecedented devastation and loss of life. In its wake, a new multilateral international organisation was created—the League of Nations—although the United States, which had played a leading role in drafting its covenant, never joined. While the League of Nations's main function was to preserve peace, the covenant also called on its members to secure and to maintain freedom of communications and transit as well as equitable treatment of commerce. It was not, however, expected to play a major role in international economic affairs. Yet the legacy of war, various revolutions, and reparations soon led to a series of financial crises in Central Europe. Economists from the League of Nations's Secretariat oversaw International Monetary Fund (IMF)-style stabilisation plans, which were widely seen as successful—although they provoked hostility in the countries affected. This facilitated an expansion in the resources of the League of Nations's Economic and Financial Organization (Clavin, 2013). Although there were no treaty commitments obliging countries to pursue particular monetary or trade policies, the Economic and Financial Organization spent the 1920s trying to coordinate a voluntary reconstruction of the pre-war economy, holding a series of conferences dedicated to restoring the gold standard and liberalising trade. This was a multilateralism-as-coordination device rather than anything binding.

The attempt to restore the gold standard was more successful than the attempt to liberalise trade, reflecting the conviction of politicians that sound money was essential to economic recovery. Importantly, a belief in the virtues of the gold standard also correlated with the conviction of balanced budgets; economic rules could be self-imposed, with this certainty the result of the prevailing idea that formal legal obligations need not dictate an economy.

International capital started flowing from the United States to Latin America and Europe, especially in the wake of the 1924 Dawes Plan, which stabilised the German currency and specified that commercial credits be senior to government debts (Ritschl, 2012). Countries, like Germany, used the money to finance reconstruction and reparation payments to Britain and France—which in turn owed the United States money as a result of loans incurred during the war. The combination of fixed exchange rates and large-scale capital flows—seen as essential by liberal internationalists and most economists—would prove to be very costly, however. The gold standard transmitted tight monetary policies in the United States and elsewhere around the globe and prohibited monetary and fiscal policies that may have prevented the slump (Temin, 1989; Eichengreen, 1992). Large-scale capital flows led to 'the mother of all sudden stops' (Accominotti and Eichengreen, 2016), as the United States ceased lending, which transformed a deep recession into a global depression in 1931.

Countries responded by abandoning all constraints on their policy independence. They left the gold standard, defaulted on their debts, and imposed capital controls. These actions worked. Leaving the gold standard was clearly associated with recovery, in part by replacing expectations of deflation with those of inflation (Temin and Wigmore, 1990; Ellison, Lee, O'Rourke, 2024). Defaulting on international debts did not appear to have hurt countries either, although they would end up paying 20 basis points extra on their borrowing when global capital markets re-opened 40 years later (Eichengreen and Portes, 1989; Özler, 1993).

There were two problems, however. While some democratic governments (e.g. Britain) chose to abandon the gold standard early, others (e.g. Germany) stuck to the rules of an out-of-date system, leaving it to demagogues to change policy direction and to reap the resultant rewards. The policy framework of the 1920s was eventually rejected everywhere, but the attempt in some countries to delay the inevitable would have fateful consequences. Where democratic parties advocated the radical reform that was needed (e.g. Sweden), they reaped the electoral rewards; where democrats failed to offer an alternative vision of how to manage the economy (e.g. Germany), they were ejected from power (Berman, 2006).

The second problem was that countries left the gold standard at different times, exacerbating the economic difficulties of those that remained pegged to gold. Britain's decision to leave the gold standard in September 1931, in particular—while beneficial in the long run both to itself and to its trading partners by spurring recovery—led to a spate of protectionism in countries fearing the consequences of overvaluation (Eichengreen and Irwin, 2010). More generally, the Great Depression led to a wave of tariff and non-tariff barriers to trade, with an increase in protectionism being most noticeable in those countries remaining on the gold standard the longest. Ironically, persisting with a monetary institution thought to symbolise a commitment to an open international economy deepened the breakdown in international trade.

The world was still connected by a web of MFN agreements, strengthened by the commitment of the United States to this unconditional principle. This made liberalising trade even more difficult; in its retrospective history of interwar trade policy, the League of Nations concluded that

> instead of facilitating [trade], the clause tended to obstruct the reduction of tariffs by means of bilateral or multilateral agreements, owing to the reluctance of governments to make concessions which would be generalised by it. This was the result, mainly, of two causes: first, the refusal of the United States to reduce its own very high tariff by negotiation while claiming to benefit from any tariff reduction negotiated between European countries; secondly, the opposition of certain countries—notably the United Kingdom, the United States and the British Dominions—to derogations from strict M.F.N. practice permitting the conclusion of regional or similar agreements for tariff reduction, the benefits of which would be limited to the participants.
>
> (League of Nations, 1942: 119)

Belgium, Luxembourg, and the Netherlands, for example, tried to negotiate mutual tariff reductions but were prevented from doing so by Britain's refusal to waive its MFN rights in this matter. Moreover, as the Economic and Financial Organization explained, the MFN clause could lead to free-rider problems that arose during the 1930s.

A legalistic insistence on other countries' MFN commitments did not imply that Britain was committed to non-discrimination; on the contrary, Britain and its colonies adopted a policy of imperial preference that would continue until Britain's accession to the European Economic Community (EEC), upsetting the United States in particular. Other empires, would-be empires, and soon-to-be empires formed similar blocs.

While MFN clauses in existing treaties were an obstacle to liberalising trade during the 1930s, the breakdown of the principle was geopolitically harmful. The shift from multilateral trade to trade increasingly channelled within mutually hostile blocs exacerbated international tension and heightened the desire to become as self-sufficient as possible—a tendency that had been evident ever since World War I, which saw the successful blockade of the Central European powers by Allied navies (Zahra, 2023). When countries did not possess the resources to become self-sufficient, a logical response was to try to become so via conquest. These tensions were clearly a contributory factor to the outbreak of World War II in Asia and played a role in Adolf Hitler's calculus as well (Tooze, 2006).

The interwar period never saw the international pre-1914 labour mobility, although in the immediate aftermath of World War I, there were attempts to institutionalise a commitment to open international labour markets. During peace negotiations, the Government of Germany submitted a proposal that would have given a right to workers to live and to work wherever they could find jobs. Several European delegations also argued that international migration should be brought under the auspices of the newly created International Labour Organization (ILO), which, in principle, had the power to enforce international conventions regarding labour standards. However, these proposals were vetoed by countries of immigration; ILO's scope remained limited to issues such as unemployment insurance, child labour, and the length of the workday. Its effectiveness to enforce even these standards would eventually collapse after the onset of the Great Depression (James, 2001).

The international economic system of the 1920s and 1930s still involved large European empires in Africa and Asia, and north-south trade focussed on the exchange of northern manufacturers for southern primary products. Colonies remained open to trade with their colonisers, although some—notably the British Dominions and India—were free to protect infant industries, and their trade policies were no longer non-discriminatory. The Great Depression marked the beginning of the end of empires, however, as falling product prices and incomes and attempts by colonisers to force the burden of adjustment onto local shoulders increased nationalist sentiments (Rothermund, 1996).

2.2.4 The Post-War World

The post-World War II era marked a decisive break with the past, in that new multilateral institutions emerged that imposed legal obligations on member states—especially in trade. To a large extent, these undertakings were designed to avoid the catastrophe of the 1930s. Thus, instead of the discriminatory trade blocs of the 1930s, Article I of the General Agreement on Tariffs and Trade (GATT) decreed that all signatories would become each other's MFN; non-discrimination was to become the central principle underpinning international trade. There were, however, a number of exceptions. Unlike in the 1930s, MFN obligations would not prevent countries from forming free trade areas or customs unions, subject to the condition that these do not increase the average level of protection facing non-members. Moreover, much to the frustration of the United States, existing empires were allowed to retain their preferential trade agreements. The empires eventually disappeared, but in 1971, the new Generalised System of Preferences emerged, under which rich countries—including the United States—agreed to unilaterally extend tariff preferences to poorer ones.

A series of negotiating rounds convened by the GATT led to tariffs being progressively revised down. Reflecting preferences of the United States, these negotiations involved commodity-specific deals and were based on the principle of reciprocity. At first, bargaining was bilateral, with concessions made by importers to their principal suppliers of particular goods being generalised to other countries via the MFN principle. The temptation to 'free ride' meant that this approach ran into diminishing returns in the late 1950s, with bargaining becoming multilateral. By the 1990s, however, with the number of GATT members rising sharply, the limitations of the latter approach were also becoming increasingly visible.

In the monetary sphere, policymakers adopted a system of fixed but adjustable exchange rates, but the experience of the Great Depression had taught them the importance of monetary policy autonomy. The logical conclusion was capital controls, which were widely adopted. IMF was set up to help manage the new fixed exchange rate system and balance-of-payments issues that could arise. Currencies were to be made convertible, although this was only achieved at the end of the 1950s. Migration was severely restricted by governments, although the 1951 Refugee Convention forbid signatories from returning refugees to countries where they may face significant threats to their lives or freedom.

While the aim was to create a new global economic order, in reality, the Cold War meant that the classic Bretton Woods mix of fixed but adjustable exchange rates, convertible currencies, capital controls, and tariff reductions was largely limited to the West and its allies. Indeed, this geopolitical context explains why the United States allowed the British to retain their imperial preferences and not only tolerated—but actively encouraged—the formation of the EEC in the 1950s. The GATT's MFN obligations did not extend to the treatment of non-members, and the Cold War implied tight controls on trade between West and East, where trade was highly controlled in line with the Communist doctrine. From 1949, the United States and its North Atlantic Treaty Organization (NATO) allies restricted the export of strategic goods to Communist countries via the Coordinating Committee on Multilateral Export Controls, an informal institution that was only disbanded in the 1990s. In addition, former European colonies often used their new-found legislative freedom to educate their workforces—as well as to pursue the same protectionist trade policies that wealthy countries had adopted in earlier decades. The 1950s and 1960s actually proved to be a period of deglobalisation when viewed in a global—as opposed to a Western—perspective (Findlay and O'Rourke, 2007).

The transformation from Bretton Woods to the present system occurred in several stages. First, beginning in the late 1960s, capital controls were progressively undermined; in the early 1970s, the fixed exchange rate regime was abandoned. Major currencies now floated against each other, although many smaller countries continued to peg. Remaining capital controls in wealthy countries were abandoned under the influence of free market doctrines, a trend that later spread to the developing world. A series of international financial crises associated with sudden stops ensued, most recently in the Eurozone. In theory, floating may have implied greater macroeconomic policy flexibility; in practice, monetary policies were increasingly delegated to independent central banks with mandates to control inflation.

Second, developing countries opened to trade and foreign investment, whether because of disillusionment with previous policies, in the hopes of emulating their peers that had successfully pursued similar policies in the past, or pressure from multilateral agencies and creditor governments in the wake of debt crises. In some cases, notably China and South-East Asia, this shift was associated with very rapid economic growth; in others, the 1980s and 1990s saw a decline in growth rates compared to the 1950s and 1960s. Third, the international economic system became truly global, with China's opening to trade and the collapse of the Soviet Union being key turning points. Democracy, capitalism, and a commitment to openness no longer were associated with each other; capitalism and autocracy occurred together in several countries, while the global economic system now spanned geopolitical divides and would, some hoped, help erase these. Fourth, bilateral trade and investment deals proliferated and increasingly involved behind-the-border provisions, leading to more fears of democratic accountability in countries where that was an issue. Fifth, the conventional wisdom regarding appropriate economic policy changed, becoming far more market oriented. While there was considerable variation across countries, marginal tax rates fell, trade unions weakened, privatisation and deregulation were encouraged, and industrial policy became taboo in many countries.

On balance, therefore, the international system evolved in a way that implied less domestic policy flexibility than had previously been seen. The macroeconomic policy constraints—implied by mobile financial capital, microeconomic policy constraints considered a requirement to attract foreign direct investment, and changing views regarding what constituted appropriate economic policy—all pulled in this direction. The COVID-19 pandemic has thus marked a significant break with the recent past in terms of the scale of government intervention involved. The Biden Administration's Inflation Reduction Act in the United States may, in time, come to be seen as a major turning point similar to the transformations of the early 1980s.

2.3 Discussion

2.3.1 Rules, Discretion, and Democracy

The rules of the gold standard and MFN treatment principle governed the international economic order of the late 19th and early 20th centuries. In the former case, these rules reflected a consensus regarding appropriate monetary policy; in the latter, they arose from a spontaneous process of bilateral treaty-making. Rules reflecting the conventional wisdom of the day can, in practice, be as binding as international legal obligations—a proposition symbolised by Sidney Webb's shocked reaction to Britain's 1931 decision to quit the gold standard: 'Nobody told us we could do that'. Heinrich Brüning's austerity budgets for Germany in the 1930s may have had devastating consequences, but he believed that he had no choice. When the conventional wisdom shifts, however, it can do so quickly. Nearly every country returned to the gold standard in the 1920s, and nearly all abandoned it again in the 1930s. Whether today's taboos concerning—for example—industrial policy will be overturned as a result of the pandemic and Inflation Reduction Act remains to be seen, but it would be unsurprising if they were.

The post-war world was novel because of the extent to which rules—particularly in the sphere of trade—were codified in multilateral (rather than bilateral) treaties that were, in principle, binding. This legalisation of economic rulemaking was further enhanced by the strengthened dispute settlement mechanisms of the World Trade Organization. In the monetary sphere, this shift towards rules took a different form. The old multilateral fixed but adjustable exchange rate regime was replaced with a floating regime managed by central banks that were independent and had tightly circumscribed inflation-fighting mandates.[2] The rules, however, were generally imposed by governments that retained the power to change them.

The shift to rules came in part from a desire to avoid a repetition of the interwar period. The United States was particularly focussed on eliminating trade discrimination; this goal was one of the eight enumerated in the 1941 Atlantic Charter signed by President Franklin Roosevelt and Prime Minister Winston Churchill. Yet the shift to rules also reflected views that democracy could not be trusted to produce market-friendly, open economic policies. Economists sometimes rationalise rules by appealing to the prisoner's dilemma, need to avoid mutually destructive behaviour, problems relating to time inconsistency, or short time horizons of democratically elected politicians. As Slobodian (2018) noted, some economists also distrust politicians and voters, as they can be seen as excessively willing to intervene in the economy in ways regarded as undesirable. For example, few, if any, economists would today use the language employed by economist Fritz Machlup in 1969, who wrote the following:

> Let me recall Mill's dictum that there can be no liberty for 'savages'. Replace this harsh word by 'politically and intellectually immature people' and reflect on the proposition that full democracy may not be the most suitable system of government for such people; that, for example, the unlimited right to vote and elect the men who will govern the country may lead to the destruction of many other freedoms and also of any real chance for economic development.
> (Slobodian, 2018: 146)

However, many probably sympathised with the former president of the European Commission, Jean-Claude Juncker, who said, in 2007, that 'We all know what to do, but we don't know how to get re-elected once we have done it'. Seen in such a perspective, the attraction of making rulemaking structural reform—or macroeconomic policy, trade policy, or even fiscal policy—democracy-proof is apparent.

The problem is that politicians such as Juncker—and the economists whose policy advice they follow—may not always know what exactly to do. The historical record suggests that in such circumstances, discretion will eventually triumph over rules, whether self-imposed or outlined in treaties.[3] The gold standard and its associated *mentalité* was once seen as inviolable, but when its destructive consequences became apparent, it was swiftly abandoned. The only issue was whether it would be abandoned by democratic politicians or by their opponents. Whenever open trade has become too costly politically, governments have eventually intervened in the market, whether during the generally liberal 19th century, generally illiberal 1930s, or generally liberal early 21st century.

Again, questions have centred on the form that the interventions would take and what kind of politicians would take them on (e.g. whether the early 21st-century return to discretionary policies with implications for international trade flows would predominantly involve politicians like President Donald Trump imposing tariffs or politicians like President Joe Biden introducing the Inflation Reduction Act). Given the increasing political strains of the last 20 years, history suggests that it would be strange if the status quo were maintained. Moreover, what has already happened in the United States will have a global impact. While many in Europe and elsewhere doubt that the Inflation Reduction Act is compatible with World Trade Organization rules, the Biden Administration will continue to pursue it, and the implicit rules governing state behaviour everywhere will change as a result.

Where rules are too constraining, they are eventually abandoned. Where inappropriate rules are maintained in place for too long, democracy can be made fragile and international cooperation discredited. In a world that needs global cooperation more than ever, it is dangerous when liberal internationalism becomes excessively identified with a particular economic policy, as during the 1930s. It is crucial to distinguish amongst rules that are essential, rules that are not, and rules that are potentially damaging, and accept that democratic governments require policy flexibility to cope with changing circumstances.

2.3.2 Geopolitics and the International Economic Order

Examples exist of multilateral conventions solving collective action problems, such as the 1999 Montreal Convention that is combatting the hole in the ozone layer. It is less clear that international trade agreements have, in fact, been adopted to rule out mutually destructive prisoner's dilemmas. Rather, as Gowa (2015) argued, they have typically been motivated by geopolitical considerations. The central role of the MFN principle in post-war planning was due to the perception of the United States that trade blocs had destabilised the interwar world geopolitically; the fact that the United States nevertheless allowed Britain to enter the GATT with its imperial preferences intact was due to the onset of the Cold War and fear that the

Soviet Union would exploit any differences amongst the major Western powers. The United States saw European integration as politically beneficial, which outweighed the economic costs to the United States of trade diversion. Subsequent European moves to deepen integration have reflected a political commitment to a closer union. Moreover, as Gowa emphasised, there is an asymmetry between trade with allies and trade with potential enemies. While the former implies positive security externalities, the latter may involve negative security externalities. Thus, trade deals are typically between allies rather than potential enemies; Western exports of sensitive goods to the Soviet bloc were restricted throughout the Cold War, and exports of certain advanced chips to China are banned today.

The globalisation of the post-1990 period is due to the collapse of the Soviet Union and China's opening to the West. It would be utopian and unrealistic to expect current levels of globalisation to survive a serious escalation of geopolitical tension. Nor does the historical record support the view that trade will prevent those tensions from escalating, as the world was extremely globalised in 1914. Indeed, once war becomes a possibility, then import dependencies can be a factor increasing tension, as was the case during the 1930s (Bonfatti and O'Rourke, 2018). This is particularly true if the post-1945 taboo on seizing other countries' territory by force is abandoned, which is one of several reasons why Russia's invasion of Ukraine is so concerning.

On the positive side, China has not completely aligned itself with Russia, which would have threatened a complete breakdown of the international economic order. Perhaps that is in part due to its economic connections with the West, which would be consistent with the liberal peace theory. Yet the world has arrived at a very dangerous juncture, and a major issue facing policymakers is how to manage a global economy straddling a widening geopolitical divide. If integration goes into reverse, what rules should all sides respect?

2.3.3 International Migration

Discussions of the global economic order typically cover trade, investment, and monetary arrangements. Migration is rarely examined, although the potential benefits of labour flows from low- to high-wage destinations are enormous not only for the individuals involved but for their families and home regions. Global remittances are over twice the level of official aid from Organisation for Economic Co-operation and Development (OECD) countries; remittances from the Gulf Cooperation Council alone are equivalent to more than half of all OECD aid.

The obvious problem is that public opinion in wealthy democracies will never accept the open borders that some economists call for. Yet policymakers can design schemes that allow a greater level of legal migration, managed in such a way that would be acceptable to public opinion. The potential gains seem significant enough that such attempts should be made.

Notes

1 At least in countries, such as India, where there had been significant industrial production.

2 As former Italian Minister of Economy and Finance Tommaso Padoa-Schioppa noted, central banking has shifted from being internationalist and Keynesian to nationalist and monetarist.

3 Furthermore, where acceding to rules would have been too constraining, governments have generally not signed onto them in the first place. This is particularly true of more powerful countries; the United States did not join the League of Nations, objected to the proposed International Trade Organization, and more recently blocked the appointment of judges to the World Trade Organization Appellate Body.

References

Accominotti, O., and B. J. Eichengreen. 2016. "The Mother of All Sudden Stops: Capital Flows and Reversals in Europe, 1919–32." *The Economic History Review* 69 (2): 469–92.

Berman, S. 2006. *The Primacy of Politics: Social Democracy and the Making of Europe's Twentieth Century*. Cambridge, UK: Cambridge University Press.

Bonfatti, R., and K. H. O'Rourke. 2018. "Growth, Import Dependence, and War." *Economic Journal* 128 (614): 2222–57.

Bordo, M. D., C. M. Meissner, and D. Stuckler. 2010. "Foreign Currency Debt, Financial Crises and Economic Growth: A Long-Run View." *Journal of International Money and Finance* 29 (4): 642–65.

Catão, L. A. V., and S. N. Solomou. 2005. "Effective Exchange Rates and the Classical Gold Standard Adjustment." *American Economic Review* 95 (4): 1259–75.

Clavin, P. 2013. *Securing the World Economy the Reinvention of the League of Nations, 1920–1946*. Oxford, UK: Oxford University Press.

Eichengreen, B. J. 1992. *Golden Fetters: The Gold Standard and the Great Depression, 1919–1939*. Oxford, UK: Oxford University Press.

Eichengreen, B. J., and D. A. Irwin. 2010. "The Slide to Protectionism in the Great Depression: Who Succumbed and Why?" *The Journal of Economic History* 70 (4): 871–97.

Eichengreen, B. J., and R. Portes. 1989. "Dealing with Debt: The 1930s and the 1980s'." In *Dealing with the Debt Crisis*, edited by I. Husain and I. Diwan, 69–88. Washington, DC: World Bank.

Ellison, M., S. S. Lee, and K. H. O'Rourke. 2024. "The Ends of 27 Big Depressions." *American Economic Review* 114 (1): 134–68.

Esteves, R., and D. Khoudour-Castéras. 2009. "A Fantastic Rain of Gold: European Migrants' Remittances and Balance of Payments Adjustment during the Gold Standard Period." *The Journal of Economic History* 69 (4): 951–85.

Findlay, R., and K. H. O'Rourke. 2007. *Power and Plenty: Trade, War, and the World Economy in the Second Millennium*. Princeton, NJ: Princeton University Press.

Gowa, J. 2015. "Explaining the GATT/WTO: Origins and Effects." In *The Oxford Handbook of the Political Economy of International Trade*, edited by L. L. Martin, 19–36. New York: Oxford University Press.

Hatton, T. J., and J. G. Williamson. 1998. *The Age of Mass Migration: Causes and Economic Impact*. Oxford, UK: Oxford University Press.

Huberman, M. 2012. *Odd Couple: International Trade and Labor Standards in History*. New Haven, CT: Yale University Press.

Huberman, M., and C. M. Meissner. 2010. "Riding the Wave of Trade: The Rise of Labor Regulation in the Golden Age of Globalization." *The Journal of Economic History* 70 (3): 657–85.

James, H. 2001. *The End of Globalization: Lessons from the Great Depression*. Cambridge, MA: Harvard University Press.

Kelly, M., and K. H. O'Rourke. 2024. "Industrial Policy in the Shadow of Conflict: Lessons from the Past." In *How Europe Should De-Risk: Economic Security in an Age of Interdependence*, edited by J. Pisani-Ferry, B. W. Mauro, and J. Zettelmeyer. Paris; London: CEPR Press.
Lewis, W. A. 1978. *The Evolution of the International Economic Order*. Princeton, New Jersey: Princeton University Press.
Nations, League. 1942. *Commercial Policy in the Interwar*. Period: International Proposals and National Policies.
O'Rourke, K. H. 2006. "The Worldwide Economic Impact of the French Revolutionary and Napoleonic Wars, 1793–1815." *Journal of Global History* 1 (1): 123–49.
O'Rourke, K. H., and J. G. Williamson. 1999. *Globalization and History: The Evolution of a Nineteenth-Century Atlantic Economy*. Cambridge, MA: MIT Press.
Özler, Ş. 1993. "Have Commercial Banks Ignored History?" *The American Economic Review* 83 (3): 608–20.
Ritschl, A. 2012. "The German Transfer Problem, 1920–33: A Sovereign-Debt Perspective." *European Review of History: Revue Européenne d'Histoire* 19 (6): 943–64.
Robertson, D. H. 1938. "The Future of International Trade." *The Economic Journal* 48 (189): 1–14.
Rothermund, D. 1996. *The Global Impact of the Great Depression, 1929–1939*. London: Routledge.
Schumpeter, J. A. 1943. *Capitalism, Socialism, and Democracy*. London: G. Allen & Unwin.
Slobodian, Q. 2018. *Globalists: The End of Empire and the Birth of Neoliberalism*. Cambridge, MA: Harvard University Press.
Temin, P. 1989. *Lessons from the Great Depression*. Cambridge, MA: MIT Press.
Temin, P., and B. A. Wigmore. 1990. "The End of One Big Deflation." *Explorations in Economic History* 27 (4): 483–502.
Tooze, J. A. 2006. *The Wages of Destruction: The Making and Breaking of the Nazi Economy*. London: Allen Lane.
Williamson, J. G. 2011. *Trade and Poverty: When the Third World Fell Behind*. Cambridge, MA: MIT Press.
Wilson, C. 1978. *Profit and Power: A Study of England and the Dutch Wars*. The Hague: M. Nijhoff.
Zahra, T. 2023. *Against the World: Anti-Globalism and Mass Politics between the World Wars*. New York: W. W. Norton and Company.

3 Rethinking Global Governance

Cooperation in a World of Power

Joseph E. Stiglitz and Dani Rodrik*

3.1 Introduction

Today, the world is highly integrated and interdependent. Climate change affects all; emissions from one country can have devastating global effects. Viruses know no international borders. For more than 200 years, a basic lesson of economics has been that lowering trade barriers contributes to higher standards of living by allowing for greater specialisation and taking advantage of comparative advantages. Knowledge produced in one country can be of benefit to the whole world.[1]

While these areas and many others demand global governance, the world possesses limited global cooperation. Policies are determined by domestic politicians based on 'national interest'; the nation-state remains the principal locus of political accountability. Taking into account such a political reality, a more circumscribed, less ambitious global agenda may be preferable. This chapter thus advances a framework for minimal global governance architecture.

First, some general principles that should govern the design of global governance are outlined, and their justifications are provided. The next section discusses the reasons—both positive and normative—for the minimal conception of global governance. In the remaining sections, implications of these ideas are drawn from a variety of arenas—intellectual property rights, trade, financial flows, monetary policy, investment agreements, and management of debt. Principles help examine the possibility of good agreements (green-lighted), areas where agreements should be widely circumscribed (red-lighted), and areas where agreements should occur under extreme caution (yellow-lighted).

3.2 Four General Principles[2]

A minimalist global governance architecture should be based on the following four principles. First, international rules should generally allow countries to do as they please as long as they do not engage in explicitly beggar-thy-neighbour (BTN) policies[3] or, in the case of advanced countries, impose significant costs on poorer countries. It is remarkable how many provisions of global agreements violate this principle. Typically, the behaviours of small developing countries have no impact

DOI: 10.4324/9781003571384-3

on the global economy, yet this is an arena in which international agreements have had perhaps the most binding effects—precisely because these countries are small and powerless. Countries may engage in actions that the West suggests are foolish (e.g., various domestic regulations, investment policies, or social policies), but they bear the consequences. Hence, the first principle restricts international discipline to policies that have a specific BTN nature.[4]

The second principle is that there are marked variations amongst countries, so any international agreement must reflect these differences in circumstances. These differences may arise from different national preferences, historical trajectories, or economic conditions (e.g., levels of income). If national regulations or standards reflect the provision of public goods, countries may differ in their ideals regarding the type of public goods. Financial regulations, for example, may entail a trade-off between promoting financial innovation and securing financial stability. Similarly, various nations will put different weights on the contending goals of privacy, convenience, and innovation when regulating new technologies such as artificial intelligence (AI).

The third principle is that global agreements should be consistent not only with global efficiency but also with global fairness. A focus on global public goods and the avoidance of BTN policies, with due regard to differences across countries, is not enough. Addressing climate change or global health, for example, requires significant resources. Poorer nations should not be asked to pay for more than their fair share—especially as in the case of carbon, the advanced economies are responsible for the bulk of historical emissions. In both cases, the standard of global fairness would require significant resource and technology transfers from the North to the South. Similarly, policies in advanced countries such as the United States can have significant adverse effects on developing countries. A minimal standard of fairness requires that such countries formulate their policies with due regard to negative spillovers, especially for poorer nations. This principle also implies that developing countries and emerging markets should be wary about signing on to agreements that give them a small share of the surplus generated—especially because of the high levels of uncertainty associated with the future evolution of the global economy. A small gain can easily be turned into a large loss.[5]

The final principle is that all economic arrangements have some sort of broad social and political consequences that must be considered. Economics does not stand outside of society. International economic arrangements can produce redistributive effects across income groups or regions that can produce unforeseen consequences. Limitations on the autonomy of national policymakers can undermine political accountability and produce a backlash against mainstream political leaders, increasing support for right-wing, authoritarian populists. Capital market liberalisation—allowing the free flow of money in and out of a country—has not only large and potentially adverse financial and economic consequences but also political consequences. Global agreements affect the policy space and democratic governance within a country. Economic arrangements may also shape individuals and social arrangements. A society where cooperatives play a more important role may lead to more accommodating individuals; neoliberal capitalism, with its emphasis on the unwavering pursuit of self-interest, may generate more selfish people and institutional arrangements that condone such behaviour.[6]

3.3 Central Tensions in Global Governance

The centre of political activity and political accountability remains the nation-state. Even in the European Union, which has witnessed a significant transfer of policy-making powers to Brussels, Frankfurt, and Strasbourg, politics takes place mostly in the national capitals. This can be—and often is—seen as a hindrance to global economic cooperation and governance in the face of common challenges such as the provision of global public goods. Furthermore, the multiplicity of sovereigns creates jurisdictional discontinuities, which produce transaction costs and impede global economic integration, reducing efficiency. Now that import tariffs and capital controls have largely—but not entirely—receded into the background, differences in legal regimes and regulatory practices are often the chief obstacles to a unified global economy.

Historically, the nation-state has played a significant and positive role in promoting economic development. It is associated with curbing local violence, expanding social solidarity beyond communities, mobilising mass education, fostering industrialisation, and spreading representative political institutions. Moreover, if the facts are accepted that (i) markets have to be embedded in non-market institutions to provide regulation and to address market failures, and (ii) there is no single, universal mapping between markets and those institutions due to historical contingencies and locally differing trade-offs amongst contending values such as equity versus efficiency, there is a strong normative case for the nation-state even in an age of globalisation. From this perspective, the nation-state can be seen in a more positive light as the site of experimentation amongst diverse institutional forms of market economies. Institutional diversity at the global level and international economic integration are both valuable. An optimum set of global arrangements would not maximise one at the expense of the other, leaving ample policy autonomy for the nation-state.

The design of global governance must consider the tension between two forces. On one hand, global governance can act as a framework to create a fair, just, and efficient world. This includes providing global public goods, limiting negative externalities, promoting positive externality-generating activities, engendering the cooperation necessary to reap the potential rewards of globalisation, and creating a global rule of law (i.e., a rules-based system where every country is treated fairly).[7] On the other hand, global governance can be a mechanism to exert power and for the powerful to extract rents from the least powerful. There is a clear parallel between the first vision of global governance and the standard arguments for the rule of law within countries—and the tensions identified globally parallel those existing within countries. Although economists have traditionally championed the rule of law, the consequences depend on whose rules and for whom the rules are designed.

The rhetoric surrounding global governance typically focuses on the first force, while the reality more often seems linked to the second force. Global agreements often propel developing countries into actions through which there is (i) no evident significant externality to justify such exertion of power and (ii) little desire to circumscribe advanced countries from actions (e.g., in their monetary policies) associated with large externalities. The absence of enforcement mechanisms means that typically, when the United States or European Union violates a global regulation or norm, there are no consequences as long as the impacts are only or mostly on the less powerful. When a small country violates a global regulation or norm, however, the consequences may be significant. Thus, in practice, the rules-based system operates markedly differently from the way it is supposed to.

3.3.1 Good and Bad Outcomes

Some countries—most notably those in East Asia—have nonetheless managed to take advantage of globalisation. They have grown rapidly, so the disparity between their incomes and that of advanced countries has markedly decreased. They did not obey the dictates of the Washington Consensus concerning the policies that countries should adopt to maximise growth; yet they still existed within the rules, which were largely written by—and for—advanced countries. Africa's experience has been different, as it experienced premature de-industrialisation under the structural adjustment programmes of the International Monetary Fund and World Bank and saw incomes stagnate for a quarter of a century, which was even worse than Latin America's lost decade.

In the Uruguay Round of negotiations establishing the World Trade Organization, advanced countries obtained most of their demands, while developing countries got few. The subsequent round—known as the Development Round—was supposed to rectify the imbalance (e.g., Stiglitz and Charlton, 2007). However, that round collapsed after 14 years of futile negotiations in December 2015.

3.3.2 The End of the Neoliberal Order

Another reason to rethink global governance centres on the fact that today's global architecture was created largely in an era of neoliberalism, where a certain set of ideas prevailed. Free trade and unfettered capital movements were desirable, but these ideas have now largely been discredited, and the policies based on them are being rethought. The benefits of free trade seem less than were claimed, and the costs that were imposed, especially on workers—including lower wages, large adjustment costs, and high levels of uncertainty and vulnerability—are greater. The same is true for capital market and financial market liberalisation.[8]

3.3.3 Self-Interest of Nations

A realistic agenda for global governance must be based on the national interests of individual countries if it is to be self-sustaining. A complication arises because the concept of self-interest is ambiguous; what may matter is not the self-interest of the country as a whole but that of powerful interests within the country.

Thus, one may argue that it is in the unilateral self-interest of the United States to abolish many tariffs, reduce emissions, and push for agreements where others do. However, producers (e.g., those in the fossil fuel industry) may have a different view, and it may be politically impossible to design compensation schemes that would induce them to go along with policies in the national interest. Those heard in international trade negotiations are typically not ordinary citizens but producers (Rodrik, 2018). After an agreement is made, it may also be those interests that determine compliance.

Sometimes, the overall gains to society are sufficiently large and broad that special interests are overcome, possibly by some form of compensation. Indeed, agreements can be viewed as ways of restraining special interests, featuring some coalescence of disparate weaker forces against more powerful special interests. Many international agreements—reflecting this battle between special interests and broader national interests—do compel countries to undertake actions in their own interests unilaterally. More commonly, however, rather than trade agreements serving to restrain special interests in favour of the general interest, powerful special interests use international agreements—typically made in secret with relatively weak public discussion—to tie the hands of governments in favour of the special interests. For example, in recent negotiations over digital trade, the digital giants have been attempting to forge agreements that would circumscribe the ability of governments to impose regulations concerning privacy, digital harm, competition, and national security.

3.3.4 Externalities

Even in areas where there are large externalities, and, in principle, global cooperation would enable better outcomes, cooperation may be difficult to achieve. Advanced countries exert negative externalities on others, and they do not want to be circumscribed in their actions; it is thus difficult—if not impossible—to obtain the cooperation of those adversely affected to compensate (i.e., bribe) the powerful countries not to exert their negative externalities in a Coasian solution.

3.4 Towards a Minimalist Global Architecture

The preceding sections provided an argument for a minimalist global architecture; this section illustrates this system of global governance. Two areas are highlighted—climate change and public health—in which the costs of global cooperation could be low, benefits large, and special interests limited under a minimalist global governance. Then, an area is examined in which an ambitious global reform agenda—multi-national taxation—has mixed results, with successes and failures consistent with pursuing a minimalist agenda. Investment agreements are then discussed, in which the world seems to be moving towards a minimalist agenda. Next, a minimalist trade agenda is outlined; finally, debt, which has long had a minimalist agenda that has failed, is reviewed. In each arena, some elements of a minimalist agenda are suggested; no agenda is comprehensive.

3.4.1 Climate Change

There is now almost universal agreement that global action is necessary to deal with climate change, most emissions going forward will come from developing countries and emerging markets, and additional finance is required if developing countries and emerging markets are to make the investments required to reduce emissions. An easy source of funds exists—the issuance of Special Drawing Rights by the International Monetary Fund (IMF). Special Drawing Rights are essentially IMF-printed money, which—as long as there is sufficient excess capacity in the global economy—are close to costless. Despite the low or no cost, however, resistance continues, perhaps because the issuance of public money may reduce the returns of those in the financial sector. A global agreement for climate change and Special Drawing Rights would be of enormous benefit.

3.4.2 Public Health

An important part of global governance concerns knowledge and intellectual property. Accordingly, since 1995, the Trade-Related Aspects of Intellectual Property Rights (TRIPS) Agreement has provided strong protections, the terms of which were set by advanced countries—as well as special interests (e.g., pharmaceutical and entertainment industries) within those countries. The provisions largely echoed those within the United States and European Union and were designed to maximise profits rather than to enhance innovation or well-being (e.g., Stiglitz, 2006). A single regime was imposed on all countries. For example, it called for compulsory licenses for health, the importance of which was reinforced during the HIV/AIDS epidemic. The pharmaceutical industry resisted and, in subsequent years, embraced multiple dilatory strategies, which resulted in millions of US dollars in profits. The deaths and suffering were only collateral damage.

The issue came to a head with the COVID-19 pandemic. There was an urgency to develop the vaccines, therapeutics, and associated products and to ensure that they were widely distributed. No one knew how long the pandemic would last, how bad the consequences would be, nor how it would mutate. Governments (especially that of the United States) spent billions of US dollars to rush research and production, building on government-supported basic research to create the mRNA platform for COVID-19 vaccines.

Due to the urgency of the moment, South Africa and India requested a waiver of intellectual property under the TRIPS Agreement to increase the manufacturing capability for vaccines, therapeutics, and associated products. Users would still have to pay royalties, but the underlying legal framework would be unchanged. US President Joe Biden appeared persuaded, but the grip of the pharmaceutical companies in Germany, Switzerland, and the United Kingdom proved to be an insurmountable barrier. The waiver was never enacted.

A minimalist trade agenda would recognise that the appropriate intellectual property regime for each country depends on its circumstances—in particular, that the TRIPS Agreement does not always advance the well-being of the global economy and society. Moreover, there needs to be, at a minimum, automatic intellectual property waivers in the presence of any pandemic declared by the World Health Organization—as well as compulsory licenses for technologies related to climate change.

3.4.3 Taxation of Multi-National Corporations

An important aspect of globalisation is multi-national corporations operating in multiple countries. Ascertaining how taxing rights should be allocated has been difficult, and corporations often strive to ensure that their income is attributed to jurisdictions with low tax rates. The transfer price system, which has been in place for a century, has been inadequate for new digital technologies. The system attempts to allocate profits to where income arises by pretending that there are arms-length prices at each stage of production. Yet as such prices do not, in fact, exist, prices can be easily made up. Profits can thus be shifted to, for example, a tax haven like Panama. The abuses of the system are enormous; for example, all of Apple's profits in Europe originate from a few employees in Ireland.

As the world sank into the Great Recession of the late 2000s, the need for more tax revenues became urgent, and the diversion of profits to tax havens became increasingly problematic. Digital giants appeared to be amongst those not paying their fair share of taxes. The Organisation for Economic Co-operation and Development (OECD) thus began working to improve the global tax regime through base erosion and profit shifting (BEPS), which has two pillars: (i) ensuring firms pay a minimum tax of 15% (yet often lowered through exceptions and exemptions to 12%–13%, less than half the rate of taxation in Latin America); and (ii) allocating tax rights for the largest firms for a small portion of their profits (based on no economic theory). In return, countries would have to forego imposing unilateral measures, like digital taxes. The revenues that most developing countries could expect from BEPS was miniscule, and when offset by the potential for growing digital taxes, almost surely negative. Although it began as an initiative to raise more revenues for developing countries, ensure that the multi-national corporations pay their fair share of taxes, and simplify the taxation of multi-national corporations, BEPS failed on all accounts, except one—guaranteeing that multi-national corporations pay at least a very low minimal tax.

OECD claimed BEPS as an important first step that would eventually generate the desired results. Yet it is undeniable that multi-national corporations from the United States and European Union—especially the digital giants—had triumphed with a minimal tax. Moreover, thanks to a small additional tax on a small portion of their income, they would be protected against additional taxation, such as digital taxes.

From this, it can be discerned that the locus of global decision-making needs to be in a venue where the voices of developing countries and emerging markets are stronger than in OECD, the club of advanced countries. The G24,[9] a group of developing countries, has put forward a coherent set of reform proposals, which was ignored in favour of those put forward by advanced countries.

A minimalist agenda that would focus on setting a minimum tax rate, curtailing tax havens, reforming the double-tax regime, and preserving rights to taxation may lead to a better global tax regime.

3.4.4 Investment Agreements

Investment agreements began as a seemingly innocuous effort to protect investors against expropriation. Investors could buy insurance against expropriation at a low cost through a branch of the World Bank Group and national insurers, but expropriations had become rare by the time that investment agreements started to proliferate.

In practice, the agreements gave foreign investors more rights than domestic investors, protected investors against changes in regulations and taxes, and compensated them exorbitantly for any losses incurred. Disagreements were settled through investor-state dispute settlements that involved highly paid private arbitrators, not subject to modern standards (e.g., concerning conflicts of interest and transparency) and without a framework for appeal. By 2016, the agreements started to be used against the United States; a critical difference between the North Atlantic Free Trade Agreement (NAFTA) and the US-Mexico-Canada Agreement that succeeded it was the elimination (for the most part) of investor-state dispute settlements. Within Europe, there has also been a move against these agreements, as it has become clear that they are likely to be an obstacle to the green transition.

Investment agreements are a clear manifestation of powerful companies advancing their interests over the well-being of society. Although it now appears unlikely that any new agreements will be signed, there is a legacy of such agreements; a minimalist global architecture would work to terminate them.

3.4.5 Trade and Industrial Policy

It is easier to specify what should not be in a good trade agreement than what should be. The principles enunciated earlier imply (i) providing more scope for countries to tailor their intellectual property regimes to their economic circumstances than the TRIPS Agreement allows; (ii) not imposing digital rules until after there is greater clarity about the regulatory regime that is appropriate for each country; and (iii) not circumscribing a country's regulatory framework unless there is compelling evidence that it is a BTN policy.

The issue is that it is not easy to classify whether industrial and/or trade policies are BTN and against international commitments. For example, industrial policies in the form of subsidies to encourage the development of particular industries, particularly those aimed at enhancing the green transition, have emerged as problematic. Reducing emissions is a global public good; actions of countries towards green production and consumption should be welcome. Yet these may distort trade patterns, giving countries a comparative advantage in the production of, for example, a particular green product. China created a marked advantage in the production of solar panels, originally through government subsidies and eventually because of it acquired technological superiority and scale economies. Other countries have not been able to compete; the United States and European Union thus have imposed tariffs on Chinese exports, including the panels. Under a minimalist approach, China's subsidies and, thus, cheaper panels would be viewed as globally welfare-enhancing, while the United States and Europe may have potential job losses in these sectors.

Another example of the US's Inflation Reduction Act (IRA) subsidies is also actually directed at enhancing green investment. Some are investments in non-tradeable sectors (e.g., energy) whose impact on the global trade regime is only indirect (e.g., subsidised electricity). The objective of the measure is to green the economy but in ways that do not cost jobs (i.e., that maintain and strengthen current competitive relations based on the current implicit carbon subsidy arising from not charging a carbon price). The same is true of green subsidies for tradables, like electric batteries. In both cases, jobs in the United States may come at the expense of jobs in developing countries. This may make the Inflation Reduction Act a BTN policy, although that is not its goal.

However, we should take note that some provisions of the Inflation Reduction Act, such as domestic sourcing requirements, are indeed BTN, which are explicitly discriminatory vis-à-vis trade partners. If the United States seeks to divert jobs that may be created elsewhere to the United States and is successful in doing so, the result would be a clear BTN practice. Green policies targeting climate change mitigation cannot be neatly separated from trade policies, and often, domestic political bargains will necessitate advanced countries adopting messy policies that are good for the climate but potentially problematic from a trade perspective. Developing countries, however, do not have the fiscal space to respond to this. Even if they could, there would be significant adverse consequences for the global distribution of income, with corporate profits increasing at the expense of everyone else. Countervailing duties would be of limited benefit since they would only affect imports into the country imposing them—not competitiveness in other countries.

Similar trade-offs exist with the CHIPS programme of subsidies for advanced technologies in the United States. To the extent that this programme targets important market failures (e.g., innovation spillovers and national security externalities), there is little reason for disciplining the United States through global rules, even if the benefits accrued primarily to the United States. The programme could be used as a source of geopolitical leverage over other nations to alter their technology-sourcing decisions, penalising them for using Chinese technology, in which case it would be more objectionable. The United States has deployed a broad range of export controls on advanced semiconductors and equipment, purportedly for national security reasons. To the extent that these controls aim to undermine the technological capabilities of China—as many observers believe they do—the policy is BTN (Rodrik and Walt, 2024).

On the other hand, the United States is clearly violating existing international agreements with impunity. In the absence of a functioning appellate body, there is no way to hold it to account; even if there were such a body, it would be a slow and drawn-out process. At the same time, the European Union is attacking developing countries that attempt to use industrial policies (i.e., Indonesia, which has banned the export of unrefined nickel). The minimalist trade agenda suggests that weighing national and global benefits against the trade-diverting effects of such subsidies is too much to ask of a global governance system ruled by power. Indeed, some fundamental assumptions of the post-World Trade Organization trade order are no longer tenable.

Moreover, China's economic growth has not led to greater convergence between its economic model and that of the West; instead, it has fuelled greater geopolitical tensions and triggered the prioritisation of national security over efficiency and comparative advantage considerations. Supply chain resilience has become a critical objective for all nations. These, along with other challenges, such as pandemic preparedness, imply that deep economic integration on the hyper-globalisation model is no longer feasible. Markets on their own do not account for concerns, and governmental interventions—including through subsidies and trade restrictions—may be warranted.

There is no longer a presumption that any governmental intervention is an unwarranted and unfair trade intervention—particularly one designed to gain an advantage over a trading partner. The focus on trade should move from stricter, common rules seeking policy harmonisation to a more minimalistic approach that expands national policy space while avoiding the worst BTN policies and ensuring the poorest countries are not systematically left behind.

3.4.6 Debt

Debt has always been a problem for the poor and for poor countries, but in the aftermath of the COVID-19 pandemic, war in Ukraine, and post-pandemic inflation, it is becoming critical. Several countries are in debt distress, and a few have gone over the brink. There is no international framework for resolving sovereign debt problems, such as bankruptcy procedures that help overindebted individuals and corporations within each country restructure their debts. These procedures help protect households and jobs and incentivise lenders from pushing excessive indebtedness. The United Nations General Assembly overwhelmingly approved the creation of such a framework in 2014 and followed this with a set of principles, again endorsed by the General Assembly in 2015. A few key creditors—the United States and the United Kingdom—voted against it, however, so it was never realised.

The G20 has recognised the problematic nature of current minimal arrangements. At the beginning of the pandemic, it created the Debt Sustainability Initiative to allow for the suspension of debt payments for those in the most distress. The arrangement proved ineffective, with private sector creditors refusing to participate and debtors being reluctant to ask for debt suspension, lest it lead to a credit rating downgrade. This initiative was thus followed by the Global Sovereign Debt Roundtable, which seems equally ineffective. Most countries do not only need a suspension of debt servicing; they need either greater access to liquidity or debt restructuring. Much literature has shown that the cost of delay can be enormous (e.g., Guzman, Ocampo, Stiglitz, 2016).

The current minimalist architecture is too little—debt negotiations have become a power game in which powerful financial interests overcome others. It is unclear if an international bankruptcy court recommended by the United Nations Commission to be established in the aftermath of the 2008 global economic crisis is achievable (Stiglitz, 2010). Therefore, a more modest mediation service, with the IMF providing benchmark calculations of how much restructuring is necessary if debt is to become sustainable, is perhaps more realistic.

3.5 Concluding Remarks

Global agreements and institutions reflect the imbalances of global power amongst countries and deficiencies in democratic governance within the major countries. Outcomes reflect the interests of large and powerful players within advanced and influential countries. While within democracies, an imperfect system of checks and balances is designed to curb the excesses of power, nothing comparable operates at the global level. There are occasions when the voice of global civil society is heard, but those are more the exception than the rule. Its inability to curb 'vaccine apartheid' during the COVID-19 pandemic illustrates the limitations.

A 'good' system of global governance must take these realities into account. Discussions have value to help define aspirations. Yet *realpolitik* entails designing a global architecture that balances the benefits of the provision of global public goods and regulation of global externalities with the risks of abuses from the exertion of power by special interests. Today, those who are engaged in trying to construct a global architecture that benefits rich and formidable companies in wealthy and dominant countries have learned how to cloak their self-interest in the language of virtue. The aspiration of a comprehensive and strong agenda for a fair and efficient global architecture has, in many respects, led to a more dysfunctional global architecture—such as premature de-industrialisation and deregulation of capital and financial markets—resulting in deeper economic and financial crises and increasing disparities between the richest and poorest within and amongst countries.

The minimalist global architecture is based on the presumption that the rich and powerful cannot be effectively constrained, so weaker countries (i.e., developing countries and emerging markets) must discern the agreements and institutions that work best for them with the knowledge that when it is convenient for the rich and powerful to break the rules or to subvert the institutions to work for their own interests, they will do so.

Rivalry between blocs of countries, particularly between the United States and China, may result in a competition for the hearts and minds of those in the developing world that will circumscribe the worst behaviours imaginable. Within democratic countries, there are strong movements in support of social and economic justice as well—not only within the boundaries of a country but extending across the globe. The stronger the competition for influence in the developing world and the more robust the movements for social and economic justice within powerful countries, the greater the possibilities for advancing beyond a minimalist global architecture.

Notes

* The author acknowledges financial assistance from the Hewlett and Sloan Foundations and valuable discussions with Martin Guzman and David Vines.

1 While climate and public health have long been recognised as global public goods, knowledge, too, is a global public good (Stiglitz, 1999).

2 Some of these principles were more fully articulated in Stiglitz (2024), Rodrik (2020), and Rodrik and Walt (2024).

3 BTN policies are defined as those that provide benefits at home only to the extent that they impose costs on other countries. They are policies whose benefits are the direct and intended result of that harm. Applying import tariffs or export restrictions to extract monopoly rents from other countries, competitive devaluations under conditions of unemployment, or paper-profit shifting through tax havens are some examples.

4 Yet countries whose policies have a disproportionate effect on the global monetary, financial, regulatory, or trade context should face a higher degree of accountability and responsibility; ideally, this should occur even under a minimalist global architecture. Arguments entailing political realism that force a focus on this minimalist vision suggest that such accountability is unlikely to occur. Advanced countries should accept some global oversight over policies that have significant and adverse effects on the economic prospects of lesser-developed nations. More expansive global governance would attempt to address externalities more generally; today, this more expansive view is necessary. As an example, the intent of those using fossil fuels is to lower their energy costs; climate change, harming everyone everywhere, is the unintended consequence. Their lowered cost of energy comes at the expense of the well-being of everyone on the planet. Within countries, actions that harm others are regulated, whether the benefits of those actions are the direct and intended result of that harm. Intentions play no role; it is only the effects of actions that matter.

5 A tax agreement recently proposed by the Organisation for Economic Co-operation and Development (OECD) illustrates this. Developing countries were offered a pittance, but in return, they would have to give up rights to impose a digital tax as well as other 'unilateral measures'. Some countries signed on, believing that even some revenues are better than nothing. Yet, almost surely, with the growth of the digital economy, what they had agreed to forego would be of increasing importance. If this OECD agreement were ever to come into force, developing countries and emerging markets would actually be worse off, with the gains from the global agreement going largely to the advanced countries.

6 This was a central theme of the recent literature on endogenous preferences and how preferences are shaped by society and, in turn, help shape it (Hoff and Stiglitz, 2016; Demeritt, Hoff, Stiglitz, forthcoming). These ideas were derived from a long tradition. See, in particular, Polanyi (1944) and Polanyi (2001), with a foreword linking his work with globalisation by Stiglitz.

7 This vision of global governance sees it as protecting small- and medium-sized countries from the arbitrary exercise of power by advanced countries.

8 Theory and evidence have long been sceptical of many neoliberal claims. See, for instance, Newbery and Stiglitz (1984), showing that in the absence of good risk markets, everyone may be worse off due to free trade; Stiglitz (2004), showing that capital market liberalisation may decrease welfare; Stiglitz (2003); and Stiglitz (2017).

9 Algeria, Argentina, Brazil, China, Colombia, Congo, Cote d'Ivoire, Ecuador, Egypt, Ethiopia, Gabon, Ghana, Guatemala, Haiti, India, Iran, Kenya, Lebanon, Mexico, Morocco, Nigeria, Pakistan, Peru, Philippines, South Africa, Sri Lanka, Syria, Trinidad and Tobago, and Venezuela.

References

Allison Demeritt, Karla Hoff, and Joseph E. Stiglitz. forthcoming. *The Other Invisible Hand: How Culture Shapes Societies and Wellbeing*. New York: Columbia University Press.

Guzman, Martin, José Antonio Ocampo, and Joseph E. Stiglitz, eds. 2016. *Too Little, Too Late: The Quest to Resolve Sovereign Debt Crises*. Columbia University Press. https://doi.org/10.7312/guzm17926.

Hoff, Karla, and Joseph E. Stiglitz. 2016. "Striving for Balance in Economics: Towards a Theory of the Social Determination of Behavior." *Journal of Economic Behavior & Organization* 126 (June): 25–57. https://doi.org/10.1016/j.jebo.2016.01.005.

Newbery, David M. G., and Joseph E. Stiglitz. 1984. "Pareto Inferior Trade." *The Review of Economic Studies* 51 (1): 1. https://doi.org/10.2307/2297701.

Polanyi, Karl. 1944. *The Great Transformation: The Political and Economic Origins of Our Time*. New York: Farrar and Straus.

Polanyi, Karl. 2001. *The Great Transformation: The Political and Economic Origins of Our Time*, 2nd beacon paperback ed. Boston, MA: Beacon Press.

Rodrik, Dani. 2018. "What Do Trade Agreements Really Do?" *Journal of Economic Perspectives* 32 (2): 73–90. https://doi.org/10.1257/jep.32.2.73.

Rodrik, Dani. 2020. "Putting Global Governance in Its Place." *World Bank Research Observer* 35 (1): 1–18. https://doi.org/10.1093/wbro/lkz008.

Rodrik, Dani, and Stephen Walt. 2024. "How to Construct a New Global Order." *Oxford Review of Economic Policy* 40 (2): 256–68. https://doi.org/10.1093/oxrep/grae011.

Stiglitz, Joseph E. 1999. "Knowledge as a Global Public Good." In *Global Public Goods*, edited by Inge Kaul, Isabelle Grunberg, and Marc Stern, 1st ed., 308–25. New York, NY: Oxford University Press. https://doi.org/10.1093/0195130529.003.0015.

Stiglitz, Joseph E. 2003. *Globalization and Its Discontents*. New York: W. W. Norton.

Stiglitz, Joseph E. 2004. "Capital-Market Liberalization, Globalization, and the IMF." *Oxford Review of Economic Policy* 20 (1): 57–71. https://doi.org/10.1093/oxrep/grh004.

Stiglitz, Joseph E. 2006. *Making Globalization Work*, 1st ed. New York: W. W. Norton & Co.

Stiglitz, Joseph E. 2010. *The Stiglitz Report: Reforming The International Monetary and Financial Systems in The Wake of The Global Crisis*. New York: New Press.

Stiglitz, Joseph E. 2017. *Globalization and Its Discontents Revisited: Anti-Globalization in the Era of Trump*, 1st ed. Erscheinungsort nicht ermittelbar: W. W. Norton & Company, Incorporated.

Stiglitz, Joseph E. 2024. *The Road to Freedom: Economics and the Good Society*, 1st ed. Erscheinungsort nicht ermittelbar: W. W. Norton & Company, Incorporated.

Stiglitz, Joseph E., and Andrew Charlton. 2007. *Fair Trade For All: How Trade Can Promote Development*. New York, NY: Oxford University Press. https://doi.org/10.1093/oso/9780195328790.001.0001.

4 Roles of Bilateral, Regional, and Plurilateral Cooperation

Shujiro Urata

4.1 Introduction

Globalisation of economic activities in the form of trade and investment expansion heavily contributed to the rapid economic growth of the global economy from the 1990s to the latter half of the 2000s, improving allocation of resources and promoting innovation and technological progress. However, economic growth slowed after the 2008 global economic crisis. Faced with this difficult economic situation, many countries implemented protectionist policies, resulting in the slowdown of trade and investment.

In the mid-2010s, the United States began to perceive challenges by China, as China continued its high economic growth, catching up to the United States. To deal with this situation as well as an increased trade deficit vis-à-vis China, US President Donald Trump imposed additional high tariffs on imports from China in 2018. Chinese President Xi Jinping retaliated by imposing additional high tariffs on imports from the United States. Several subsequent rounds of additional tariff imposition from both countries have resulted in a tariff war. The US-China conflict accelerated as both countries also began to restrict bilateral trade and foreign direct investment (FDI) to protect their economies, particularly technological capability. The United States has also asked its allies and other countries to follow its policy towards China. The US-China trade war not only has had a negative impact on global trade but has damaged the world trading order under the World Trade Organization (WTO), as both of their actions have violated WTO rules without consequences.

The COVID-19 pandemic, which began in China in 2020 and quickly spread throughout the world, resulted in the further slowdown of trade and FDI, as restriction of people's mobility reduced economic activity—particularly in the distribution sector, a key sector in conducting trade. Furthermore, the trade and FDI environment has been damaged by increasing geopolitical tensions in several other parts of the world in the 2020s, most notably US-China confrontation in the Indo-Pacific and Russia's invasion of Ukraine.

Furthermore, the United States, China, and many other countries have begun to pursue inward-oriented nationalistic economic and industrial policies under the auspices of protecting national security. One notable example is the development

DOI: 10.4324/9781003571384-4

of the semi-conductor industry, including by the United States, China, the European Union, Japan, and South Korea through government subsidies. These policy developments have resulted in the division of the global economy into the US-led group and China-led group, further hindering global trade and FDI. If the confrontation between the two groups escalates, the global trade and investment system may break down, potentially resulting in a dire situation, such as occurred before World War II.

Faced with this contemptuous global trade and FDI environment, various types of trade and FDI cooperation schemes—as well as bilateral, plurilateral, and regional schemes—have been created to avoid the destruction of the global trade and FDI system and to achieve healthy and sustained economic growth. This chapter reviews these schemes, specifically regional trade agreements (RTAs) and plurilateral trade agreements, and presents several policy recommendations towards their use. Moreover, an alternative dispute settlement mechanism, known as the Multi-Party Interim Appeal Arbitration Arrangement (MPIA), has also been proposed and is examined in this chapter.

Section 4.2 studies the problems of the current global trading system under WTO with a focus on the dysfunction of the Appellate Body in the dispute settlement mechanism. Section 4.3 reviews two types of emerging international cooperation activities on trade and FDI—RTAs and plurilateral trade agreements. RTAs cover a wide range of policy areas and involve a limited number of members, while plurilateral trade agreements involve a large number of participants and focus on one policy area. Section 4.4 assesses the development of the MPIA, an alternative to the Appellate Body. Section 4.5 concludes by providing some policy recommendations.

4.2 Dysfunction of the World Trade Organization

The General Agreement on Tariffs and Trade (GATT) entered into force in 1948; eight multilateral trade negotiations were concluded under it, resulting in a freer and more open world trading system. The Uruguay Round, the last multilateral trade negotiation under the GATT, concluded in 1994.

Under the GATT, WTO was established in 1995 and has subsequently contributed to strengthening the world trade system. While the GATT is an agreement, WTO is an international organisation. Indeed, the GATT was created due to the failure to develop the International Trade Organization after World War II, which had been expected to provide a free and open world trading system to promote international trade with an aim of avoiding protectionism, a factor that led to World War II.

Many 'improvements' were incorporated into WTO to solidify and to strengthen the world trading system. They may be classified into two groups: (i) introduction of new rules and (ii) strengthening of existing rules. Regarding new rules, reflecting the increased importance of intellectual property, services, and investment in international economic activities, the rules of intellectual property rights (i.e. the Trade-Related Aspects of Intellectual Property Rights [TRIPS] Agreement), trade in services (i.e. General Agreement on Trade in Services [GATS]), and investment (i.e. Agreement on Trade-Related Investment Measures [TRIMS]) were added to the GATT, which covers trade in goods.

Another improvement was the strengthening or facilitation of the dispute settlement mechanism.[1] Under the GATT, first, a complainant must query the dispute settlement body for consultation. If the issue is not resolved within 60 days, then the complainant can request the dispute settlement body to establish a panel, which can only be established if all contracting parties agree. The panel then submits a report, and the adoption of the report requires a positive consensus as does the authorisation of countermeasures against a non-implementing respondent. Because of this method, a respondent can block the process, making it difficult to resolve disputes efficiently. During 1948–1994 under the GATT, the number of consultations, establishment of panels, issuance of panel reports, and adoption of the reports were 317, 158, 136, and 96, respectively.[2]

Under WTO, two fundamental changes were made: (i) adoption of a negative consensus and (ii) establishment of the Appellate Body, creating a two-tier dispute settlement system. The Appellate Body was established to receive an appeal from a complainant that disagrees with the conclusion of the panel. The Appellate Body, consisting of seven persons, can uphold, modify, or reverse the conclusions of the panel. In addition, by adopting a negative consensus, the dispute settlement body automatically establishes panels and adopts both panel and Appellate Body reports, unless there is a consensus not to do so. The number of consultations and establishment of panels thus increased substantially under WTO. During 1995–2023, the number of consultations and panels were 621 and 372 , respectively. However, currently, the Appellate Body is not functioning due to vacancies.[3]

Today, WTO has two important functions for managing the global trading system to promote trade: (i) rulemaking and (ii) dispute settlement. Rulemaking includes market opening or trade liberalisation, while dispute settlement is associated with monitoring and enforcement of rules. WTO has not been performing these two functions well, however.

Multilateral trade negotiation—the Doha Development Agenda (DDA)—began in 2001 on various points, including agriculture, non-agriculture market access, services, rules (e.g. anti-dumping and subsidies), trade facilitation, development, TRIPS, and trade and the environment. At the beginning of the DDA, investment, competition, trade facilitation, and transparency in governmental procurement (i.e. Singapore issues) were the focus of the negotiations. Since that time, however, the DDA has not progressed smoothly because of differences in opinions amongst WTO members. As of December 2023, only two negotiations have been concluded, those on trade facilitation and fisheries subsidies.[4] The Trade Facilitation Agreement was established in 2017, and the Agreement on Fisheries Subsidies was adopted in 2022.[5]

In addition, the dispute settlement mechanism of WTO is not functioning as expected. As noted, the Appellate Body stopped functioning in December 2019 due to vacancies, which occurred because the United States refused to approve candidates due to its dissatisfaction with the performance of the Appellate Body. For more than 20 years, the United States has noted that the Appellate Body has diminished WTO members' rights—which are protected under the WTO Agreement—by repeatedly failing to apply the rules of various WTO agreements in a manner that adheres to the text of those agreements (USTR, 2020). Indeed, the Appellate Body has strayed far from the limited role that WTO members assigned to it. Through this persistent overreaching, the Appellate Body has increased its own power and seized from sovereign nations and other WTO members an authority that it was not provided.

USTR (2020) provided several cases to support its criticism, including those related to procedural discretion and erroneous interpretations of WTO agreements. One example of procedural discretion is ignoring the deadline of proceedings. The text of Article 17.5 of Dispute Settlement Understanding is clear in its requirement that the Appellate Body complete appeals 'as a general rule' within 60 days, and that '[i]n no case shall the proceedings exceed 90 days' (USTR, 2020: 4–5; WTO, 2024). However, the Appellate Body has routinely violated Article 17.5 and ignored the deadline mandated by WTO members, without consulting the parties to an appeal. This conduct has grown worse over time, with some appeals taking more than 1 year to complete.

Moreover, USTR (2020) highlighted a case where the Appellate Body adopted an erroneous interpretation of the term 'public body'. WTO agreements discourage certain subsidies provided 'by a government or any public body'. The Appellate Body has adopted a narrow interpretation of 'public body', which requires an entity to possess, exercise, or be vested with governmental authority for it to constitute a public body. Yet this requirement is not found in the agreed text nor is it consistent with the ordinary meaning of the term 'public body'. The Appellate Body's narrow interpretation fails to capture a vast number of government-controlled entities, such as state-owned enterprises, undermining the ability of members to counteract subsidies that are injuring their workers and businesses. Although WTO was created by and for market economies, the Appellate Body's public body interpretation favours non-market economies at the expense of market economies and sowed confusion amongst WTO panels and members.

Another reason for the dysfunction of WTO is its consensus decision-making. With 164 members, reaching a consensus on any issue is difficult. One of the most contentious divisions is found between developed and developing members. As an example, some developed members argue that some developing members that enjoy preferential treatment should be treated as developed members.

4.3 New Trade Agreements

To deal with the current dysfunction of WTO in regard to promoting trade liberalisation and rulemaking, WTO members have formed new trade agreements, which include RTAs and plurilateral trade agreements.

4.3.1 Regional Trade Agreements

One of the first regional trade agreements[6] in the post-World War II period was the European Economic Community (EEC) formed in 1958.[7] The EEC was a customs union under which import tariffs on trade with customs union members were eliminated, and members applied common tariffs to imports from non-members.[8] The EEC was not consistent with the basic principle of non-discrimination in the GATT, but it was accepted as an exception with several conditions because the economic development and reconstruction of Western European countries was viewed as important to protect democracy and a free market economy from the threat of Communism. Some conditions related to the EEC, which had to be satisfied to be accepted into the GATT, included (i) not raising tariffs on imports from non-members, (ii) eliminating tariffs on all products, and (iii) completing these processes within a reasonable time period. The EEC was later expanded in membership and scope, transforming into today's European Union. The European Union has 27 member countries and allows free movement of goods, services, capital, and people amongst its members.

RTAs were not established until the end of the 1980s (Figure 4.1). Many between the end of 1950s and the latter half of the 1980s involved developing countries, including the Central America Free Trade Area (formed in 1959), European Free Trade Association (1960), Central America Common Market (1961), African Common Market (1963), Arab Common Market (1965), and Caribbean Free Trade Agreement (1968). A main objective was to promote economic development by creating a larger market, as many RTA members are constrained by small domestic markets.

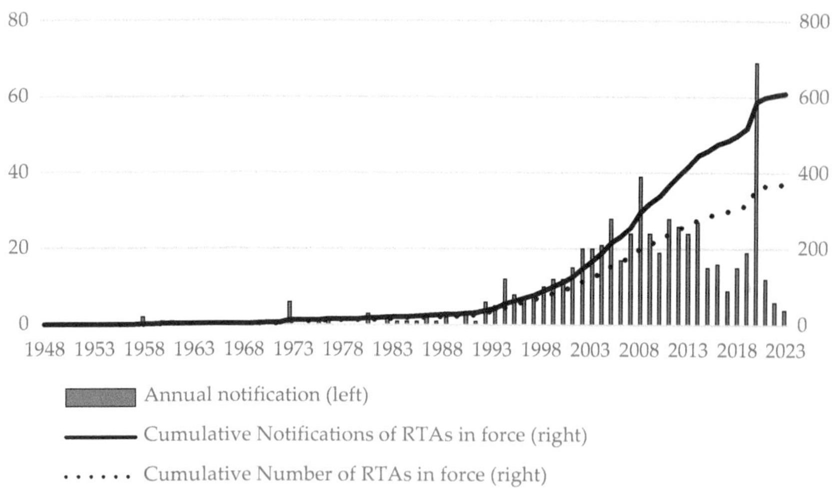

Figure 4.1 Evolution of Regional Trade Agreements in the World

RTA = regional trade agreement.

Source: WTO, Regional Trade Agreements Database, https://rtais.wto.org/UI/charts.aspx#.

The latter half of the 1980s saw a rapid increase in RTAs, including the Canada-US Free Trade Agreement (CUSFTA) in 1989. Several reasons may be identified for the rapid expansion of RTAs. First, the EEC expanded its membership from 6 to 12 countries[9] by 1986, and members were successful in achieving high economic growth, signalling that forming an RTA is beneficial to members. Second, the Uruguay Round, which began in 1986, was deadlocked. Thus, GATT members that were eager to promote trade liberalisation to achieve economic growth decided to form RTAs with like-minded members; reaching an agreement with a limited number of countries is easier than reaching a consensus amongst a large number. Third, RTAs triggered a domino effect, resulting in a sharp increase in their number. An RTA—a discriminatory trade policy with preference given to its members—presents a disadvantage to non-RTA members in international competition. Often, non-RTA members tried to join existing RTAs or to set up new RTAs to deal with disadvantageous positions, increasing the number of RTAs. The creation of the CUSFTA had a significant impact on the expansion of the number of RTAs because it signalled to the world that the United States—a champion of the multilateral trading system of the GATT—opted for a discriminatory and preferential trade policy over its tradition of encouraging multilateral and non-discriminatory trade practices.[10]

In the 1990s, the trend of establishing RTAs continued. They included the Association of Southeast Nations (ASEAN) Free Trade Area in 1993 with six ASEAN members (i.e. Brunei Darussalam, Indonesia, Malaysia, Philippines, Singapore, and Thailand)[11] and the North American Free Trade Agreement (NAFTA) in 1994 with Canada, Mexico and the United States. The increase in the number of RTAs persisted after the establishment of WTO, mainly because of the difficulty in starting multilateral trade negotiation under WTO.

The difficulty in multilateral trade negotiations has often been due to the differences of the views between developed and developing countries. Developed countries are eager to introduce new rules on various international economic activities, such as e-commerce and competition policy, while developing countries are more reluctant to do so. In fact, WTO members took 6 years to start a multilateral trade negotiation after WTO establishment. The DDA, which began in 2001, is still underway; as already noted, very little progress has been achieved so far.

Faced with little progress on multilateral trade negotiations, countries interested in promoting trade have opted for RTAs with like-minded countries. There is a tendency for countries to establish bilateral RTAs first and then to participate in plurilateral RTAs. Obviously, it is easier for two countries to come to an agreement than more than three countries. This pattern may be observed in Figure 4.2, which shows the cumulative number of bilateral and plurilateral RTAs in Asia.

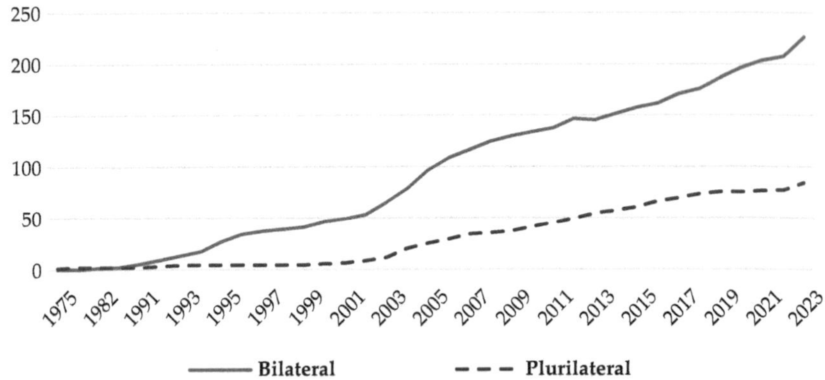

Figure 4.2 Bilateral and Plurilateral Free Trade Agreements in Asia

Source: Asian Development Bank, Free Trade Agreements, Asia Regional Trade Center, https://aric.adb.org/fta.

The progression from bilateral to plurilateral RTAs is found in many countries. For example, Japan established bilateral RTAs with Singapore (entry into force in 2002), Mexico (2005), Malaysia (2006), Chile (2007), Thailand (2007), Indonesia (2008), and Brunei Darussalam (2008) before a plurilateral RTA with the 10 ASEAN member states—the ASEAN-Japan Comprehensive Economic Partnership Agreement—in 2008 (Mattoo, Rocha, Ruta, 2020). Japan then helped establish the Comprehensive and Progressive Trans-Pacific Partnership Agreement (2018) involving 11 countries, the Japan–EU Economic Partnership Agreement (2019) involving 28 countries, and the Regional Comprehensive Economic Partnership (2022) Agreement involving 15 countries. Similar patterns of progression from bilateral to plurilateral agreements is observed for South Korea and the United States. For South Korea, a bilateral RTA with Chile was the first RTA in 2004, which was followed by Singapore (2006) and plurilateral RTAs with ASEAN (2010) and the European Union (2011). For the United States, the first RTA was bilateral with Israel (1985), followed by CUSFTA in 1989 and then NAFTA, a plurilateral RTA with Canada and Mexico in 1994. The number of policy areas covered by RTAs has increased in the last 2 decades as well (Figure 4.3).[12]

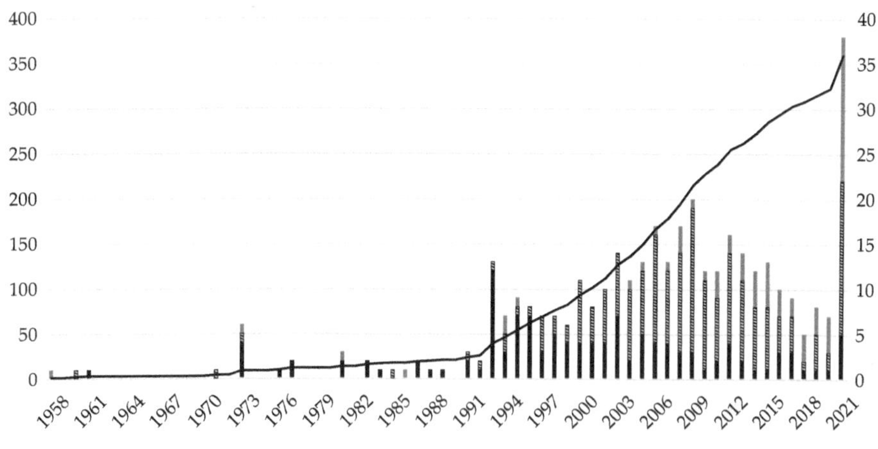

Figure 4.3 Deep Integration—Policy Areas Covered by Regional Trade Agreements

Note: The study considered 52 policy areas. See Mattoo, Rocha, Ruta (2020) for policy areas.

Source: World Bank, Deep Trade Agreements, https://datatopics.worldbank.org/dta/dashboard.html.

Table 4.1 shows the changes in the policy coverage of RTAs over time. For RTAs enacted from 1958 to 2000, two-thirds (66%) contained 1–9 policy areas. The corresponding shares for RTAs enacted in 2001–2010 and 2011–2021 were significantly lower at 27.4% and 16.7%, respectively. By contrast, the shares of RTAs with 10–20 policy areas increased from 26.5% for those enacted during 1958–2000 to 65.9% and 50.0% for those enacted during 2001–2010 and 2011–2021, respectively. The share of RTAs with 20 or more policy areas increased from 7.1% and 6.7% during 1958–2000 and 2001–2010, respectively, to 33.3% during 2011–2021.

Table 4.1 Changes in the Policy Coverage in Regional Trade Agreements (%)

Years Enacted	*Number of Policy Areas*			
	<10	*10–20*	*>20*	*Total*
1958–2000	66.3	26.5	7.1	100.0
2001–2010	27.4	65.9	6.7	100.0
2011–2021	16.7	50.0	33.3	100.0

Source: World Bank, Deep Trade Agreements, https://datatopics.worldbank.org/dta/dashboard.html.

Many RTAs are found to be deep in terms of policy coverage and have become deeper over time. Hofmann, Osnago, Ruta (2017) examined the policy coverage of 279 active RTAs signed by 189 countries between 1958 and 2015. They found that many RTAs include provisions on core policy areas, including WTO+[13] and four of the WTO-extra[14] provisions (i.e. competition policy, investment, movement of capital, and intellectual property rights) (Table 4.2). More than 90% of RTAs include provision on tariffs and customs, and one-third include legally enforceable provisions covering all core policy areas.

Table 4.2 Coverage of Core Policy Areas in Regional Trade Agreements

Policy Area	*Included*	*Legally Enforceable*
FTA industrial	100.0	98.6
FTA agriculture	99.6	98.2
Customs	90.4	81.8
Export taxes	78.6	76.4
Anti-dumping	75.7	67.9
Competition policy	74.6	66.1
Technical barriers to trade	70.4	54.3
Sanitary and phytosanitary standards	66.8	52.5
State aid	65.7	57.9
General Agreement on Trade in Services	65.0	50.7
Countervailing measures	63.9	58.2
TRIPS	57.1	55.4
Public procurement	56.4	42.9
Investment	55.0	38.9
Movement of capital	53.9	50.4
State enterprises	52.5	49.3
Intellectual property rights	47.5	39.6
TRIMS	32.5	31.1

FTA = free trade agreement, TRIMS = trade-related investment measures, TRIPS = trade-related aspects of intellectual property rights.

Note: Percentage of regional trade agreements covering the policy area in total number of regional trade agreements (279).

Source: Hofmann, Osnago, Ruta (2017).

They also found that that the depth of RTAs increased as the number of both border (e.g. industrial and agricultural tariffs, anti-dumping, countervailing measures, TRIMS, TRIPS, customs, export taxes, sanitary and phytosanitary measures, and technical barriers to trade) and behind-the-border (e.g. state enterprises, state aid, competition policy, intellectual property rights, investment, public procurement, and GATS) measures in RTAs rose. Futher, they found that both discriminatory/preferential and non-discriminatory measures increased over time.

Several factors may be identified for an increase in deep RTAs. One is the rapid expansion of international economic activities in the form of cross-border movement of goods, services, capital, people, and data, resulting in an increase in the degree and magnitude of contact with foreign firms and people. This trend has been facilitated by liberalisation policies in trade and investment, deregulation, and technological progress. Another factor behind the expansion of deep RTAs is the absence of well-established international rules regulating these movements to achieve free and fair competition by establishing level playing fields. These factors have made policymakers realise the need for deep trade agreements.

4.3.2 Plurilateral Agreements: Joint Statement Initiatives

The rulemaking functions of WTO have been stalled due to the lack of progress of the DDA; thus, like-minded groups of WTO members issued various joint statements on advancing discussions on e-commerce; developing a multilateral framework on investment facilitation; launching a working group on micro, small, and medium-sized enterprises (MSMEs); and advancing ongoing talks on domestic regulation in services trade at the WTO's 11th Ministerial Conference in December 2017.[15] Recognising the importance of inclusiveness, these groups have been open to all WTO members.

E-commerce

E-commerce or cross-border trade in data plays an important role in today's digitalised economy. E-commerce contributes to economic growth in various ways—it not only improves the efficiency and resilience of trade in goods and services online and on the ground but also promotes innovation and improves productivity and/or competitiveness. While e-commerce has beneficial impacts on economic growth, it also generates sensitive challenges, which include its impact on national security and privacy protection. Despite the rapid growth of e-commerce, several bilateral and plurilateral frameworks on e-commerce exist—but there are no globally agreed on rules. Developed countries tend to favour free and open e-commerce frameworks and are concerned about dominance by big tech companies; developing countries call for less open frameworks to maintain their power to regulate their own markets.[16]

At the 11th Ministerial Conference, a group of 71 WTO members agreed to initiate exploratory work towards future WTO negotiations on trade-related aspects of e-commerce.[17] Exploratory work on future WTO e-commerce rules began in

March 2018. By the end of 2018, more than 110 member countries participated in meetings on a wide range of issues, including electronic signatures, electronic payments, online consumer protection, and data flow.

In January 2019, Australia, Japan, and Singapore[18] hosted an unofficial ministerial-level meeting on e-commerce in Davos, Switzerland. Representatives exchanged views on the significance of associated rulemaking at WTO. After the meeting, a joint statement was issued confirming the intention to start negotiations on e-commerce involving 76 member countries, representing approximately 90% of international trade. As a result, in June 2019, during the G20 Osaka Summit, the Special Event on the Digital Economy was attended by leaders from 27 countries, including China, Japan, and the United States. These leaders—along with 78 countries and regions participating in the WTO e-commerce joint statement initiative—agreed to aim for substantive progress in e-commerce negotiations by the 12th Ministerial Conference scheduled for December 2021.

In December 2021, a joint chair's ministerial statement was issued, noting substantive progress, including consensus on eight articles covering online consumer protection and open government data (WTO, 2021b). Then, one of the important agreements reached at the 12th Ministerial Conference in June 2022 was to maintain the current practice of not imposing customs duties on electronic transmissions until the 13th Ministerial Conference. In December 2022, a new consolidated negotiation text reflecting consensus on 10 articles was compiled. In January 2023, a joint chair's ministerial statement was issued, confirming the acceleration of discussions and aiming for a substantive conclusion by the end of 2023. After the final round of e-commerce negotiations in 2023, Australia, Japan, and Singapore delivered a statement that negotiations reached a substantial conclusion on several global digital trade rules, covering digital trade facilitation, an open digital environment, and business and consumer trust (WTO, n.d.-h.). Members expect to conclude negotiations in early 2024.

Investment Facilitation for Development[19]

A joint initiative on investment facilitation for development was launched by a group of developing and least-developed WTO members in 2017. Recognising the importance of investment in promoting economic development as well as the need for closer international cooperation to create a more transparent and predictable environment for facilitating cross-border investment, this joint initiative aims to develop a multilateral agreement on investment facilitation for development that will improve the investment and business climate in developing WTO members. Specific measures for discussions include improving the transparency and predictability of investment measures; streamlining and speeding up administrative procedures and requirements; and enhancing international cooperation, information sharing, exchange of best practices, and relations with relevant stakeholders, including dispute prevention. The initiative does not cover market access, investment protection, and the investor-state dispute settlement.

Investment has been incorporated into WTO through the GATS and TRIMS, but these only cover certain aspects. The GATS has rules on services provided by foreign suppliers through a commercial presence in member countries, while the TRIMS has rules on investment measures related to international trade. Investment was originally included in the DDA but later dropped because of the differences in the opinions of WTO members.

Negotiations on IFD were formally launched in September 2020.[20] Participating members have made significant progress on key pillars of a future investment facilitation for development agreement, such as on the transparency of investment measures. It also reported that they have been working to advance discussions on remaining topics, including improving the predictability of investment measures; simplifying and speeding up investment-related administrative procedures; strengthening the dialogue between governments and investors; promoting the uptake by companies of responsible business conduct practices, including preventing and fighting corruption; and ensuring special and differential treatment, technical assistance, and capacity building for developing and least-developed countries.

Micro, Small, and Medium-Sized Enterprises[21]

At the 11th Ministerial Conference in December 2017, 88 WTO members signed a statement declaring their intention to create an informal working group on MSMEs to explore ways in which WTO members could better support MSMEs' participation in global trade.[22] Behind this movement was a recognition that MSMEs' participation in global trade has remained limited due to several obstacles (e.g. a lack of relevant skills, lack of knowledge about international markets, non-tariff barriers, cumbersome regulations and border procedures, and limited access to finance, particularly trade finance) and that their participation should be increased.

The MSME group met for the first time in March 2018. Since its establishment, the MSME group has produced various recommendations and declarations aimed at addressing challenges that MSMEs face when they trade internationally. Specifically, recommendations include providing data and information on policies related to MSMEs through the WTO Trade Policy Review process; promoting the compilation of information on platforms regarding tariffs, non-tariff measures, rules of origin, and trade procedures; encouraging transparency through the implementation of trade facilitation agreements; advocating for capacity building and technical assistance; and improving access to trade finance.

The MSME group continues to discuss a wide variety of topics including cross-border payments; digitalisation, with a particular focus on cyber-readiness and paperless trade through recognition of e-documents and standards to digitalise trade; informality; intellectual property and innovation; low-value shipments; MSME financing; sustainability; trade facilitation; and RTAs.

Domestic Regulation of Services

A group of 59 WTO members established the Joint Initiative on Services Domestic Regulation in December 2017 and began negotiations, with the aim of developing disciplines to facilitate services trade and to mitigate the unintended trade-restrictive effects of measures relating to licensing requirements and procedures, qualification requirements and procedures, and technical standards.[23] In September 2021, participants finalised their text-based negotiations. The disciplines agreed by the participants focus mainly on the transparency, predictability, and effectiveness of procedures with which businesses must comply to obtain authorisation to supply their services. They have been designed to apply to all sectors where participants have undertaken commitments in their schedules for trade in services under the GATS.

In December 2021, 67 WTO members adopted a declaration announcing the successful conclusion of negotiations on domestic regulation of services. The participants proceeded with the process of incorporating a reference document as additional commitments in the GATS schedule. In December 2022, they initiated WTO procedures towards the entry into force. In February 2024 and following the conclusion of certification procedures under the GATS, the disciplines have entered into force for 46 WTO members.[24]

Research has found that the benefits from implementing the new rules on domestic regulation of services would result in significant reductions in trade costs amounting to USD150 billion annually, particularly in some of the most crucial services sectors such as finance and business services (WTO and OECD, 2021). Implementation is likely to generate broader trade benefits for economies, such as increased services trade and further participation in global value chains.

4.4 Multi-Party Interim Appeal Arbitration Arrangement

The WTO dispute settlement mechanism is not functioning as intended because the Appellate Body stopped its operation due to vacancies in December 2019. The United States blocked appointment of new Appellate Body members, as discussed in Section 4.2. In response to this, 47 WTO members created the MPIA in April 2020 to serve as a provisional solution during the suspension of the Appellate Body's function.[25] Instead of appealing to the non-functional Appellate Body when dissatisfied with panel decisions, the MPIA establishes a framework for dispute resolution through arbitration. Any WTO member can join the MPIA by notifying the dispute settlement body.

4.5 Conclusion

Groups of WTO members have established new types of trade agreements, RTAs and plurilateral trade agreements, and an alternative dispute settlement mechanism, the MPIA. These developments reflect the view of many WTO members that establishing and managing a rules-based trade system is crucial for maintaining an open, stable trade and investment environment. Such a system will also help avoid the division of the world economy in light of the tensions between the United States and China, which has resulted in reduced trade and investment by fragmenting the world economy.

Many countries, especially small and developing countries, are losing growth opportunities. Thus, groups of middle-power countries such as Australia, Canada, Japan, and South Korea, and groups of countries belonging to the European Union, ASEAN, and the Global South headed by India, must play active roles in maintaining and strengthening the rules-based trade system under WTO by promoting and effectively using new trade agreements. It is also crucial for them to engage the United States and China bilaterally, plurilaterally, and regionally in their attempt to rebuild the global trade system under WTO.

Notes

1 On the dispute settlement mechanism of the GATT/WTO, see WTO. "Dispute Settlement." https://www.wto.org/english/tratop_e/dispu_e/dispu_e.htm
2 WTO. "GATT Disputes." https://gatt-disputes.wto.org/
3 WTO. "Dispute Settlement Activity—Some Figures." https://www.wto.org/english/tratop_e/dispu_e/dispustats_e.htm
4 The Information Technology Agreement, which reduces or removes tariffs on information technology products such as computers, telecommunications equipment, and semi-conductors, entered into force in July 1997, after reaching an agreement in December 1996 before the launch of the DDA. The product coverage of Information Technology Agreement expanded in 2015.
5 This agreement has not been enacted. For it to be operational, two-thirds of WTO members must deposit their 'instruments of acceptance' with WTO. "WTO, Agreement on Fisheries Subsidies." https://www.wto.org/english/tratop_e/rulesneg_e/fish_e/fish_e.htm
6 In the GATT, RTAs include customs unions and free trade agreements (FTAs). More accurately, the term 'economic integration agreement' is used for services trade instead of FTAs. However, in policy and research discussions, the term 'FTA' is generally used to cover both trade in goods and in services. In addition, partial scope agreements, which have been adopted by developing members and are small in number, are included.
7 The EEC was signed in 1957 with six members: Belgium, France, Italy, Luxembourg, the Netherlands, and West Germany, and entered into force in 1958.
8 An FTA is a trade policy under which tariffs on imports from FTA members are eliminated, like a customs union. Unlike a customs union, however, FTA members apply their own tariff rates on imports from non-FTA members.
9 New members were Denmark, Ireland, and the United Kingdom in 1973; Greece in 1981; and Spain and Portugal in 1986.
10 Others believe that the US-Israel FTA in 1985 signalled a shift in US trade policy from one based on multilateral and non-discriminatory rules to one with bilateral and discriminatory rules. Mainly political reasons—not economic reasons—led to the formation of the US-Israel FTA, however.
11 The ASEAN FTA was enlarged later by accepting new ASEAN members including Viet Nam (1995), the Lao People's Democratic Republic and Myanmar (1997), and Cambodia (1999).
12 The World Bank uses the expression 'trade agreements' in its analysis. This chapter uses 'RTAs' instead. There are other expressions including preferential trade agreements and FTAs. Technically, there are differences amongst these expressions, but to simplify the discussion, the term 'RTA' is used.
13 WTO+ provisions are some policy areas that fall under the current mandate of WTO. These provisions (referred to as 'WTO plus' or 'WTO+' in the literature) include areas such as customs regulations, export taxes, anti-dumping, countervailing measures, technical barriers to trade, or sanitary and phytosanitary standards (Hofmann, Osnago, Ruta, 2017).

14 'WTO-extra provisions' are those outside of the WTO mandate and include a wide-ranging set of policy areas from investment to environmental laws to nuclear safety (Hofmann, Osnago, Ruta, 2017).
15 WTO. "Joint Statement Initiative on E-commerce." https://www.wto.org/english/tratop_e/ecom_e/joint_statement_e.htm
16 See, for example, Miura and Urata (2023) about different attitudes towards e-commerce amongst major countries.
17 See WTO. "Joint Initiative on E-commerce News Archives." https://www.wto.org/english/news_e/archive_e/jsec_arc_e.htm for the development of working groups and negotiation at WTO.
18 Australia, Japan, and Singapore became co-conveners of the working group.
19 WTO. "Investment Facilitation for Development." https://www.wto.org/english/thewto_e/minist_e/mc12_e/briefing_notes_e/bfinvfac_e.htm
20 WTO. "Investment Facilitation for Development." https://www.wto.org/english/thewto_e/minist_e/mc12_e/briefing_notes_e/bfinvfac_e.htm. The number of participating members increased from 70 to over 110, and the co-coordinating countries are Chile and South Korea.
21 WTO. "Informal Working Group on Micro, Small and Medium-sized Enterprises (MSMEs)." https://www.wto.org/english/tratop_e/msmes_e/msmes_e.htm
22 As of March 2023, 98 WTO members were participating in the initiative.
23 WTO. "Services Domestic Regulation." https://www.wto.org/english/tratop_e/serv_e/jsdomreg_e.htm
24 WTO. "Services Domestic Regulation." https://www.wto.org/english/tratop_e/serv_e/jsdomreg_e.htm
25 On MPIA, for example, see Geneva Trade Platform. "Multi-Party Interim Appeal Arbitration Arrangement (MPIA)." https://wtoplurilaterals.info/plural_initiative/the-mpia/ and WTO (2020).

References

Asian Development Bank. n.d. "Free Trade Agreements." *Asia Regional Integration Center*. Accessed December 24, 2024. https://aric.adb.org/fta.

Hofmann, Claudia, Alberto Osnago, and Michele Ruta. 2017. "Horizontal Depth: A New Database on the Content of Preferential Trade Agreements." *World Bank, Policy Research Working Paper*, no. 7981. https://documents1.worldbank.org/curated/en/700771487791538589/pdf/WPS7981.pdf.

Mattoo, Aaditya, Nadia Rocha, and Michele Ruta. 2020. *Overview: The Evolution of Deep Trade Agreements*. Washington, DC: World Bank. https://doi.org/10.1596/978-1-4648-1539-3.

Miura, Hideyuki, and Shujiro Urata. 2023. "Establishing Multilateral and Regional Rules on Digital Trade: The Role of Japan and Middle Powers." In *Great Power Competition and Middle Power Strategies: Economic Statecraft in the Asia-Pacific Region. The Political Economy of the Asia Pacific*, edited by Vinod K. Aggarwal and Margaret A. T. Kenney, 185–207. Berlin: Springer Nature Switzerland. https://doi.org/10.1007/978-3-031-38024-2_9.

United States Trade Representative (USTR). 2020. *Report on the Appellate Body of the World Trade Organization*. Washington, DC: United States Trade Representative. https://ustr.gov/sites/default/files/Report_on_the_Appellate_Body_of_the_World_Trade_Organization.pdf.

World Bank. n.d. "Deep Trade Agreements (DTAs): Data, Analysis and Toolkits." Accessed December 24, 2024. https://datatopics.worldbank.org/dta/dashboard.html.

World Trade Organization (WTO). 2020. "Statement on a Mechanism for Developing, Documenting and Sharing Practices and Procedures in the Conduct of WTO Disputes."

https://docs.wto.org/dol2fe/Pages/FE_Search/FE_S_S009-DP.aspx?language=E&CatalogueIdList=263504.

World Trade Organization (WTO). 2021a. "Services Domestic Regulation." https://www.wto.org/english/tratop_e/serv_e/jsdomreg_e.htm.

World Trade Organization (WTO). 2021b. "WTO Joint Statement Initiative on E-Commerce." https://www.wto.org/english/news_e/news21_e/ji_ecom_minister_statement_e.pdf.

World Trade Organization (WTO). 2024. "Analytical Index DSU Article 17." In *WTO Analytical Index*. Geneva. https://doi.org/10.30875/0000709a-en.

World Trade Organization (WTO). n.d.-a. "Agreement on Fisheries Subsidies." *World Trade Organization (WTO)*. https://www.wto.org/english/tratop_e/rulesneg_e/fish_e/fish_e.htm.

World Trade Organization (WTO). n.d.-b. "Dispute Settlement." Accessed December 24, 2024. https://www.wto.org/english/tratop_e/dispu_e/dispu_e.htm#top.

World Trade Organization (WTO). n.d.-c. "Dispute Settlement Activity—Some Figures." Accessed December 24, 2024. https://www.wto.org/english/tratop_e/dispu_e/dispustats_e.htm.

World Trade Organization (WTO). n.d.-d. "GATT Disputes Database." Accessed December 24, 2024. https://gatt-disputes.wto.org/.

World Trade Organization (WTO). n.d.-e. "Informal Working Group on Micro, Small and Medium-Sized Enterprises (MSMEs)." Accessed December 24, 2024. https://www.wto.org/english/tratop_e/msmes_e/msmes_e.htm.

World Trade Organization (WTO). n.d.-f. "Investment Facilitation for Development." Accessed December 24, 2024. https://www.wto.org/english/thewto_e/minist_e/mc12_e/briefing_notes_e/bfinvfac_e.htm.

World Trade Organization (WTO). n.d.-g. "Joint Initiative on E-Commerce." Accessed December 24, 2024. https://www.wto.org/english/news_e/archive_e/jsec_arc_e.htm.

World Trade Organization (WTO). n.d.-h. "Joint Statement Initiative on E-Commerce." Accessed December 24, 2024. https://www.wto.org/english/tratop_e/ecom_e/joint_statement_e.htm.

World Trade Organization (WTO). n.d.-i. "Regional Trade Agreements Database." Accessed December 24, 2024. https://rtais.wto.org/UI/PublicMaintainRTAHome.aspx.

WTO and OECD. 2021. "Services Domestic Regulation in the WTO: Cutting Red Tape, Slashing Trade Costs, and Facilitating Services Trade." *Brief. OECD-WTO Trade Policy Brief.* https://www.wto.org/english/tratop_e/serv_e/oecd_wto_trade_policy_2021.pdf.

5 Correlated Trade and Geopolitics Driving a Fractured World Order

*Danny Quah**

5.1 Introduction

In the 2020s, public discourse, international relations scholarship, and global policymakers have all noted that geopolitical rivalries are worsening global fragmentation. The friend-shoring, de-risking, and decoupling emerging from US-China geopolitical rivalry have caused trade barriers to increase everywhere. From 2019 to 2022—coincident with the COVID-19 pandemic that also exacerbated geopolitical tensions—international trade restrictions rose three-fold (Georgieva, 2023). From this, a considerable loss in global well-being is possible; indeed, fragmentation over the long term could reduce global gross domestic product (GDP) by up to 7% (USD7.4 trillion), equivalent to the combined GDPs of France and Germany and more than three times the size of the entire sub-Saharan African economy (Georgieva, 2023).

A leading international relations scholar, Joseph Nye, noted of US decoupling that 'it would be foolish to think [that] we can separate our economy completely from China without enormous costs' (Nye, 2021). These enormous costs can be viewed as the price of fragmentation, but when the price is sufficiently high, rational agents will not undertake actions that incur those costs. Accordingly, International Monetary Fund (IMF) Managing Director Kristalina Georgieva wrote a 2023 *Foreign Affairs* article entitled, 'The Price of Fragmentation' (Georgieva, 2023). IMF Deputy Managing Director Gita Gopinath used the same reasoning to argue that if geopolitical-driven fragmentation produces individual gains, when set against real costs, those gains are illusory. Individual gains from fragmentation are, at best, only relative in that 'even those who benefit from fragmentation could be left with a larger slice of a much smaller pie . . . . [E]veryone could lose' (Gopinath, 2024).

This chapter investigates the relationship between geopolitics and economics as forces jointly driving world order. Have geopolitics and economics always driven world order in opposite directions, one splintering and the other coalescing? How accurate is the IMF (and indeed conventional) belief that geopolitical rivalries are fragmenting the world, but economics holds the global economy—and thus world order—together? This chapter argues that conventional wisdom is at odds with the global experience of the last 5 decades. The last 50 years can be divided

DOI: 10.4324/9781003571384-5

into two periods: (i) the centripetal era of 1980–2010, when both geopolitics and economics drove world order to ever-greater coalescence; and (ii) centrifugal era, from 2011, when both geopolitics and economics drove world order to ever-greater fragmentation.

If the current era is indeed centrifugal and economic ties are splintering world order, then seeking to develop greater economic interconnectedness—without recalibrating underlying fundamentals—is doomed to fail. Increasing trade ties will produce only perverse results, further fracturing the world. Instead, more effective and better-targeted policies are needed. This chapter suggests drawing on mechanisms that target repairing fragmentation beyond just strengthening trade ties. Such policies are (i) seek inadvertent cooperation; (ii) identify and shelve zero-sum propositions with prisoner's dilemma or epic fail outcomes (Armstrong and Quah, 2023; Quah, 2024b); and (iii) build systems around plurilateral principles or pathfinder multilateralism, and when first-best multilateralism is unavailable, seek second-best solutions in restricted problem domains.

This chapter is organised as follows. Section 5.2 documents how convergence due to geopolitical and economic forces in the early part of the last half-century produced the centripetal era and coalesced world order. Section 5.3 describes how after the centripetal era, both geopolitical and economic forces reversed direction so that the two drove fragmentation in the international system. It also examines reasons for the parallel reversal in both geopolitical and economic forces.[1] Section 5.4 advances three proposals to mitigate further global fracture, given that trade—the large, already extant natural glue to the international system—may no longer be effective. Section 5.5 provides a brief conclusion.

5.2 Convergence

In the 1980s, conceptualisation of world order and the global economy were powered by three critical ideas—political convergence, economic efficiency, and comparative advantage. These drove the coalescence of world order in this period of the centripetal era.

Political convergence refers to the hypothesis that as incomes rise and economic development progresses, societies tend naturally to become more democratic (Lipset, 1959). This provided an easy resolution to the challenge noted by US President John F. Kennedy of the 'long twilight struggle' between democracy and freedom, and totalitarianism and tyranny.

Economic efficiency does not entail high productivity or advanced technology. Instead, it refers to an imperative to seek efficiency in the sense that economists understand, Pareto optimality. Outcomes have to be, rationally, win-win. Coupled with the idea of political convergence, every victory on economic efficiency during this time also meant a further advance in the march to democracy worldwide.

Finally, comparative advantage references another key concept in economics, that all nations—no matter how differentially resourced and under-developed—would gain in some manner from participating in the global system of trade and capital flows. Globalisation—the construct that sought to make anything produced anywhere available to everyone everywhere—was therefore the appropriate objective for the emerging international system.

These three ideas formed a self-reinforcing, globally consistent, virtuous cycle of policy and practice, driving both prosperity and democracy.[2] The system did not promise that everyone would achieve the same levels of well-being, only that the norm would be win-win outcomes and a tendency towards democracy. The imperatives of economic efficiency and comparative advantage drove more intense and widespread globalisation, so that cross-country flows of trade and foreign direct investment rose.

In retrospect, the 1980s and 1990s appear to confirm success in a coalescent international system, at least along particular dimensions. Economically, the big success was the rise of China and East Asia. These are obviously outside of the usual Transatlantic locus of economic success; that they both became richer meant there was convergence for the world. Moreover, there were significant poor parts of the world that converged upwards to become richer, and modernity arrived in these places where previously it had been absent.

However, convergence failed in several significant dimensions. For instance, many studies of cross-country income dynamics revealed persistent income disparities (e.g. Pritchett, 1997); a middle-income trap (e.g. ADB, 2011) in that poor countries remained bounded away from reaching the same levels of economic achievement as rich countries; and even twin-peakedness in the cross-country distribution of incomes (e.g. Quah, 1996, 1997), where distinct clusters of convergence emerged, with at least one grouping of countries stagnating at lower income levels.

All of these studies, however, were of per capita incomes, treating each nation as a distinct data point. This meant that China, with over 1 billion people, was treated on equal basis with, for example, Haiti, which has under 10 million people. Data at a more disaggregated level provided more insight on economic convergence. Quah (2011) calculated the world's economic centre of gravity based on urban cities and rural centres and used dynamics of that centre of gravity to map out a dramatic change in the world's economic landscape since the 1980s. The key finding was that the rapid rise of incomes outside of the Transatlantic region had, by 2008, pulled the world's economic centre of gravity 5,000 kilometres east from its traditional 20th-century resting point in the Atlantic Ocean (i.e. midway between the United States and Western Europe). Over this same period, China's economic growth lifted nearly 700 million out of extreme poverty (Chen and Ravallion, 2010). Thus, as a narrative of individual incomes and economic well-being in the 3 decades after 1980, the overarching story was, indeed, convergence.

In parallel with these technical findings, a narrative on political convergence appeared. Fukuyama (1992) reported two key conclusions: (i) a 'consensus on the legitimacy of liberal democracy as a system of government emerged throughout the world'; and (ii) market mechanisms targeting economic efficiency and leveraging comparative advantage had produced 'unprecedented levels of prosperity in developed countries and in countries that had been, at the close of World War II, part of the impoverished Third World'.

US President Bill Clinton (2000) provided one of the most vivid and memorable depictions of confidence in political convergence during this centripetal era. He spoke on how China might try to buck the trend on political convergence by seeking to contain the flow of information on the internet: 'Good luck! That's sort of like trying to nail Jell-O to the wall'. He also made clear the prevailing thinking on economic and geopolitical alignment:

> China is not simply agreeing to import more of our products. It is agreeing to import one of democracy's most cherished values, economic freedom. The more China liberalizes its economy, the more fully it will liberate the potential of its people—their initiative, their imagination, their remarkable spirit of enterprise. And when individuals have the power, not just to dream, but to realize their dreams, they will demand a greater say.
>
> (Clinton, 2000)

Alongside these global successes in world order, one nation—the United States—emerged as the key player in the international system. It had become the de facto leader in a unipolar world order. An economic historian, Charles Kindleberger, described this kind of international leadership on the basis of the hegemonic stability theory. This is the idea that the international system—like any macroeconomy—naturally undergoes bouts of instability, for which a sufficiently large agent must be the consumer and lender of last resort or, more generally, provide the global public good of international policy-making (Kindleberger, 1996, 2013). Indeed, even beyond Keynesian countercyclical stabilisation, a hegemon is needed to provide security, maintain the rules of world order, and support global institutions that monitor and correct deviations. This allows the emergence of equitable openness in international trade and gives rise to the idea of multilateralism—a rules-based order, a level playing field in economic engagement, commitment to peaceful resolution of disputes, cooperation in problem-solving, and equal treatment of nations. At the time, the United States was the only economy powerful and rich enough to provide these global public goods (Kindleberger, 2013). As some political scientists described so vividly, US unipolarity produced world order (Ikenberry, 2005).

In conclusion, the 3 decades following 1980 saw remarkable success in political convergence, economic efficiency, and comparative advantage driving a coalescent, converging world order. The centrifugal era was, overall, a success, establishing with ever-greater firmness an integrated global economy. There were, of course, notable exceptions to this view in the literature (e.g. Rodrik, 2006). It is not that geopolitics no longer mattered (e.g. Luce, 2023), but geopolitical and economic forces aligned to produce convergence in the international system.

5.3 Shifts

By the late 2010s, it had become obvious that China was demonstrating no democratic tendencies even as it modernised, grew rich, and developed advanced technologies. This was not just a data point inconsistent with an academic hypothesis (Fukuyama, 1992; Lipset, 1959). Instead, this failure of convergence grew to become a driving force in modern Great Power rivalry. Because of its sheer size, China's political non-convergence presented, in some policymakers' views, an unacceptable threat and ideological challenge to the incumbent hegemonic Great Power, the United States. The United States' policy towards China thus shifted from engagement—increasing trade and investment and people-to-people ties—to balancing or undertaking actions to protect itself against China's present and future capabilities.

Under a regime of geopolitical engagement, China's actions might have been viewed as innocent or ambiguous. However, in the new atmosphere of balancing, they elevated concerns. Such markers included China's emplacement construction and heightened territorial claims in the South China Sea, aggressive wolf warrior diplomacy, concerns over the 'two Xs' (i.e. Xinjiang Uygur Autonomous Region, representative of China's 'ethnic management' policies, and President Xi Jinping for his centralisation of political power, including Xi's assumed association with Document No. 9, which warned of seven 'dangerous' Western values [Buckley, 2013]), restrictions on information flow during the COVID-19 pandemic, and China's dramatically rising military power. Obviously, comparable actions are seen elsewhere—including in the United States itself—but in China's case, these attracted elevated scrutiny because they appeared to represent a change in China's geopolitical stance. Taken with the fear that China's stubborn political non-convergence represented a statement of international intent, these markers reinforced the new vicious cycle of suspicion of China.[3]

By 2018, the US position on China had concretised into policy statements such as those by the US Secretary of Defense James Mattis, who stated, 'Great Power competition, not terrorism, is now the primary focus of US national security' (DOD, 2018). On China, he stated that the United States and the West

> face growing threats from revisionist powers . . . that . . . seek to create a world consistent with their authoritarian models, pursuing veto authority over other nations' economic, diplomacy, and security decisions . . . . [China persists] in taking outlaw actions that threaten regional and even global stability. Oppressing their own people and shredding their own people's dignity and human rights, they push their warped views outward.
>
> (DOD, 2018)

Such views are much more jarring in comparison to Clinton's 2000 'Jell-O to the wall' understanding of the disruptive or commanding power of states such as China. These views also stand in stark contrast to earlier positions held by US leadership in the centripetal era and earlier, which strove to bring China into the international system. US President Richard M. Nixon, for instance, wrote in 1967 that the United States

> cannot afford to leave China forever outside the family of nations, there to nurture its fantasies, cherish its hates and threaten its neighbors . . . . [t]here

> is no place on this small planet for a billion of its potentially most able people to live in angry isolation.
>
> (Nixon, 1967)

Circumstances had thus reversed the train of argument in political convergence, and geopolitics had turned into a force for fragmentation rather than coalescence.

All nations are, of course, increasingly empowered by technology to be able to undertake 'outlaw actions that threaten regional and even global instability' (DOD, 2018). Yet what are the incentives of different nations to do so? When Nixon wrote the passage cited, China was indeed a dangerous country. The nation was in the throes of the Cultural Revolution that caused over 1 million deaths and the arbitrary persecution of millions; it was feared to be actively exporting a Communist revolution around the globe. Today's China does none of these things; it is known for bringing 700 million out of poverty and helping the world reach Sustainable Development Goals. China's most notable exports are still feared—but for their competitiveness and economic impact on other nation's industries, not for their incompatible ideology.

In this reversal from coalescence to fragmentation, China's role is not just a counterexample to political convergence. China has also become the source—for the United States and other Western economies—of 'China shock', or the idea that one's trading partner is stealing one's jobs, dismantling one's industry, and turning one's thriving middle-class communities into ghost towns. How can trade do all this when it is supposed to bring mutual benefits?

In the IMF view described previously, economic efficiency and comparative advantage give rise to outcomes that benefit all sides. This happens at the level of aggregate well-being; thus, they remain forces for coalescence through the perspective of international policy-making. The costs of decoupling are high. However, at the level of individual agents in the United States or other developed countries, the lived experience from trade differs from the positive effects at the aggregate level. Trade does not bring economic efficiency nor the welfare impact of comparative advantage; instead, it shifts price ratios. When trade occurs, relative prices change—otherwise, trade would have no effect. Yet any change in relative prices means some agent somewhere experiences reduced prices for what they produce and sell (Quah, 2024a). For affected individuals, this translates into perceptions of China shock—falling employment, shuttered industries, and displaced communities.

It is this price disturbance that matters—not the aggregate welfare improvement, income inequality, or aggregate bilateral trade deficits.[4] The relevant negative price shock can affect those at the top of income distribution as easily as it can those at the bottom. Thus, an effect on income inequality is neither necessary nor sufficient for political resistance to trade. Even if inequality falls, those at the top of income distribution can find cause to rally against trade. By the same reasoning, a negative price shock from trade can worsen the well-being of those affected, whether the trade balance is in surplus or deficit or a trade deficit is large or small. Such a price shock is, of course, not inconsistent with standard concerns over inequality and trade deficits, but it can take effect regardless of what happens to inequality and trade deficits. Neither inequality nor the trade deficit are sufficient statistics for understanding the impact of trade.

Research on prices and the political consequences of trade is not as widely available as that on inequality or trade balances. Figure 5.1 shows the dynamics of US import prices; imports from China, Mexico, and Canada; and the US Consumer Price Index.[5]

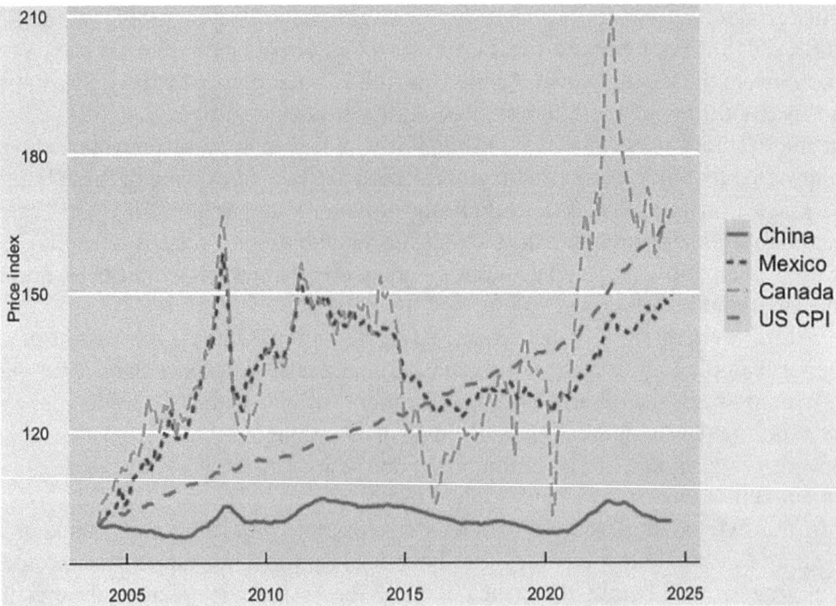

Figure 5.1 United States Import and Domestic Prices, 2003–2024

US CPI = United States Consumer Price Index.

Note: The graph shows, from 2003 to 2024, prices of imports into the United States from China, Mexico, and Canada, alongside the US CPI. In the 2 decades plotted, China's import prices into the United States have remained flat, only 0.5% higher at the end than at the beginning. In contrast, imports from Canada have seen price inflation higher even than in the US Consumer Price Index, ending the 2-decade period with prices 68% higher than at the beginning. Imports from Mexico, similarly but not as extreme, had prices ending 49% higher than at the start. The US CPI inflated 65% over this sample.

Source: United States Census Bureau, International Trade Data, https://www.census.gov/foreign-trade/data/index.html.

A first observation is that import prices do not uniformly remain low. In the figure, in the normalisation adopted, all price indexes begin at 100 in 2003. Both Mexico and Canada import prices show inflation rates higher than that in the US Consumer Price Index. This is not unexpected or unusual; compositions of import bundles change, and when those bundles shift into containing higher-technology products, import price inflation can be high. Indeed, over the entire time sample, import prices from Mexico and Canada have, separately, shown both acceleration and slowdown in cycles over time.

The most striking observation, however, is that concerning imports from China. China's move from low-tech to high-tech exports barely moved how much the United States had to pay for imports from China generally. Price inflation in China imports has been zero over the entire 2 decades in contrast to that in the US Consumer Price Index of 65%, Canada import prices of 68%, and Mexico import prices of 49%. China imports into the United States have remained dramatically cheap, although by 2024, almost half of that flow had become machinery and mechanical appliances, no longer low-quality toys and textiles. Keeping import prices low in this way is remarkable for the compositional change that must have occurred in this time. Towards the beginning of this time period, the view on China's production had been that with a per capita income at the same level as Guyana and the Philippines; most of the Chinese population did not have enough money to buy advanced technological products or have the resources to invent them (Allison et al., 2021).

Two concrete implications are notable. First, China's exports to the United States have strongly benefited US consumers, keeping prices low and the cost of living down. Second, however, by exactly the same observation, the China shock is significant for US workers in the same industries. These price dynamics are why those workers see jobs vanishing, industries being dismantled, and ghost towns emerging where middle-class communities once thrived.

The broader geo-economics dimension, too, turned in the late 2010s. The earlier themes of economic efficiency and comparative advantage were ones where every participant could find agreement with the outcome, as the exchange gave advantages to everyone (i.e. win-win). In the late 2010s, China grew rich; other countries did as well, spreading economic prosperity and thus increasing agency and capability to more parts of the world. The world thus became more multipolar, moving away from US unipolarity. This did not mean other parts of the world were growing to become direct rivals of the global hegemon; a decline in unipolarity does not mean automatically a rise in bipolarity. It meant that the distribution of power across the global landscape had become more diffuse. This growing multi-polarity—a shift in the distribution of economic and military capabilities towards a more uniform distribution rather than remaining single-peaked in only the United States—is, of course, another way to characterise economic convergence. There is lessening prominence of poles in the distribution of power.

Multilateralism—the idea that there is a level playing field and that all players obey the same set of rules—emerged from the principles of economic efficiency and comparative advantage. Multilateralism has allowed economic convergence to occur from the early 2010s and produce multi-polarity. Paradoxically, this combination of multilateralism and multi-polarity has generated a pull-back from further coalescence, however. Increasing multi-polarity means that the benefits advanced economies derive from supporting global public goods, such as international trade, are shared more with other countries (Gaspar, Hagan, Obstfeld, 2018). Turning away from continuing to support the provision of global public goods, like the international trading system, denotes a retreat from the globalisation and multilateralism that had been so powerful for coalescing the global economy. Maintaining multilateralism is difficult and especially challenging when others start to win as well.

5.4 Proposals

With both geopolitics and economics now centrifugal, the global challenge is no longer choosing the incorrect point on a trade-off locus. Instead, the danger is that nations end up in a prisoner's dilemma or epic fail gridlock. Armstrong and Quah (2023) and Quah (2024b) suggested that in such a situation, there are three policy options.

First, look for inadvertent cooperation. Obviously, in a prisoner's dilemma outcome, if all players decide to collaborate, equilibrium could shift to an outcome where all improve their well-being. A fragmented world order, however, is unlikely to be one where contractual obligations are trusted. The international community should thus seek cooperation without binding contracts; economists are familiar with such arrangements. Adam Smith characterised that 'it is not from the benevolence of the butcher, the brewer, or the baker that we expect our dinner, but from their regard to their own interest'. An example of such unplanned cooperation occurred the 2020s in the South China Sea, where individual nations have overlapping territorial claims. Instead of giving in to an all-out rivalry, South-East Asian nations have been able to agree on a code of conduct for that body of water and continue to seek China's participation in that agreement.

Second is the possibility of navigating a fractured international system by looking to Third Nations—those that are not Great Powers in direct contention—to nudge Great Powers out of prisoner's dilemmas (Quah, 2024b). Through small side payments—that, in the cooperative outcome, may not be needed but whose availability is guaranteed—gridlock can be averted, and the usual prisoner's dilemma outcome removed as a possible equilibrium.

Third are options that recognise how a fragmented global economy makes it impossible to have universal multilateral solutions. Yet the spirit of multilateral problem-solving can be maintained in smaller subsets of the international community for restricted problem domains. These solutions can be thought of as providing pathfinder, plurilateral outcomes in the absence of full and complete multilateralism. An example of this is the World Trade Organization's Multi-Party Interim Appeal Arbitration Agreement (MPIA). In March 2020, with the World Trade Organization Appellate Body understaffed and non-functioning, 16 WTO members set up the MPIA to decide on cases between members of the group itself.

5.5 Conclusion

When observers and policymakers acknowledge the risks of a fractured global economy and world order, it is often assumed that geopolitics is to blame. The typical accompanying hypothesis is that economics can hold world order together. IMF and many others believe in the view that economic exchange across nations makes mutual benefits to trade apparent and notes the tremendous costs of economic decoupling and deglobalisation.

This chapter has argued that large geopolitical and economic forces do, indeed, drive world order. However, their direction does not support the hypothesis that economics can provide a centripetal force for the international system. Between 1980 and 2010, both geopolitical and economic forces powered the coalescing of world order. However, after 2010, both forces reversed direction and contributed, instead, to the current fragmentation of the international system.

That economics can be a centrifugal force hinges on effects similar to two familiar ideas: (i) trade increases inequality and (ii) trade deficits attract political objections. In the United States and the developed West, such effects are commonly thought of as the China Shock, as China is a large trading economy that attracts the greatest political attention. The China Shock mechanism proposed in this chapter is centred on price change and is thus simpler and more direct than in narratives of inequality or trade deficits.

That economics no longer holds the global economy together means that fragmentation risks to the global economy cannot be mitigated by recalibrating trade patterns. The problem instead rests on how trade itself is perceived to be the problem. Three recommendations would help mitigate these problems of geopolitical and economic fracture: (i) inadvertent cooperation, (ii) Third Nations nudging the Great Powers away from gridlock, and (iii) pathfinder or plurilateral adjustments to multilateralism.

Notes

* The author thanks members of the International Economic Association (IEA) New World Order group for helpful comments.

1 World order—the international economic system, together with the norms and conventions determining relations across nations—is a point in a high-dimensional topological space. Over time, world order evolves as a function of its past values with a vector of driving variables, including geopolitical and economic forces. The latter may be exogenous or causally prior with respect to world order or, more typically, be jointly determined (i.e., world order with geopolitical and economic forces can be viewed as a vector autoregression in an appropriately defined topological space). This chapter describes the features of the propagation mechanism and impulses determining that vector autoregression, and hence the dynamics of world order.

2 Popular writing in the 1990s sometimes associated variants of this thinking with neoliberalism, the Washington Consensus, and other labels. Many of the central ideas in those, however, vary from those in the current chapter. This chapter considers outcomes but does not comment on the pathways to achieve those goals. There is, for instance, no suggestion in this chapter that free markets and fiscal discipline—key components of neoliberalism—are the only means to achieve efficiency and to leverage comparative advantage. Nor does it suggest that increasing democracy is a precondition needed to guarantee economic success. The Washington Consensus was not a plank for building world order; instead, it sought to provide concrete policy proposals for specific problems facing, mainly, Latin American economies. More detailed analyses are available that unpack the differences across neoliberalism, the Washington Consensus, and other similar labels, such as Naim (1999), Rodrik (2006), Spence (2021), and Williamson (2002).

3 An illustration of both the ambiguity and extreme risk lies in China's August 2021 demonstration of its Fractional Orbital Bombardment System (FOBS) capabilities. FOBS, initially developed by the Soviet Union in the 1960s, refers to the launch of a nuclear warhead off of a hypersonic glide vehicle in low earth orbit. China's approach to FOBS sacrifices accuracy for range, speed, and undetectability; this renders FOBS less suited

for first-strike actions but improves its second-strike retaliatory capability (Kaushal and Cranny-Evans, 2021). Indeed, China's own public announcements confirm this general perception of retaliation, in that FOBS allows 'using nuclear forces [so] US forces cannot crush China' and that 'when the Chinese people have this weapon . . . , nuclear blackmail toward the people of the world will be completely destroyed' (Fravel, 2019). China may be responding endogenously to US action and seeking only to achieve equilibrium, or China may be actively seeking primacy in a way that needs to be countered. The centrifugal era favours the second view.

4 This corresponds to Adão et al. (2022); Autor, Dorn, Hanson (2013); and others. However, it also emphasises price effects directly rather than the impact of trade working through inequality or aggregate trade balances.

5 United States Census Bureau. "International Trade Data." https://www.census.gov/foreign-trade/data/index.html. Import prices are monthly import price indexes by origin, all industries, for China, Mexico, and Canada, respectively, while the US Consumer Price Index is for all items less food and energy taken as the US city average for all urban consumers. The series are normalised to all begin at 100 in December 2003, the earliest date for which China and Mexico data are available.

References

Adão, Rodrigo, Paul Carrillo, Arnaud Costinot, Dave Donaldson, and Dina Pomeranz. 2022. "Imports, Exports, and Earnings Inequality: Measures of Exposure and Estimates of Incidence." *The Quarterly Journal of Economics* 137 (3): 1553–614. https://doi.org/10.1093/qje/qjac012.

Allison, Graham, Kevin Klyman, Karina Barbesino, and Hugo Yen. 2021. *The Great Tech Rivalry: China vs the U.S.* The Belfer Center for Science and International Affairs, Harvard Kennedy School. https://www.belfercenter.org/publication/great-tech-rivalry-china-vs-us.

Armstrong, Shiro, and Danny Quah. 2023. "Economics for the Global Economic Order: The Tragedy of Epic Fail Equilibria." *Lee Kuan Yew School of Public Policy Working Papers*, October. https://doi.org/10.48550/arXiv.2310.18052.

Asian Development Bank. 2011. *Asia 2050: Realizing the Asian Century*. Manila: Asian Development Bank. https://www.adb.org/publications/asia-2050-realizing-asian-century.

Autor, David H, David Dorn, and Gordon H Hanson. 2013. "The China Syndrome: Local Labor Market Effects of Import Competition in the United States." *American Economic Review* 103 (6): 2121–68. https://doi.org/10.1257/aer.103.6.2121.

Buckley, Chris. 2013. "China Takes Aim at Western Ideas." *The New York Times*, August 19, 2013, sec. World. https://www.nytimes.com/2013/08/20/world/asia/chinas-new-leadership-takes-hard-line-in-secret-memo.html.

Chen, S., and M. Ravallion. 2010. "The Developing World is Poorer than We Thought, But No Less Successful in the Fight Against Poverty." *The Quarterly Journal of Economics* 125 (4): 1577–625. https://doi.org/10.1162/qjec.2010.125.4.1577.

Clinton, William Jefferson. 2000. "Trade is the Smart Thing." *The New York Times*, March 9, 2000, sec. World. https://www.nytimes.com/2000/03/09/world/clinton-s-words-on-china-trade-is-the-smart-thing.html.

Fravel, M. Taylor. 2019. *Active Defense: China's Military Strategy Since 1949. Princeton Studies in International History and Politics*. Princeton, NJ: Princeton University Press.

Fukuyama, Francis. 1992. *The End of History and the Last Man*. New York; Toronto: Free Press; Maxwell Macmillan Canada; Maxwell Macmillan International.

Georgieva, Kristalina. 2023. "The Price of Fragmentation." *Foreign Affairs*, August 22, 2023. https://www.foreignaffairs.com/united-states/price-fragmentation-global-economy-shock.

Gopinath, Gita. 2024. "How Policymakers Should Handle a Fragmenting World." *Foreign Policy (blog)*. 2024. https://foreignpolicy.com/2024/02/06/how-policymakers-should-handle-a-fragmenting-world/.

Ikenberry, G. J. 2005. "Power and Liberal Order: America's Postwar World Order in Transition." *International Relations of the Asia-Pacific* 5 (2): 133–52. https://doi.org/10.1093/irap/lci112.

Kaushal, Sidharth, and Sam Cranny-Evans. 2021. "China's New Hypersonic Capability." *Royal United Services Institute (blog)*. October 26, 2021. https://rusi.org.

Kindleberger, Charles P. 1996. *World Economic Primacy, 1500 to 1990*. Oxford, UK: Oxford University Press.

Kindleberger, Charles P. 2013. *The World in Depression, 1929–1939*, 40th anniversary ed. Berkeley, CA: University of California Press. https://www.ucpress.edu/books/the-world-in-depression-1929-1939/paper.

Lipset, Seymour Martin. 1959. "Some Social Requisites of Democracy: Economic Development and Political Legitimacy." *American Political Science Review* 53 (1): 69–105. https://doi.org/10.2307/1951731.

Luce, Edward. 2023. "The New Washington Consensus." *Financial Times*, April 19, 2023. https://www.ft.com/content/42922712-cd33-4de0-8763-1cc271331a32.

Mattis, James N. 2018. "Remarks by Secretary Mattis on the National Defense Strategy." *U.S. Department of Defense*, January 19, 2018. https://www.defense.gov/News/Transcripts/Transcript/Article/1420042/remarks-by-secretary-mattis-on-the-national-defense-strategy/https%3A%2F%2Fwww.defense.gov%2FNews%2FTranscripts%2FTranscript%2FArticle%2F1420042%2Fremarks-by-secretary-mattis-on-the-national-defense-strategy%2F.

Naim, Moises. 1999. *Fads and Fashion in Economic Reforms: Washington Consensus or Washington Confusion?* Washington, DC: Foreign Policy Magazine. https://www.imf.org/external/pubs/ft/seminar/1999/reforms/naim.htm.

Nixon, Richard M. 1967. "Asia After Viet Nam." *Foreign Affairs*, October 1, 1967. https://www.foreignaffairs.com/articles/united-states/1967-10-01/asia-after-viet-nam.

Nye Jr, Joseph S. 2021. "With China, a 'Cold War' Analogy is Lazy and Dangerous." *The New York Times*, November 2, 2021, sec. Opinion. https://www.nytimes.com/2021/11/02/opinion/biden-china-cold-war.html.

Pritchett, Lant. 1997. "Divergence, Big Time." *The Journal of Economic Perspectives* 11 (3): 3–17. https://www.jstor.org/stable/2138181.

Quah, Danny. 1996. "Twin Peaks: Growth and Convergence in Models of Distribution Dynamics." *The Economic Journal* 106 (437): 1045. https://doi.org/10.2307/2235377.

Quah, Danny. 1997. "Empirics for Growth and Distribution: Stratification, Polarization, and Convergence Clubs." *Journal of Economic Growth* 2 (1): 27–59. https://www.jstor.org/stable/40215931.

Quah, Danny. 2011. "The Global Economy's Shifting Centre of Gravity: Global Economy's Centre of Gravity." *Global Policy* 2 (1): 3–9. https://doi.org/10.1111/j.1758-5899.2010.00066.x.

Quah, Danny. 2024a. "Economic Principles for A New World Order of Multipolarity and Multilateralism." *Lee Kuan Yew School of Public Policy Working Papers*, April. https://dannyquah.github.io/Storage/2024.03-Danny.Quah-Small-Poor-Trade-Technology.pdf.

Quah, Danny. 2024b. "'Export-Led Growth': The Trade-Technology Relation in Small and Poor Economies." *Lee Kuan Yew School of Public Policy Working Papers*, May. https://dannyquah.github.io/Storage/2024.03-Danny.Quah-Small-Poor-Trade-Technology.pdf.

Rodrik, Dani. 2006. "Goodbye Washington Consensus, Hello Washington Confusion? A Review of the World Bank's Economic Growth in the 1990s: Learning from a Decade of Reform." *Journal of Economic Literature* 44 (4): 973–87. https://doi.org/10.1257/jel.44.4.973.

Spence, Michael. 2021. "Some Thoughts on the Washington Consensus and Subsequent Global Development Experience." *Journal of Economic Perspectives* 35 (3): 67–82. https://doi.org/10.1257/jep.35.3.67.

US Census Bureau. n.d. "International Trade Data." Accessed December 24, 2024. https://www.census.gov/foreign-trade/data/index.html.

Vitor Gaspar, Sean Hagan, and Maurice Obstfeld. 2018. "Steering the World Toward More Cooperation, Not Less." *IMF Blog (blog)*. September 6, 2018. https://www.imf.org/en/Blogs/Articles/2018/09/06/blog-global-cooperation.

Williamson, John. 2002. "Did the Washington Consensus Fail?" *Peterson Institute for International Economics (blog)*. 2002. https://www.piie.com/commentary/speeches-papers/did-washington-consensus-fail.

6 Economic Transformation and the New Economic Order

Lili Yan Ing and Justin Yifu Lin

6.1 Introduction

World economic governance was dominated by major developed countries in the 20th century, with their economic power contributing about half of the global economy. The combined share of seven advanced countries—the United States, United Kingdom, Germany, France, Italy, Canada, and Japan—in world gross domestic product (GDP), measured by purchasing power parity, was 45.9% in 1900, 50.9% in 1950, and 44.9% in 2000 (Maddison, 2010). Due to this economic strength, these seven countries formed the Group of Seven (G7), which was the most influential economic governance in the world in the latter half of the 20th century.

Entering the 21st century, the world economic landscape changed dramatically. The G7's economic weight in the world economy dropped to 36.1% in 2010 and to 30.8% in 2020. As result of this significant change, the G7 was replaced by the G20 in 2008 during the global economic crisis as the leading global economic governance body. In this chapter, this changing global economic order is studied, causes for the change are analysed, and lessons from the change are provided. Section 6.2 depicts the changing landscape across various metrics amongst developed and developing countries. Section 6.3 explores the determinants of economic structure and causes for ongoing structural transformation. Section 6.4 offers conclusions and draws policy recommendations.

6.2 Economic Shifts

Over the past half-century, the global economic landscape has undergone significant transformation, driven by shifts in economic output, trade, manufacturing, and foreign direct investment (FDI).

6.2.1 Economic Output

From 1970 to 2022, the share of developed nations in the global GDP markedly decreased. As previously stated, for example, G7 countries saw their contribution drop from 56.0% to 30.4%. Meanwhile, emerging economies rose in prominence, with China's share jumping from 5.5% to 18.4%. Other significant contributors include South Korea, India, and Association of Southeast Asian Nations (ASEAN) Member States, collectively rising from 6.9% to 15.5% in the global GDP (Figures 6.1a and 6.1b).

DOI: 10.4324/9781003571384-6

(a)

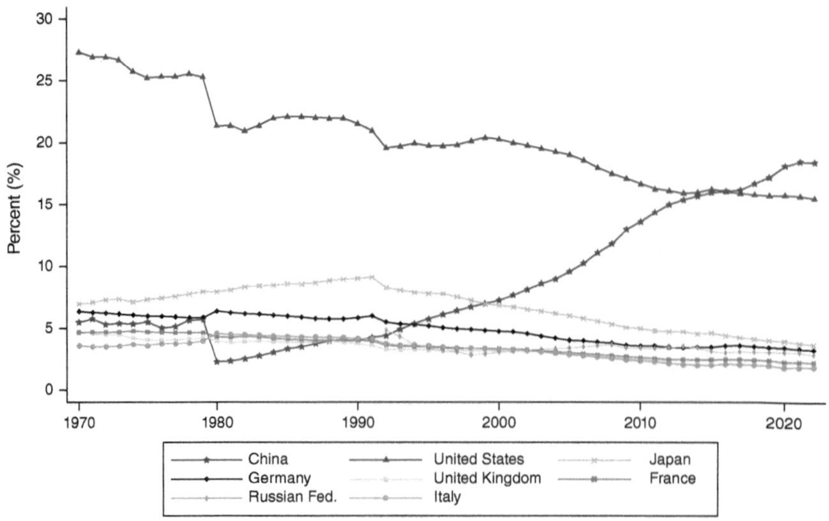

(b)

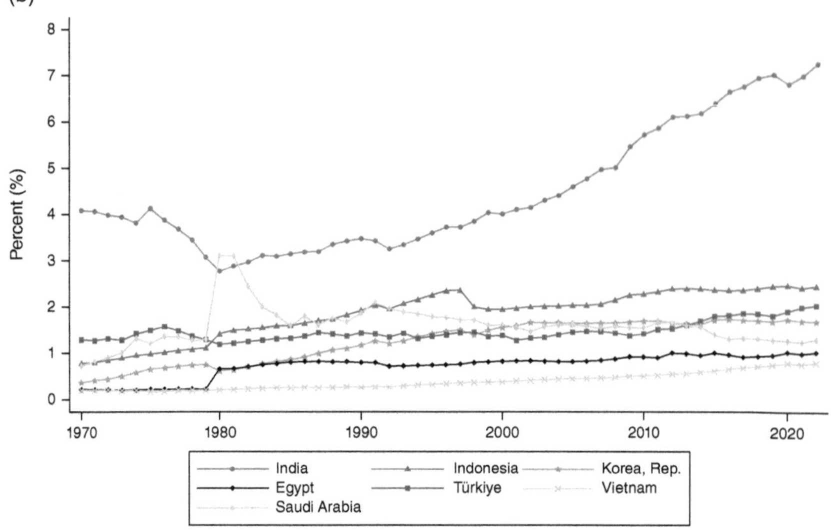

Figure 6.1 Share in World GDP by PPP, 1970–2022 (%): (a) Top 7 Decliners, except China; (b) Top 7 Gainers, excluding China

GDP = gross domestic product, PPP = purchasing power parity

Source: Authors' calculations from University of Groningen, Penn World Table Version 10.01 (1970–79), https://www.rug.nl/ggdc/productivity/pwt/?lang=en [accessed February 2024]; and IMF, GDP Based on PPP, Share of World, https://www.imf.org/external/datamapper/PPPSH@WEO/OEMDC/ADVEC/WEOWORLD [accessed February 2024].

6.2.2 Trade

A shifting dynamic is also evident in global trade. Developed economies' share of trade in goods in the world fell from 81.6% in 1970 to 57.1% by 2022, while high-income developing economies almost tripled their share from 11.5% to 33.4%. China's entry into the World Trade Organization in December 2001 significantly accelerated this shift, showcasing its growing influence in global market (Figures 6.2a and 6.2b).

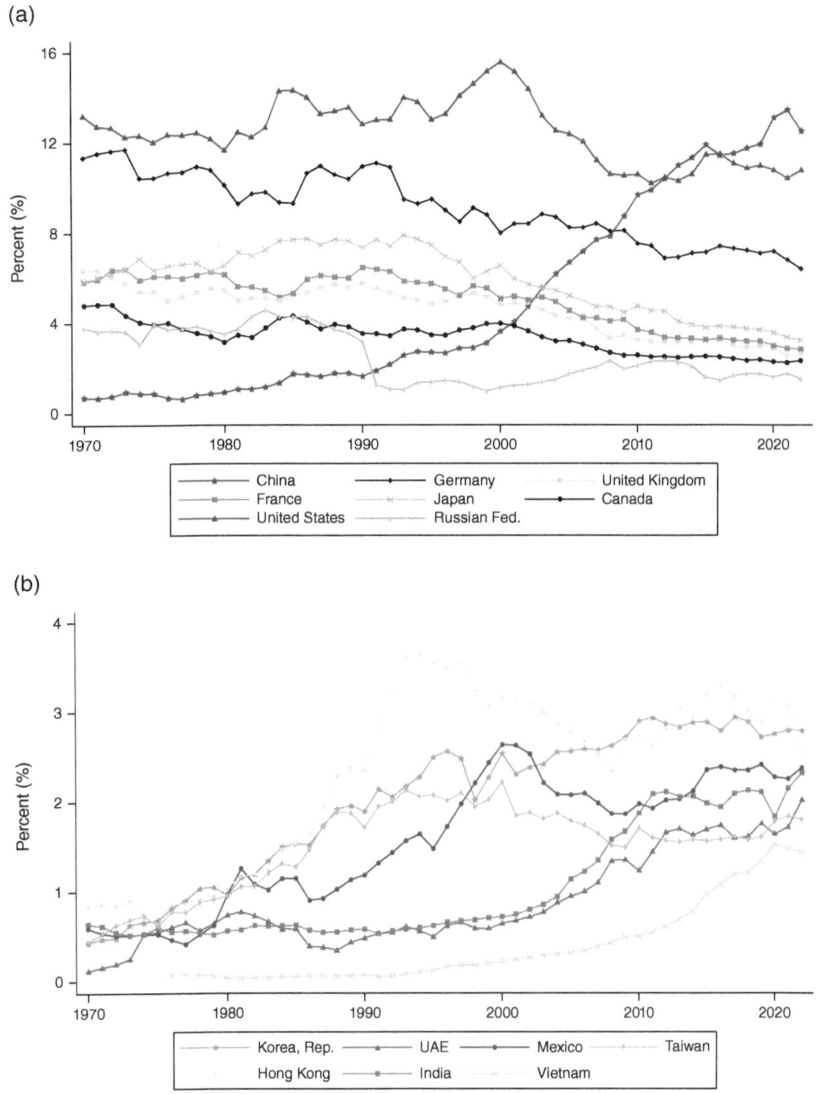

Figure 6.2 Share in World Trade in Goods, 1970–2022 (%): (a) Top 7 Decliners, except China; (b) Top 7 Gainers, excluding China

Source: Authors' calculations from UN Trade and Development, UNCTAD Stat, https://unctadstat.unctad.org/EN/ [accessed December 2022].

6.2.3 Manufacturing

The manufacturing sector has reflected a similar trend, with notable gains in global shares by countries predominantly in Asia, including India, Indonesia, and South Korea. China's share alone has increased by more than 28% since 1970. Conversely, traditional industrial powers such as the United States, Germany, and Japan have seen declines in their shares of global manufacturing value added, underscoring the redistribution of manufacturing strength across the globe (Figures 6.3a and 6.3b).

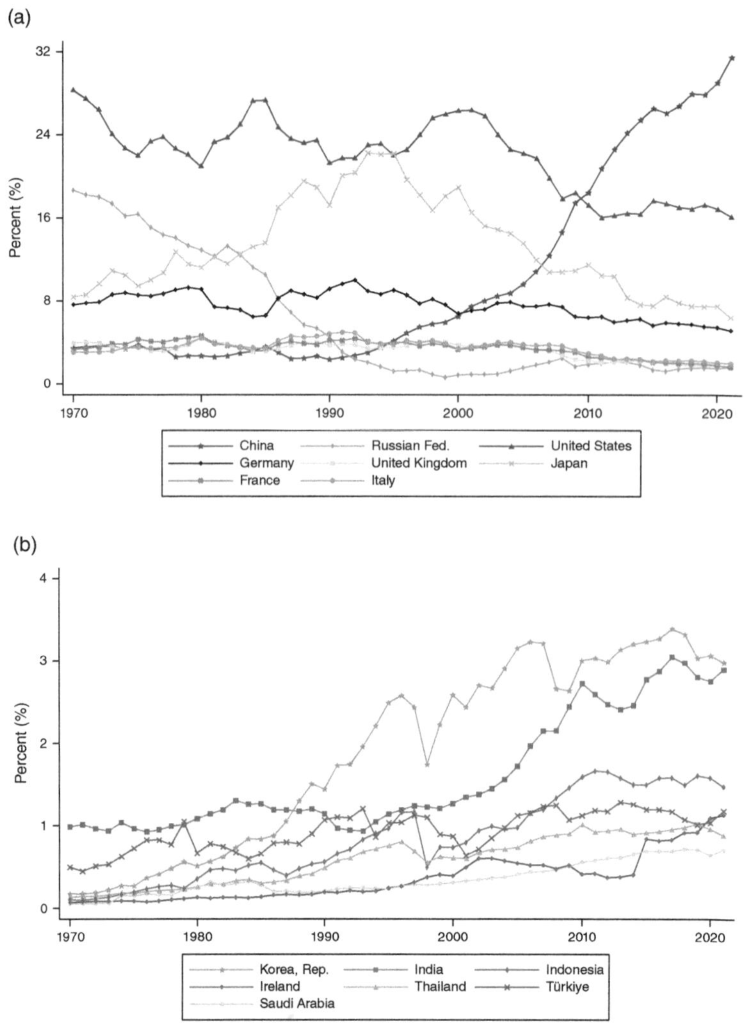

Figure 6.3 Share in World's Manufacturing Value Added, 1970–2022 (%): (a) Top 7 Decliners, except China; (b) Top 7 Gainers, excluding China

Source: Authors' calculations from UN Trade and Development, UNCTAD Stat, https://unctadstat.unctad.org/EN/ [accessed December 2022].

6.2.4 Foreign Direct Investment

In terms of FDI, developed countries' share of global inflows has halved, from 50.4% in 1970 to 25.8% by 2020. Conversely, the Asia Pacific region, including China, India, and ASEAN Member States, has seen significant growth, capturing a larger portion of global FDI inflows. The shift towards these regions reflects their rising importance in the global economic order and decline of traditional economic powerhouses (Figures 6.4, 6.5a, and 6.5b).

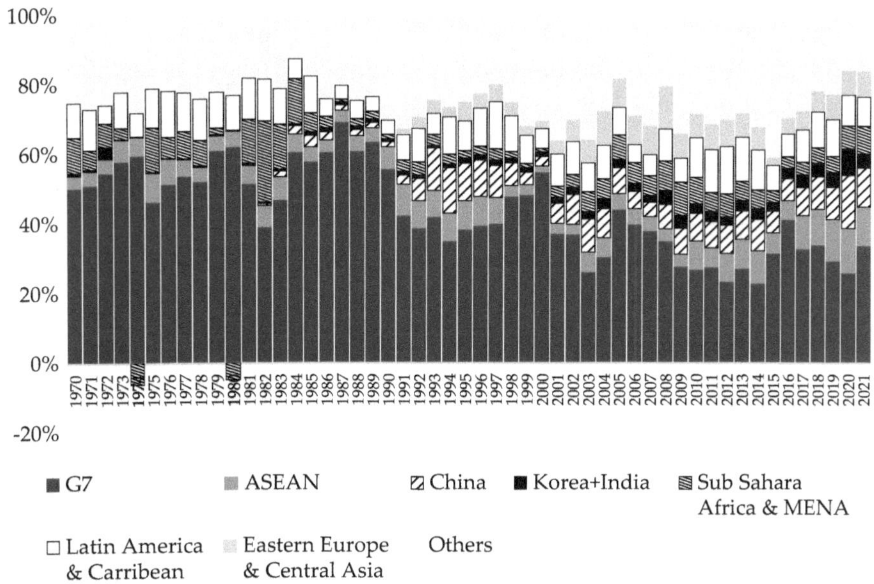

Figure 6.4 Share in World's FDI Inflow of Various Regions: 1970–2021 (%)

ASEAN = Association of Southeast Asian Nations, FDI = foreign direct investment

Source: Authors' calculations from UN Trade and Development, UNCTAD Stat, https://unctadstat.unctad.org/EN/ [accessed December 2022].

Traditionally dominated by the G7 countries, global FDI outflows have also seen a shift. While these developed nations accounted for over 80.0% of global FDI outflows in the 1970s, their share declined to 53.1% by 2021. In contrast, Asia Pacific nations like China, India, and South Korea have increased their contributions. China's FDI outflows, for instance, rose from virtually zero in the 1970s to 19.7% by 2020. This reflects their transition from primarily receiving investments to actively investing abroad, highlighting their growing economic influence and integration into the global market (Figures 6.6, 6.7a, and 6.7b).

The past 50 years have witnessed a reconfiguration of the global economic order, characterised by the decline of the West's economic dominance and rise of emerging economies.

(a)

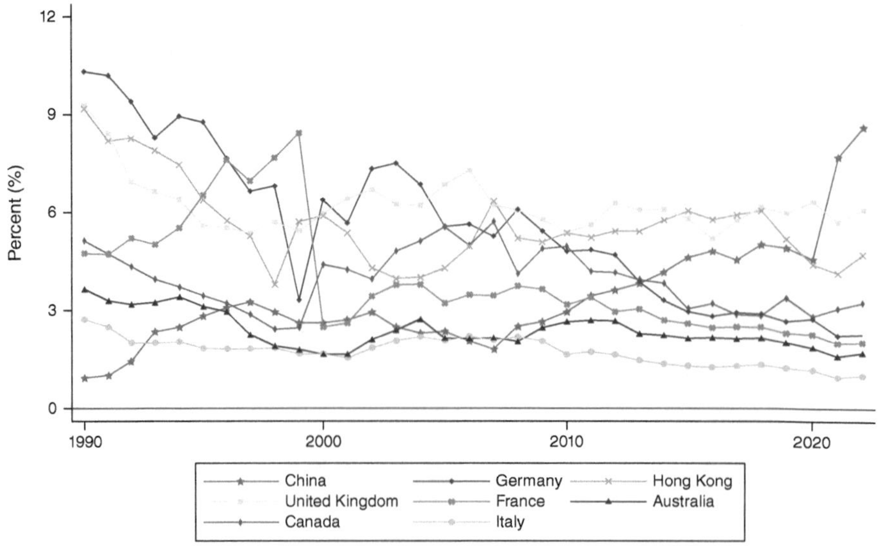

(b)

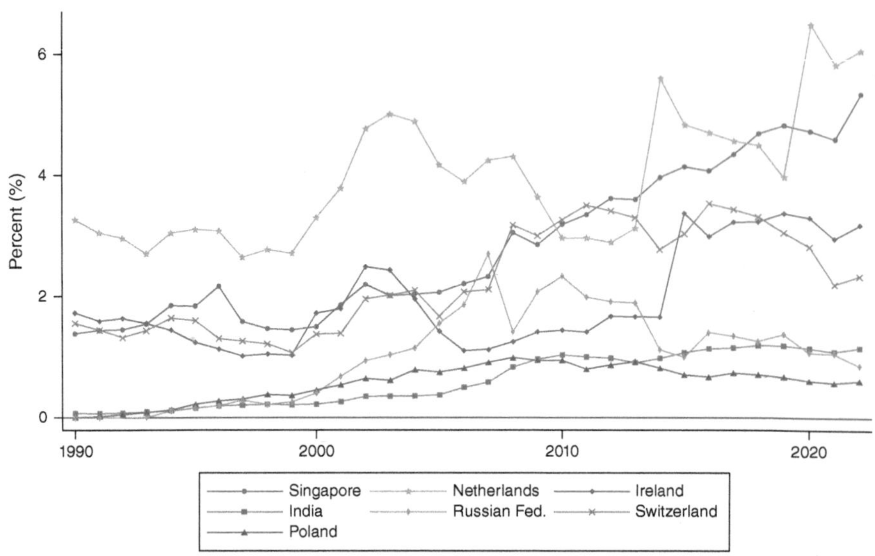

Figure 6.5 Share in World's Inward FDI Stock, 1990–2022 (%): (a) Top 7 Decliners, except China; (b) Top 7 Gainers, excluding China

FDI = foreign direct investment

Source: Authors' calculations from UN Trade and Development, UNCTAD Stat, https://unctadstat.unctad.org/EN/ [accessed December 2022].

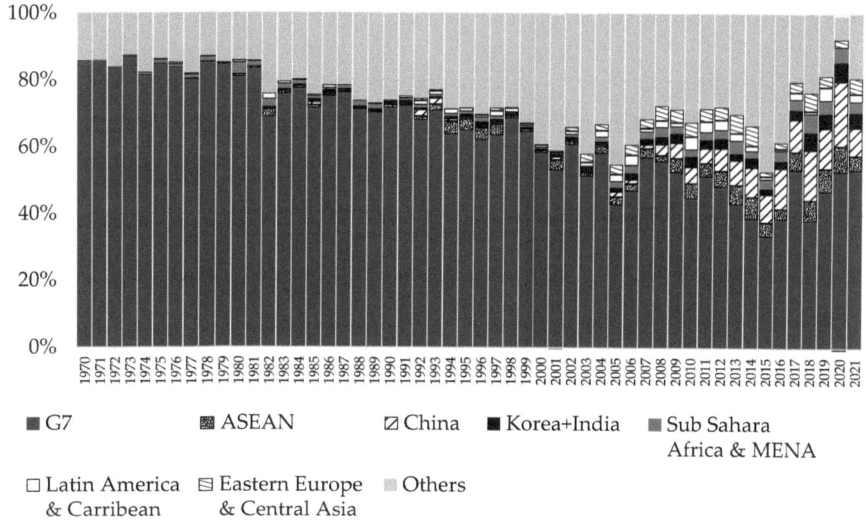

Figure 6.6 Share in World's FDI Outflow of Various Regions, 1970–2021 (%)

ASEAN = Association of Southeast Asian Nations

Source: Authors' calculations from UN Trade and Development, UNCTAD Stat, https://unctadstat.unctad.org/EN/ [accessed December 2022].

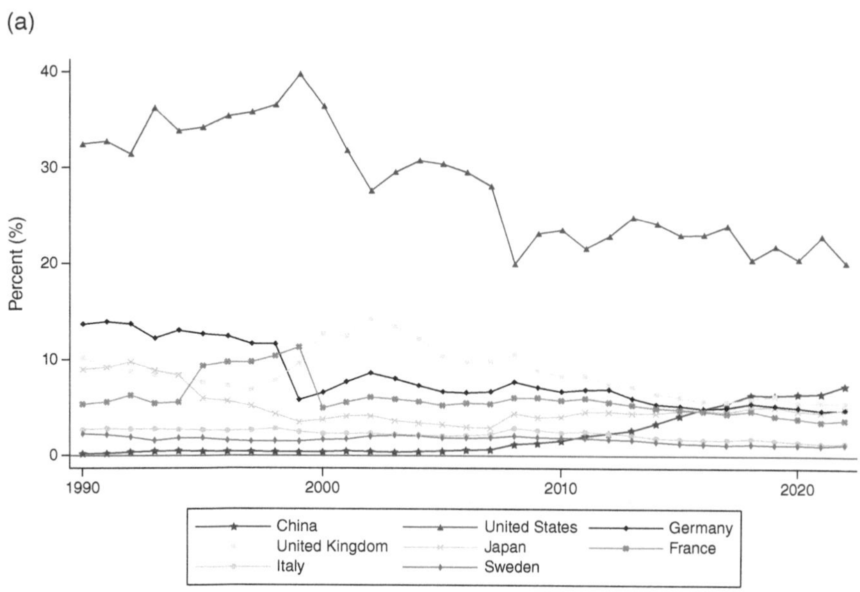

Figure 6.7 Share in World's Outward FDI Stock, 1990–2022 (%): (a) Top 7 Decliners, except China; (b) Top 7 Gainers, excluding China

FDI = foreign direct investment

Source: Authors' calculations from UN Trade and Development, UNCTAD Stat, https://unctadstat.unctad.org/EN/ [accessed December 2022].

(b)

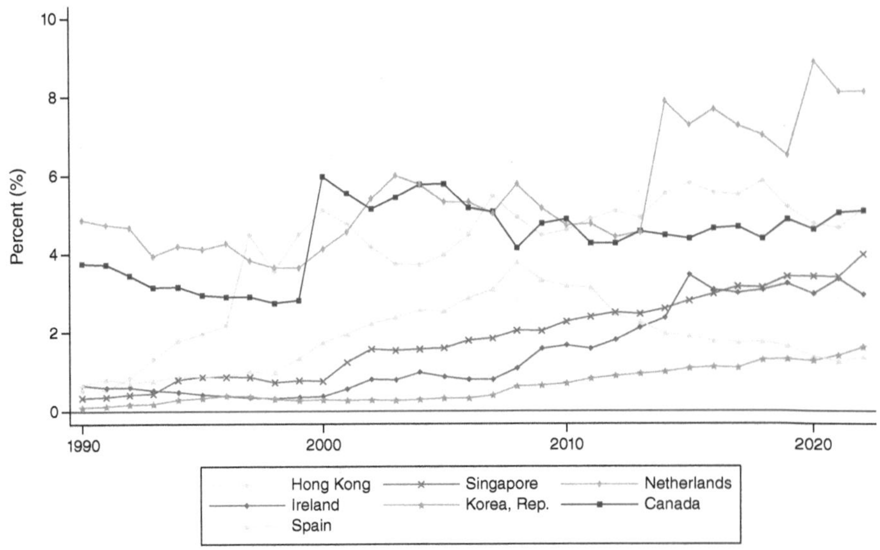

Figure 6.7 (Continued)

This shift has been influenced by a combination of globalisation, capital accumulation, technological advancements, human capital, infrastructure development, and strategic policy implementations by developing nations to harness their economic potential. These trends are likely to continue shaping the economic landscape, with developing economies playing increasingly critical roles in the global economy (Ing and Yu, 2018).

6.3 Economic Structure and Structural Transformation

To obtain a more comprehensive understanding of economic transformation, an extended period must be examined. Substantial transformations, as reflected in GDP, trade, manufacturing value added, and FDI amongst developed and emerging countries from 1970 to 2022 (as reported in Section 6.2) are not primarily caused by significant changes in the growth performance of developed countries but rather by the rapid catch-up of a few developing countries.

As illustrated in Figures 6.8 and 6.9, the average annual growth rates of per capita real GDP and aggregate real GDP in developed economies remained largely stable across the periods 1900–1970 and 1970–2022. Notable exceptions include Italy and Japan, both of which experienced a marked deceleration in real GDP growth—declining by approximately 44% in the latter period.[1] In contrast, the United Kingdom defied this broader trend, exhibiting a significant acceleration in

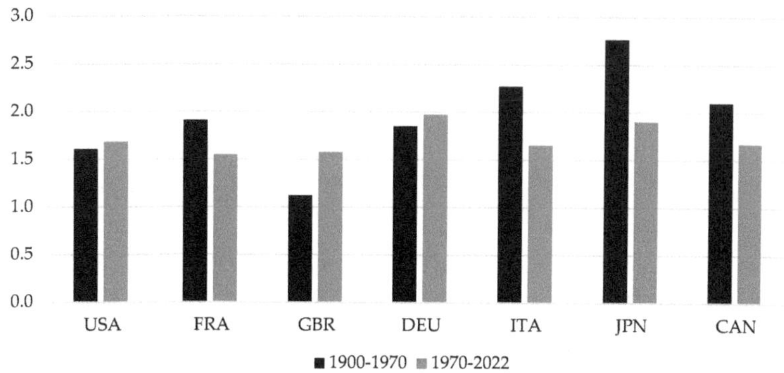

Figure 6.8 Average Annual per Capita GDP Growth Rate in the G7 (%)

CAN = Canada, DEU = Germany, FRA = France, GBR = Great Britain, ITA = Italy, JPN = Japan, USA = United States

Source: Authors' calculations from University of Groningen, Maddison Project Database 2023, https://www.rug.nl/ggdc/historicaldevelopment/maddison/releases/maddison-project-database-2023.

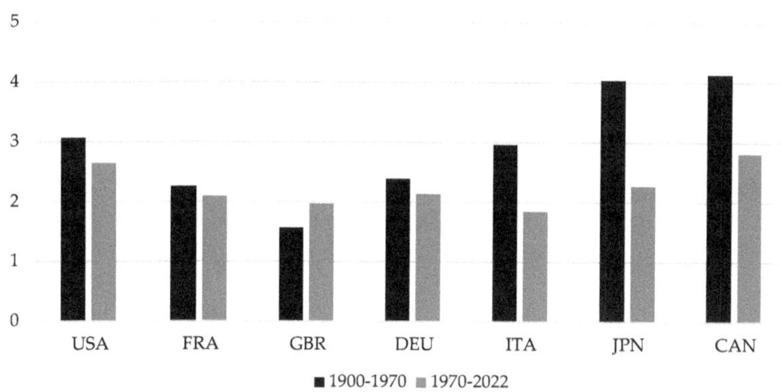

Figure 6.9 Average Annual GDP Growth Rate in the G7 (%)

CAN = Canada, DEU = Germany, FRA = France, GBR = Great Britain, ITA = Italy, JPN = Japan, USA = United States

Source: Authors' calculations from University of Groningen, Maddison Project Database 2023, https://www.rug.nl/ggdc/historicaldevelopment/maddison/releases/maddison-project-database-2023.

per capita GDP growth, which was nearly 50% higher in 1970–2022 compared to the preceding seven decades (Figure 6.8).

The profound shifts in the global economic order over this period were primarily driven by the extraordinary rise of select emerging economies—most notably China, India, Indonesia, and South Korea—whose rapid economic transformation reshaped global production, trade, and investment flows. Meanwhile, several least-developed and developing countries struggled to achieve sustained growth. Some, despite possessing considerable demographic potential, such as Argentina and Brazil in Latin America and Nigeria in Africa, remained ensnared in the middle-income trap. Others, including the Russian Federation, faced severe economic contraction. The divergence in growth trajectories among developing economies during this period underscores the critical role of national development strategies and economic transformation policies in determining long-term economic success.

6.3.1 Endowment Structure, Comparative Advantage, and Production and Trade Structure

Sustainable economic growth is a continuous process of technological innovation, elevating labour productivity, and industrial upgrading, which entails a shift from low-value-added industries to higher-value-added ones in a sustainable manner. However, harnessing the potential of technologies and new industries necessitates well-functioning hard and soft infrastructure. This includes reliable electricity for the application of most modern technology as well as road and port facilities for efficient product transport to large domestic and foreign markets, enabling the full exploitation of economies of scale. As trade sizes increase, market exchanges occur at arm's length, requiring robust contracts and legal systems for contract enforcement.

Additionally, with the scaling and risks associated with technological and industrial upgrading, the financial structure must adapt. Consequently, the entire soft infrastructure of institutions needs improvement (Kuznets, 1966; Lin, 1989; Lin and Nugent, 1995; Harrison and Rodríguez-Clare, 2010). Therefore, while modern economic growth may seem like a process of rising labour productivity, it is, in reality, a continuous process of structural changes encompassing technologies, industries, and both hard and soft infrastructure.

In general, developed countries have capital-intensive industries, while developing countries have land- and/or labour-intensive industries. This difference in industrial structure reflects variations in their factor endowments (i.e. the amounts of capital, labour, and natural resources available at a given time). Developing countries typically face a relative scarcity of capital, while labour and often natural resources are relatively abundant. Conversely, developed countries enjoy an abundance of capital, while labour is relatively scarce. Although an economy's factor endowments, which are the smallest elements for forming any economic activity and determine the economy's total allocable resources, are fixed at any particular time, they can change over time. Furthermore, the structure of endowments determines the relative prices of factors. Prices of relatively abundant factors are low, while prices of relatively scarce factors are high. This implies that the relative prices of capital, labour, and natural resources differ in countries at different development stages. These price differences play a crucial role in determining a country's comparative advantages, production pattern, and trade pattern at each stage of development.

In developed countries, high income and labour productivity result from their relative capital abundance and high total factor productivity, leading to capital-intensive industries and technologies. For a developing country aspiring to match the income and industrial structure of developed nations, the initial step is to elevate the relative abundance of capital in its factor endowment structure to the level seen in advanced countries. The ultimate objective of economic development is to increase a country's income. The intermediate goal involves developing capital-intensive industries as a means, not an end, while the immediate focus should be on swiftly accumulating capital to shift the country's comparative advantages towards more capital-intensive industries (Box 6.1). In essence, elevating a country's income necessitates industrial upgrading, and achieving industrial upgrading requires a transformation to the country's endowment structure (Ju, Lin, Wang, 2015).

Box 6.1 How Can a Country Quickly Accumulate Capital?

To accumulate capital quickly, a country can employ the following strategies:

i. *Align industries with comparative advantages.* Ensure that the country's industries align with its comparative advantages, as determined by its endowment structure, in a market economy with a facilitating state to overcome market failures in the improvements of hard and soft infrastructure. The country must have an open economy, exporting goods and services of its comparative advantages and importing goods and services of other countries' comparative advantages. It must also attract inward foreign direct investment (FDI) from countries with more abundant capital or advanced technologies than its own while providing outward FDI to other countries with relatively less capital or lower technologies. This alignment enhances competitiveness in both domestic and international markets, leading to the generation of the largest possible economic surplus.
ii. *Optimal investment allocation.* Direct investments into industries consistent with the comparative advantages derived from the country's endowment structure. By doing so, returns on investment can be maximised, resulting in a higher propensity to save.
iii. *Maximise returns on investment.* By focussing on industries that leverage the country's comparative advantages, the returns on investments are optimised. This, in turn, encourages higher savings rates, contributing to the rapid accumulation of capital.

iv. *Enhance surplus generation.* Ensure that the economic surplus generated by the country is maximised. When industries are in line with comparative advantages, they are more likely to operate efficiently, leading to increased surplus generation.
v. *Create incentives for savings.* Establish policies and incentives that encourage savings. This can be achieved by fostering a favourable environment for investment in industries aligned with the country's comparative advantages.
vi. *Facilitate changes in industrial infrastructure.* Recognise that changes in endowment structure and comparative advantages lay the groundwork for alterations in industrial structure. Ensure that the accompanying hard and soft industrial infrastructure evolves to support these changes.

By adopting these measures, a country can create conditions conducive to rapid capital accumulation, fostering economic development and growth.

Source: Authors

6.3.2 Role of Market and State in Structural Transformation

A comparative advantage is an economic concept. How is it translated into the choices of technologies and industries made by entrepreneurs? Entrepreneurs pursue profits; they will invest in industries in which a country has a comparative advantage if relative factor prices reflect the relative scarcities of factors in the country's endowments (Lin, 2009; Lin and Chang, 2009). If capital is relatively scarce, the price of capital should be relatively high; if labour is relatively scarce, the price of labour (i.e. wages) should be relatively high. With such a price system, profit-maximising entrepreneurs will use an inexpensive factor to substitute for an expensive factor in their choice of production technologies, investing in industries that require more of an inexpensive factor and less of an expensive factor. A price system with these characteristics can arise only in a competitive market, which is why successful economies are either market economies or on their way to becoming one.

While markets play a crucial role in allowing a country to align with its factor endowments and to determine comparative advantages for technology adoption and industrial development, the government's role in economic development is equally vital. Economic development entails a process of structural transformation characterised by continuous technological innovations, industrial upgrading, and improvements in infrastructure and institutions. As the factor endowment structure evolves, economies necessitate first movers—enterprises willing to embrace new technologies and venture into industries consistent with changing comparative advantages. Nevertheless, the risks for these pioneers are substantial; if they fail, they bear all the losses, and if they succeed, other firms are likely to follow suit. The resulting competition eliminates any monopoly profits (Romer, 1990; Aghion, 2009). An asymmetry exists between the losses of failures and the gains of successes for the first movers (Hausmann and Rodrik, 2003). Regardless of success or failure, first movers provide valuable information to society.

The government's role should be to encourage and to facilitate first movers for the information externality that they generate. Otherwise, there will be little incentive for firms to be pioneers in technological innovation and industrial upgrading (Rodrik, 2004; Lin, 2009, 2011; Lin and Monga, 2011; Harrison and Rodríguez-Clare, 2010). The success or failure of first movers also depends on whether improved hard and soft infrastructure matches the needs of new technologies and industries. Since improving infrastructure and institutions is beyond the capacities of individual firms, the government needs to coordinate firms' efforts in this regard or to provide the necessary improvements for avoiding the middle-income or poverty trap (Lin, 2017).

6.3.3 Dynamic Transformation, Structural Stagnation, and Premature De-Industrialisation

The First Industrial Revolution—according to Clark (2010), the singular event in human history—commenced in the United Kingdom in the mid-18th century, marking a significant turning point in the economic progress of nations. Rapid technological innovation following the advent of the Industrial Revolution created new tools with higher productivity and new industries with higher values, not only breaking the Malthusian trap but also leading to a dramatic increase in per capita income (Kuznets, 1966). From the 18th century to the mid-19th century, the annual growth rate of per capita GDP surged 20 times to 1% in Western Europe and its offshoots in North America and Australia (Maddison, 2001). This rate further doubled to around 2% per year thereafter.

Today, developing countries have the advantage of backwardness in technological innovation, potentially enabling them to grow faster than developed countries (Gerschenkron, 1962). As shown in Figure 6.10, 'successful' developing countries—such as China, India, Indonesia, and South Korea—saw double or

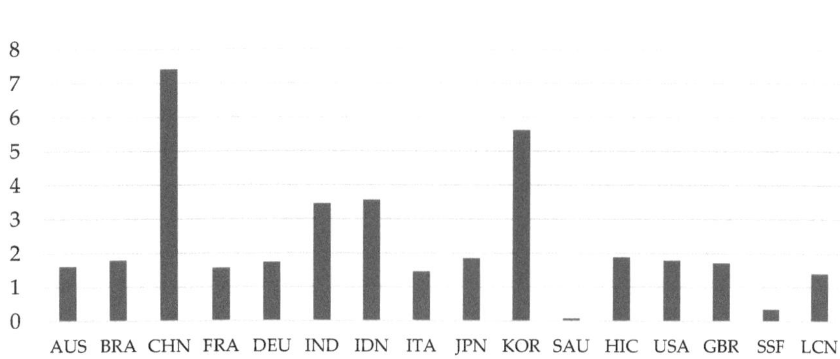

Figure 6.10 Growth Rate of GDP per Capita, 1970–2022 (%)

AUS = Australia, BRA = Brazil, CHN = China, DEU = Germany, FRA = France, GBR = Great Britain, HIC = high-income countries, IDN = Indonesia, IND = India, ITA = Italy, JPN = Japan, KOR = South Korea, LCN = Latin America and the Caribbean, SAU = Saudi Arabia, SSF = Small States Forum, USA = United States

Source: Authors' calculations from World Bank, World Development Indicators, https://databank.worldbank.org/source/world-development-indicators [accessed December 2022].

even triple the annual growth rates of high-income countries from 1970 to 2022. However, countries in Latin America and the Caribbean, as well as in Sub-Saharan Africa, experienced lower annual per capita GDP growth rates of 1.38% and 0.32%, respectively, compared to the 1.86% rate observed in high-income countries during the same period.

The diverse growth performances of developing countries have largely stemmed from differences in the development ideas that they embraced. Post-World War II, developing nations shared a common aspiration—catching up with developed countries to ensure that their populations could attain similar income levels. To achieve this goal, most developing and least-developed countries—regardless of their alignment with socialist or non-socialist ideologies—adopted a structuralist state-led import-substitution strategy. This approach aimed to develop capital-intensive industries akin to those in developed countries.

Under this approach, a country may have latent comparative advantages in certain industries but is unable to produce them due to a lack of adequate soft or hard infrastructure. If the government plays a facilitating role in removing the soft or hard infrastructure bottlenecks for these industries, however, the goods of these industries can turn from imports to domestic production and then start to be exported. Such import substitution is the nature of industrial upgrading, aligning with the change in a country's comparative advantages.

Such import-substitution policies did not work well in many countries, however, as the selection of prioritised industries (i.e. a 'picking winners' strategy) often contradicted their actual comparative advantages. This resulted in firms in those sectors being non-viable in an open and competitive market. Governments thus resorted to various price distortions and direct interventions to allocate resources for the development of advanced modern industries and to shield them from foreign competition (i.e. infant industry policy). Consequently, several economies faced stagnation and frequent crises, leading to a widening income gap between developed and developing countries.

The failure of such import-substitution approaches led to the emergence of neoliberalism in the 1970s and 1980s, which viewed governmental interventions as the primary reason for the failure of developing countries to catch up economically with developed nations. Neoliberalism advocates for a minimal state, advising developing countries to institute well-functioning market institutions similar to those in developed countries through shock therapy. It believes that dynamic growth and structural transformation will happen spontaneously once a well-functioning market is in place.

However, the results for developing countries embracing neoliberalism were disappointing. Growth rates in the 1980s and 1990s were lower than those in the 1960s and 1970s, and the frequency of crises was even higher than in the 1960s and 1970s (Easterly, 2001). Many countries in Latin America and Africa also encountered premature de-industrialisation (Felipe, Mehta, Rhee, 2014; Palma, 2005; Rodrik, 2016). The income gap between developed and developing countries further widened.[2]

As noted previously, before the implementation of market-oriented reforms, many non-viable firms existed in sectors that defied comparative advantages in transition countries. Without governmental support, these firms could not have survived in an open and competitive market. Such support mechanisms were endogenous to the viability issue of protected firms (Lin and Tan, 1999) and often took the form of second-best arrangements. If there were only a limited number of non-viable enterprises—and they were not related to essential services like power, tele-communications, or national security—the output value and employment of those firms were constrained. In such cases, shock therapy, which eliminates all governmental interventions at once, was applicable. With the abolition of governmental protection and subsidies, these non-viable enterprises would have gone bankrupt; however, the originally suppressed labour-intensive industries thrived, and the newly created employment opportunities in these sectors outweighed the losses from the bankruptcy of non-viable firms. As a result, the economy experienced dynamic growth soon after implementing the shock therapy, which was what economist Jeffrey Sachs recommended to and succeeded with in Bolivia in the 1980s.

On the contrary, if the number of non-viable firms were large, their employment constituted a significant share of the national economy, such as capital-intensive industries in the socialist-planned economies. Their services were essential for normal economic operations in the economy (e.g. firms in the power, energy, and telecommunications sectors). Shock therapy, instead of achieving the intended first best result, exacerbated the economic performance due to the second-best nature of those protections and subsidies (Lipsey and Lancaster, 1956). Governments often adopted other more disguised and costly measures after the shock therapy, and many owners of telecommunications and other large enterprises became oligarchic, leading to the lost decades observed in many transition economies in Eastern Europe, the former Soviet Union, and Latin America (Lavigne, 1995; Easterly, 2001). Moreover, these countries also encountered premature de-industrialisation because many of the comparative-advantage-defying industries collapsed after the government's removal of subsidies and protections of the non-viable firms in those industries. The government failure to help new industries turn from latent to actual comparative advantages by removing bottlenecks in hard and soft infrastructure for the industries also contributed.

Therefore, it is most desirable to have a strategy focussed on providing transitional support to non-viable firms in old priority sectors while facilitating private firms' entry into sectors consistent with a country's comparative advantages. Economic stability and dynamic growth can be achieved simultaneously via this measure. With dynamic growth, capital will accumulate; factor endowment structure as well as comparative advantages will change; and many firms in the previous priority sectors will turn from non-viable to viable, making protections and subsidies unessential. By that time, the economy will be ready to eliminate distortions and subsidies and to transit to a well-functioning market economy (Lin, 2009, 2015).

Overall, a developing country with the right development and transition strategies can grow faster than developed countries and thus increase its weight in the global GDP. In the catching-up process, it can move up the industrial ladder from resources- and/or labour-abundant industries to capital- and technology-intensive manufacturing industries. With the increase in its economic size, the country's weights in global trade can also increase. Moreover, the country can attract inward FDI towards utilising the country as a production base for export as well as to penetrate its increasingly large domestic market. Meanwhile, in its structural transformation process, the country can provide outward FDI to relocate comparative advantage-losing industries to other lower-income countries and to help industries with the country's comparative advantages enter the markets of other countries.

6.4 Policy Recommendations

Drawing insights from the growth and structural transformation patterns observed in both developed and developing countries, and considering the emerging opportunities and challenges posed by the Fourth Industrial Revolution—particularly in the context of digitalisation, which is poised to exert a substantial influence on growth performance and the global economic order in the future—certain policy recommendations come to the forefront.

i. Optimise Comparative Advantages and Effective Infrastructure

A critical element of economic transformation involves a country's capacity to optimise its comparative advantages and to implement effective interventions, focussing on both hard and soft infrastructure. It is crucial to strike a balance between interventions by the state and market forces. Emphasising the state's role is essential in creating a favourable trade and investment environment that facilitates entrepreneurs in developing industries with latent comparative advantages. This involves identifying and addressing externalities that the market may not correct on its own, such as removing infrastructure bottlenecks, and, if necessary, incentivising first movers, particularly in research and development.

Effective infrastructure development extends beyond physical structures such as roads, bridges, and special economic zones to soft infrastructure, encompassing education systems, health care, public services (e.g. electricity and information and communications technology, clean water, and waste management), digital connectivity, and a robust legal and financial framework. Well-developed hard and soft infrastructure significantly enhance a country's global competitiveness by reducing the cost of doing business, improving efficiency, attracting FDI, and increasing trade, thereby allowing firms to operate at optimal levels of economies of scale.

Note that a country's comparative advantages are not static but evolve over time. Dynamic economic growth alters the economy's endowment structure and comparative advantages. Policymakers must remain vigilant and adaptive, ready to shift focus as the economy grows and changes, adopting realistic and context-specific strategies.

ii. Adopt a Gradual Transition Strategy

It is inherent in economic cycles that many countries inherit various distortions due to a government's past political situation or development strategy, or a combination of both. The effectiveness of transition policies often depends on their phased implementation. A gradual transition strategy may be desirable, which involves providing necessary support to non-viable firms in industries that defy comparative advantages while offering support to new industries aligned with latent comparative advantages. Such a strategy may help a country achieve stability and dynamic growth simultaneously during the transition process.

Gradual transformation—both in political and economic spheres—will help a transition be successful. First, governments should establish clear timelines and exit strategies for any incentives and facilities provided to specific sectors or industries. This ensures that support is phased out systematically. Second, recognising that a country's comparative advantages are dynamic, it is crucial to ensure that all sectors keep pace with new developments and technologies. Regular assessments should guide adjustments in the focus of support. Third, beyond the active promotion of special economic zones, governments should focus on developing human capital capable of adapting to new technologies. This includes initiatives to enhance the skills of the workforce, enabling mobility across sectors. By addressing these aspects, governments can facilitate a smooth and manageable transition, minimising disruptions while steadily integrating the economy into the global market.

iii. Optimise the Use of Digital Transformation

Digitalisation, which involves using internet-of-things information systems to digitise and to create intelligent logistics, supply chains, manufacturing, delivery, sales, personalised customer preferences, and all management tasks, ultimately aims to achieve fast, effective, and personalised product supply. The Fourth Industrial Revolution offers unparalleled opportunities for economic transformation in both developed and developing countries.

Similar to structural transformation driven by technological innovation and industrial upgrading in previous industrial revolutions, governments play a pivotal role in harnessing the opportunities presented by digitalisation. This requires a multi-faceted strategy that includes the development of digital infrastructure, fostering digital literacy and skills, and creating a regulatory environment conducive to digital innovation.

Digitalisation should be integrated into broader economic development strategies, recognising digital technology not merely as a sector but as a key enabler across all sectors of the economy, including agriculture, manufacturing, and services. Effective digital transformation necessitates collaboration between the public and private sectors. Governments can play a role in facilitating this collaboration, ensuring that the private sector's innovation and efficiency align with public goals, including customer security, inclusivity, and sustainability.

Investing in digital infrastructure should go beyond traditional physical infrastructure as well. It involves the development of broadband networks, mobile connectivity, and digital platforms that are accessible to all segments of society. This infrastructure forms the backbone of a modern digital economy, enabling businesses and individuals to participate fully in digital activities. Special attention should be given to rural and underserved areas to ensure equitable access to digital infrastructure; indeed, bridging the urban–rural digital divide is crucial for inclusive economic growth. Part of digital infrastructure development also includes enhancing e-government services. Making government services more accessible and efficient through digital means can significantly improve public sector efficiency and transparency.

Governments should formulate policies and legal frameworks that establish a conducive environment and a level playing field for digital innovation. This involves regulatory structures that not only encourage entrepreneurship but also safeguard intellectual property and facilitate investments in the digital sector. Small and medium-sized enterprises and startups are often at the forefront of digital innovation, and governments should establish support systems for these entities. This support can include access to finance, mentorship programmes, and the creation of innovation hubs. Additionally, governments should develop robust policies and regulations to ensure customer protection, data privacy, and cybersecurity (Ing, Grossman, Christian, 2022).

As economies undergo digitalisation, the skills required by the workforce undergo a transformation. Governments must accordingly adapt their education and training systems to meet these changing demands. This adaptation involves not only integrating digital skills into curricula but also cultivating an educational environment that fosters creativity, critical thinking, and adaptability. The rapid pace of technological change underscores the importance of focussing on lifelong learning and continuous skills development. Governments should actively promote and support ongoing education and re-skilling opportunities for workers to remain relevant in the evolving job market. Collaborating with the industry to develop education and training programmes is crucial to ensure that the skills taught align with market needs. This collaboration can take the form of partnerships with tech companies, industry-led training programmes, and apprenticeships.

In essence, digital technology paves the way for economic diversification. Embracing digital technology enables countries to forge new sectors and to revitalise existing industries, fostering more diversified and resilient economies. The transformative power of digitalisation extends to traditional industries, rendering them more efficient, innovative, and competitive. This transformative process involves the integration of digital technologies into sectors like agriculture, manufacturing, and services, amplifying productivity and expanding market reach. Simultaneously, the development of high-value digital services—such as software development, digital content creation, and data analytics—creates new economic avenues and propels nations up the value chain in the global economy.

Notes

1 The slight declines in the latter period in these developed countries reflect the failures to fully recover from the 2008 global economic crisis.
2 Interestingly, a few countries that successfully accelerated their growth and narrowed the gap with developed nations did not adhere to the approaches proposed by the dominant development thinking of that time. In the 1950s and 1960s, Japan and the four 'Asian Tigers'—Hong Kong, Singapore, South Korea, and Taiwan—caught up with developed countries. These newly industrialising economies experienced rapid growth from the 1950s to the 1970s by adopting export-oriented development strategies. They initially focussed on labour-intensive, small-scale industries and gradually climbed the industrial ladder to larger, more capital-intensive sectors (Amsden, 1992; Wade, 1990; Lin, 2009; Chang, 2021). Their approach contradicted the prevailing structuralism, which advocated for import substitution to immediately build up large, heavy industries (World Bank, 1993).

References

Aghion, Philippe. 2009. "Some Thoughts on Industrial Policy and Growth." *Observatoire Français Des Conjonctures Économiques, Document de Travail 2009-09*, April. https://www.ofce.sciences-po.fr/pdf/dtravail/WP2009-09.pdf.

Amsden, Alice H. 1992. *Asia's Next Giant: South Korea and Late Industrialization. Oxford Paperbacks*. New York: Oxford University Press. https://doi.org/10.1093/0195076036.001.0001.

Chang, Ha-Joon. 2021. *Kicking Away the Ladder: Development Strategy in Historical Perspective. Anthem Studies in Development and Globalization*, 1st ed. London: Anthem Press. https://anthempress.com/kicking-away-the-ladder-pb.

Clark, Gregory. 2010. *A Farewell to Alms: A Brief Economic History of the World. The Princeton Economic History of The Western World*. Princeton, NJ: Princeton University Press. https://press.princeton.edu/books/paperback/9780691141282/a-farewell-to-alms?srsltid=AfmBOoqgUebCjN-a6tBDURMts93KocBZliwgga1Ij6tgSxx6UaiSPLGI.

Easterly, William. 2001. "The Lost Decades: Developing Countries' Stagnation in Spite of Policy Reform 1980–1998." *Journal of Economic Growth* 6 (2): 135–57. https://www.jstor.org/stable/40215870.

Felipe, Jesus, Aashish Mehta, and Changyong Rhee. 2014. "Manufacturing Matters . . . But It's The Jobs That Count." *Asian Development Bank, ADB Economics Working Paper Series, no. 420*. https://doi.org/10.1093/cje/bex086.

Gerschenkron, Alexander. 1962. *Economic Backwardness in Historical Perspective: A Book of Essays*. Cambridge, MA: Belknap Press of Harvard University Press.

Harrison, Ann, and Andrés Rodríguez-Clare. 2010. "Trade, Foreign Investment, and Industrial Policy for Developing Countries." In *Handbook of Development Economics*, edited by Dani Rodrik, Vol. 5, 4039–214. Elsevier. https://doi.org/10.1016/B978-0-444-52944-2.00001-X.

Hausmann, Ricardo, and Dani Rodrik. 2003. "Economic Development as Self-Discovery." *Journal of Development Economics, 14th Inter-American Seminar on Economics* 72 (2): 603–33. https://doi.org/10.1016/S0304-3878(03)00124-X.

Ing, Lili Yan, Gene Grossman, and David Christian. 2022. "Digital Transformation: 'Development for All'?" In *New Normal, New Technologies, New Financing*, edited by Lili Yan Ing and Dani Rodrik, 76–88. Jakarta: ERIA and IEA. https://www.eria.org/uploads/media/Books/2022-G20-New-Normal-New-Technology-New-Financing/11_Ch.7-Digital-Transformation-new2.pdf.

Ing, Lili Yan, and Miaojie Yu. 2018. *World Trade Evolution: Growth, Productivity and Employment*, 1st ed. London: Routledge. https://doi.org/10.4324/9781351061544.

International Monetary Fund. n.d. "GDP Based on PPP, Share of World." *World Economic Outlook*, October 2024. Accessed December 26, 2024. https://www.imf.org/external/datamapper/PPPSH@WEO.

Ju, Jiandong, Justin Yifu Lin, and Yong Wang. 2015. "Endowment Structures, Industrial Dynamics, and Economic Growth." *Journal of Monetary Economics* 76 (November): 244–63. https://doi.org/10.1016/j.jmoneco.2015.09.006.

Kuznets, Simon. 1966. *Modern Economic Growth: Rate, Structure, and Spread*. New Haven, CT: Yale University Press. http://archive.org/details/moderneconomicgr0000kuzn_z5q7.

Lavigne, Marie. 1995. *The Economics of Transition: From Socialist Economy to Market Economy*. New York: St. Martin's Press. http://archive.org/details/economicsoftrans0000lavi.

Lin, Justin Yifu. 1989. "An Economic Theory Of Institutional Change: Induced And Imposed Change." *Cato Journal* 9 (1): 1–33. https://www.cato.org/sites/cato.org/files/serials/files/cato-journal/1989/5/cj9n1-1.pdf.

Lin, Justin Yifu. 2009. *Economic Development and Transition: Thought, Strategy, and Viability*, 1st ed. Cambridge, UK: Cambridge University Press. https://doi.org/10.1017/CBO9780511805622.

Lin, Justin Yifu. 2011. "New Structural Economics: A Framework for Rethinking Development." *The World Bank Research Observer* 26 (2): 193–221. https://doi.org/10.1093/wbro/lkr007.

Lin, Justin Yifu. 2015. "The Washington Consensus Revisited: A New Structural Economics Perspective." *Journal of Economic Policy Reform* 18 (2): 96–113. https://doi.org/10.1080/17487870.2014.936439.

Lin, Justin Yifu. 2017. "Industrial Policies for Avoiding the Middle-Income Trap: A New Structural Economics Perspective." *Journal of Chinese Economic and Business Studies* 15 (1): 5–18. https://doi.org/10.1080/14765284.2017.1287539.

Lin, Justin Yifu, and Ha-Joon Chang. 2009. "DPR Debate: Should Industrial Policy in Developing Countries Conform to Comparative Advantage or Defy It?" *Development Policy Review* 27 (5): 483–502. https://doi.org/10.1111/j.1467-7679.2009.00456.x.

Lin, Justin Yifu, and Célestin Monga. 2011. "Growth Identification and Facilitation: The Role of the State in the Dynamics of Structural Change." *Development Policy Review* 29 (3): 264–90. https://doi.org/10.1111/j.1467-7679.2011.00534.x.

Lin, Justin Yifu, and Guofu Tan. 1999. "Policy Burdens, Accountability, and the Soft Budget Constraint." *American Economic Review* 89 (2): 426–31. https://doi.org/10.1257/aer.89.2.426.

Lipsey, R. G., and Kelvin Lancaster. 1956. "The General Theory of Second Best." *The Review of Economic Studies* 24 (1): 11. https://doi.org/10.2307/2296233.

Maddison, Angus. 2001. *The World Economy: A Millennial Perspective. Development Centre Studies*. Paris: OECD Publishing. https://doi.org/10.1787/9789264189980-en.

Maddison, Angus. 2010. "Historical Statistics of The World Economy: 1–2008 AD." https://www.rug.nl/ggdc/historicaldevelopment/maddison/releases/maddison-database-2010.

Palma, José Gabriel. 2005. "Four Sources of 'De-Industrialization' and a New Concept of the 'Dutch Disease.'" In *Beyond Reforms: Structural Dynamics and Macroeconomic Vulnerability*, edited by José Antonio Ocampo. https://openknowledge.worldbank.org/bitstreams/5ba9ec64-7c60-56a3-a0e6-28ed0968b449/download.

Rodrik, Dani. 2004. "Industrial Policy for the Twenty-First Century." *Harvard University Press*, November. https://doi.org/10.2139/ssrn.617544.

Rodrik, Dani. 2016. "Premature Deindustrialization." *Journal of Economic Growth* 21 (1): 1–33. https://doi.org/10.1007/s10887-015-9122-3.

Romer, Paul M. 1990. "Endogenous Technological Change." *Journal of Political Economy* 98 (No. 5, Part 2): S71–102. https://www.journals.uchicago.edu/doi/10.1086/261725.

UN Trade and Development. n.d. "UNCTAD Data Hub." *Statistical Data*. https://unctadstat.unctad.org/EN/.

University of Groningen. n.d.-a. "Maddison Project Database 2018." Accessed December 26, 2024. https://www.rug.nl/ggdc/historicaldevelopment/maddison/releases/maddison-project-database-2018.

University of Groningen. n.d.-b. "Penn World Table (1970–79)." Accessed December 26, 2024. https://www.rug.nl/ggdc/productivity/pwt/.

Wade, Robert. 1990. *Governing the Market: Economic Theory and the Role of Government in East Asian Industrialization*. Princeton University Press. https://doi.org/10.1515/9780691187181.

World Bank. 1993. *The East Asian Miracle: Economic Growth and Public Policy, Vols. 1 and 2, World Bank Policy Research Reports*. Washington: World Bank. http://documents.worldbank.org/curated/en/975081468244550798/Main-report.

World Bank. n.d. "World Development Indicators." https://databank.worldbank.org/source/world-development-indicators.

Yifu Lin, Justin, and Jeffrey B. Nugent. 1995. "Institutions and Economic Development." In *Handbook of Development Economics*, edited by Jere Behrman and T. N. Srinivasan, Vol. 3, 2301–70. Amsterdam: Elsevier. https://doi.org/10.1016/S1573-4471(05)80010-5.

Appendix: Inclusion and Exclusion of Countries

This chapter presented the results from an examination of top gainers and decliners in the global share across five selected economic metrics. Several details were applied in the data-cleaning process. First, only countries were considered with a minimum global share of 0.4% in a particular metric in the most recent available year, either 2021 or 2022. Then, countries widely recognised as tax havens were omitted from the analysis to prevent potential distortions, especially in metrics related to foreign direct investment (FDI). Second, data-cleaning treated the Russian Federation and the Union of Soviet Socialist Republics (USSR) as the same entity due to data limitations. Essentially, this involved merging the data of the USSR prior to 1990 with that of the Russian Federation from 1990 onwards. It was treated as a single, unified observation named the Russian Federation. The changes in each economic metric since the 1970s were then compared with those of all other countries. It is crucial for readers to consider this caveat when interpreting the figures related to either the Russian Federation or the Eastern Europe and Central Asia (EECA) region throughout this study.

7 A New Growth Strategy for Developing Nations

Dani Rodrik and Joseph E. Stiglitz

7.1 Introduction

Not long ago, the development community was brimming with optimism about the developing world's economic prospects. Economic growth was up, extreme poverty was sharply down, and a clear consensus seemed to have emerged on a broad growth strategy based on integration into the world economy. There were plenty of debates on the particulars of the strategy, of course. The experience of China, which had engineered history's most spectacular poverty reduction, gave ammunition to advocates of both market-oriented and more state-directed approaches to development alike. Yet both sides agreed that, however achieved, export-oriented industrialisation was the right path.

This consensus has been recently shattered by several developments, however. In particular, technological changes have made manufacturing skills- and capital-intensive—and less and less labour-absorbing—undercutting the efficacy of industrialisation as a growth strategy. The ability to absorb labour was reduced at the same time as the comparative advantage of developing countries was attenuated. As Figure 7.1 shows, economic growth rates in the developing world were already dropping in the years preceding the COVID-19 pandemic.

The pandemic itself accelerated and exposed other, more subtle trends. With lower growth, the debt problems of developing countries became crushing, and low- and lower-middle-income countries lost precious access to financial markets. Geopolitical competition between the United States and China as well as the creeping backlash against hyper-globalisation transformed the global economic landscape and rendered the world economy less hospitable to growth through trade. As incomes in developed countries increased, there was a shift away from manufactured goods to services, so the share of global output in manufacturing was in decline. The impending climate-change crisis, and the requisite green transition, affected agricultural sectors in many developing countries adversely. It also reduced global demand for material goods, especially those with a high carbon footprint, and made the development of new technologies imperative—further disadvantaging developing countries.

DOI: 10.4324/9781003571384-7

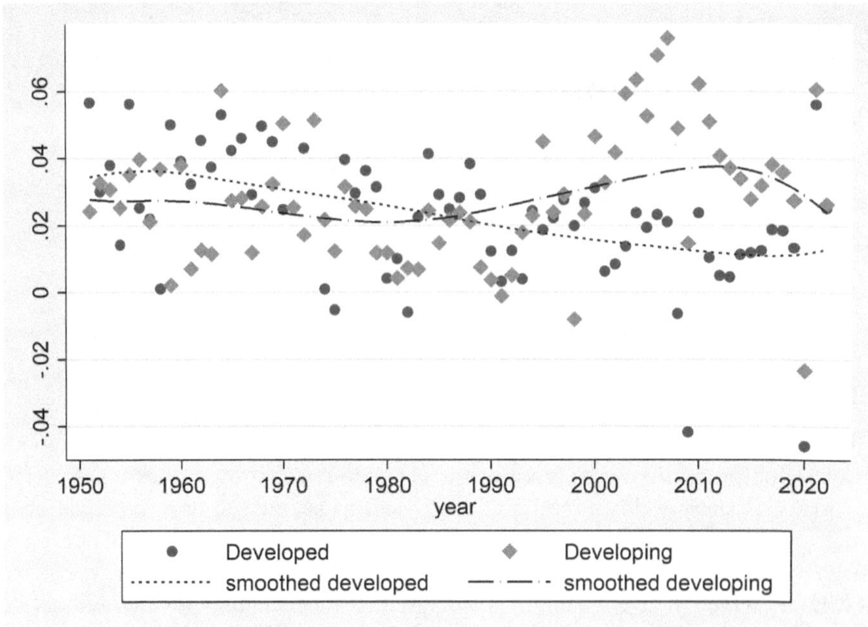

Figure 7.1 Growth Rates of Developed and Developing Countries Since 1950

Sources: University of Groningen (2017), Maddison Historical Statistics, https://www.rug.nl/ggdc/historicaldevelopment/maddison/?lang=en [accessed February 2024]; and World Bank, World Development Indicators, https://databank.worldbank.org/source/world-development-indicators [accessed February 2024].

This chapter argues that we are at a turning point in development strategy. Strategies that worked well in the past are unlikely to do so in the decades ahead. In particular, the manufacturing- and export-based growth strategies that drove East Asia's development miracles are no longer suited for today's low-income countries; at the very least, they are insufficient. New technologies, the climate challenge, and reconfiguration of globalisation require a new approach for development, emphasising two critical areas—the green transition and labour-absorbing services. Unfortunately, policymakers do not have ready-made formulas or successful models to emulate. Confronting this challenge head-on will require building greater capacity to understand new opportunities, constraints, and what works and does not as governments experiment with new policies on a number of fronts.

7.2 A Strategic Approach to Economic Development

The fundamental source of economic development in the long term is learning. Learning occurs at the level of the individual, reflected in the accumulation of human capital and learning-to-learn (Stiglitz, 1987). It also happens at higher, broader levels through organisational and societal learning, including improved governance, which entails not just understanding the principles of what makes for good governance but overcoming the impediments to their implementation. Sustainable economic growth requires patience in building up these fundamentals, including steady investment in education and skills and the quality of institutions.

While the accumulation of these fundamental capabilities is indispensable for development, it is not sufficient; it is not a substitute for a strategy of economic development focussed on structural transformation.[1] In all successful cases of economic growth, in East Asia and elsewhere, these fundamentals improved alongside rapid economic growth. They are as much a result of growth as they were a precondition. Sustained rapid growth, in turn, requires structural transformation; countries that experienced rapid growth (e.g. based on natural resources) and did not have structural transformation saw that growth evaporate at the end of the commodity boom. Moreover, countries that have focussed solely on fundamentals and invested in education and governance without promoting successful structural change have reaped meagre rewards in terms of economic growth.[2] The supply of human capital and good institutions yield little growth without simultaneous changes on the demand side of the economy, which typically come from the promotion of new, modern economic activities and the structure of production, which comes from the industrial policies discussed later.

Still another essential element of the strategy focusses on macroeconomics. Small, open economies need to ensure that they have exchange rates that are competitive, maintaining an overall balance between aggregate supply and demand, without leaving the country dependent on short-term foreign capital (and hence subject to 'sudden stops'[3]) and at as high a level of employment as possible. This has been a key failure of many resources-rich countries, as well as a reason that many countries following Washington Consensus policies failed to thrive economically. Larger economies must ensure adequate aggregate demand to maintain high levels of capacity and employment.

The current focus of development economics on randomised controlled trials (RCTs) and other rigorous methods of causal inference has obscured the importance of structural change and the need for an explicit strategy to promote it. RCTs have yielded many important policy insights in public health, education, and delivery of social services, and no doubt have contributed significantly to poverty reduction. Yet ultimately, long-term and sustainable economic development requires more than a series of local interventions restricted to policy domains where such experimental methods are applicable. The most spectacular growth miracles have been the result of sectoral or economy-wide policy reforms that fostered new economic activities without the prior benefit of RCTs. As an example, China explicitly experimented by trying new policy arrangements in some provinces before launching them elsewhere. Learning from policy successes and failures is possible even when policymakers' causal inference standards fall short of RCTs or other econometric techniques of 'evidence-based policymaking'. It would have been impossible to conduct RCTs to inform the significant strategies that really mattered; policymakers gleaned what they could by making inferences based on theory, history, econometric studies, and the limited experiments that could be conducted.

Rapid, sustained economic development thus requires an explicit strategy targeting structural transformation.[4] The common element running through all of the rapid and sustained growth cases has been the strategy of industrialisation. During the early post-World War II era, this strategy was import-substituting industrialisation. Combining heavy state intervention with import barriers, import-substituting industrialisation focussed on building domestic manufacturing capacity—initially consumer goods, followed by intermediate and capital goods industries. While not every country did well under this strategy, many countries in Latin America, the Middle East, and Sub-Saharan Africa experienced rapid economic growth until the oil shock of the second half of the 1970s.

East and South-East Asian countries—led by Taiwan in the late 1950s and South Korea in the early 1960s—also heavily promoted industrialisation through a wide variety of measures, including access to credit and tax incentives, but pushed their nascent manufacturing enterprises early on to export. This export-oriented industrialisation model proved more sustainable and eventually became the one to emulate for countries adopting more market-oriented approaches under the influence of the Washington Consensus. True to its market focus and aversion to governmental intervention, however, the Washington Consensus remained focussed on 'fundamentals'—investments in education, governance, and macroeconomic stability—and downplayed structural transformation strategies that were central to the success of East Asia, including the role of explicit trade and industrial policies to foster learning and new industries. Largely as a result, the growth payoff for Washington Consensus policies proved disappointing.

China was the most significant success story of the East Asian model. Once the government prioritised economic growth after 1978, its strategy combined market incentives with highly unconventional institutional arrangements—the household responsibility system, dual-track pricing in agriculture, township and village enterprises, and special economic zones—to foster structural change, productive diversification, and new capabilities. Industrial policies promoting new manufacturing activities were a critical part of China's economic success. China was also a beneficiary of increased globalisation, but it became one largely through its own terms.

By the 1990s, globalisation had reached new heights. Under the new model of hyper-globalisation, removing or at least reducing transaction costs on international trade, finance, and investment—'deep integration'—became a primary objective of economic policy. Reduction in these costs, along with technological advances, rendered global value chains (GVCs) the predominant force shaping global production. Joining GVCs, in turn, became the main vehicle for promoting economic growth. Entering GVCs, the thinking went, would help promote new industries, increase productivity, and generate the structural change needed for growth.[5]

However, just as global economic integration, export-oriented industrialisation, and GVCs became the foundations of a new economic development strategy, their benefits were being undermined by a process of 'premature de-industrialisation' in developing countries. The primary culprit was skills- and capital-biased technological changes in manufacturing, which increased labour productivity substantially in advanced economies where innovations originate. They also undercut the comparative advantage of low-income economies in labour-intensive manufacturing. The quality and technological standards set by leading firms in GVCs rendered labour-intensive production in export-oriented sectors even less viable (Rodrik, 2016, 2022a).[6]

The result was that globally competitive formal manufacturing sectors in developing countries ceased being labour-absorbing sectors. They turned into 'enclave' sectors where low amounts of these economies' excess low-skilled workforce could be employed.[7] In countries where manufacturing output was sustained, manufacturing employment still shrank as a share of total employment. In the few cases where manufacturing employment registered an increase, the rise was concentrated in small, informal, and low-productivity enterprises, while large, internationally competitive firms generated little demand for labour (Diao et al., 2021).

Manufacturing employment matters. Historically, structural transformation in the form of industrialisation has been the key dynamic that has driven rapid economic growth.[8] As workers moved from low- to higher-productivity sectors, they increased their earnings, aggregate productivity rose, and economic growth occurred. The key strategic question for the future is where the better, more productive jobs will come from.[9] While manufacturing will remain an important sector for most countries, it cannot be the protagonist of economic growth as it was in East Asia and other successful economies of the past, because the global share of employment in manufacturing will decline, both because of the shift in global gross domestic product (GDP) away from manufacturing and the decreased labour intensity of manufacturing employment due technological change.[10] Green industries and services must play an important role in filling the void, especially in the next few decades.[11]

7.3 The Green Transition

Climate change imposes a significant cost on low-income countries. Often, they are especially vulnerable because of their location in areas that are most affected. Their low resources and limited fiscal space make large-scale spending necessary for adaptation and response to the damage of climate change difficult, if not impossible. Their exposure to extreme weather events has also increased, resulting in losses to crops and livestock. The drag on growth is already evident in many cases and is reflected in higher borrowing spreads and reduced access to private finance in many countries.

In a world with complete, efficient markets and where governmental efforts are already optimised, the constraints imposed by climate change and requisite adjustments will reduce well-being and almost certainly growth. However, policy reforms—in part induced by the need to respond to climate change—can reduce the costs imposed by climate change and potentially produce better outcomes relative to the business-as-usual scenario. In particular, the climate challenge can become a growth opportunity if developing countries are able to turn it into an investment strategy.[12] As several large-scale global models have shown, it is possible for well-designed climate actions to boost growth in developing countries (Lankes et al., 2024). However, a plausible and desirable path towards a green transition will require large up-front investments. It will also have to go beyond investment in climate-change mitigation to build cumulative and enduring capabilities in new productive domains (e.g. renewables and green industries).

There are multiple key investment priorities related to the green transition.[13] The first is the transformation of the energy system, which entails moving from fossil fuels to renewable sources of energy. Without decarbonisation in developing countries—and the phasing out of coal-fired power plants in particular—it is difficult to see how the world can reach a target of net-zero emissions by the middle of the 21st century. Rapid technological progress and the sharp decline in prices of renewable energy have made this goal more attainable. Yet it will require massive new investments in infrastructure and electrification and in new sources of energy such as solar, wind, and green hydrogen.

There will also be requisite investments in each of the other systems that constitute a developing economy, and implementing some will be difficult because of the decentralised nature of the investments required. Transforming agriculture could lead to more productivity and higher standards of living for the large fractions of the population still dependent on that sector. Developing countries are also home to significant carbon sinks; by ensuring their restoration and protection, they can make a substantial contribution to mitigating climate change. This will require a wide range of public investments in agriculture, forests, soils, and oceans.[14] Redesigning cities, with modern transport systems and efficient housing, could also contribute to lowering emissions and greater productivity.[15]

Another area is reducing the vulnerability of developing countries to damage from climate change. There are significant needs in building defences against rising sea levels, desertification, and extreme heat. Governments will need to increase investments in food and water systems, resilience of infrastructure and urban areas, and disaster risk management.

The total investment needed for such a strategy amounts to an additional 2% of global GDP per year by 2025 and an additional 4% of global GDP per year by 2030 (excluding China) (Songwe et al., 2022). Many of these incremental expenditures reflect the up-front costs of replacing capital goods that would otherwise have to be replaced earlier. Some of these incremental costs arise from the fact that many green technologies are more capital-intensive than corresponding non-green technologies; that is, more labour is needed now, but with the benefit of less labour needed in the future. This is evident in the case of electric vehicles, where maintenance and driving costs are a fraction of those associated with internal combustion engines.

The feasibility of these actions depends on the availability of external financial support. Assuming half of the investment needs is met through domestic resource mobilisation, developing countries as a group would require an additional 2%–4% of GDP of external resource flows. Short of concerted global action by leading creditors and multilateral lenders, it is difficult to see how this could be achieved.

The COVID-19 pandemic and rising food and fuel costs have left the developing world with severe debt problems. While only a few countries have defaulted, scores of developing countries are currently illiquid. Net financial transfers to Africa have slowed down to a trickle, and low- and lower-middle-income countries have essentially lost access to bond markets.

Bridging the investment gap will require a new growth-oriented liquidity facility to allow the resumption of financial flows to these countries as well as speedier debt resolution (Rodrik and Diwan, 2023). These will have to be supplemented with domestic mechanisms to ensure adequate access to finance by households and firms, regardless of size, for green investments. Action on this front is in the interests of advanced economies as well since the climate transition is a global public good.[16]

If financing becomes available—and if the investment is deployed wisely—this ramping-up of investment for the climate transition could be an important element of the new growth strategy. Such an investment could yield additional growth of 0.5%–1.0% per year for developing countries, assuming an incremental capital output ratio of 4.[17]

From a global perspective, the timing of the green transition may be ideal, as there is a surplus of labour available to make the investments. Some are worried about a savings glut or secular stagnation, suggesting a surfeit of savings; yet the global real interest rate has been low despite recent increases in the nominal rate. A key problem is the risk premium imposed on developing countries—and even on relatively safe investments within those countries.

7.4 Better Jobs in Services

Investment in the green transition would turn a cost for developing countries into a growth opportunity. Yet it is not clear where the better, more productive jobs will come from. The climate transition could create new jobs in building solar and wind facilities, infrastructure, and climate-change mitigation activities. It will also destroy actual—and potential—jobs in fossil fuel-dependent activities and brown manufacturing. Even if, on net, it increases labour demand, developing countries still face the challenge of absorbing large amounts of additional labour from the agriculture and informal sectors into modern, productive sectors.

The problem of job creation in Africa is particularly acute. The working-age population in Sub-Saharan Africa will increase by 740 million by 2050, more than doubling its current level of 630 million people (World Bank, 2023). In the absence of job creation in more productive sectors, the bulk of this labour supply will be absorbed by precarious, unproductive informal activities in urban areas, as is the case at present. It is unlikely that decarbonisation-led structural transformation will produce the many jobs needed, which would have been created in the past by industrialisation.

The same could be said for agriculture. Agricultural modernisation, including the use of new technologies and diversification into cash crops, has significant potential in many developing countries. Yet it is difficult to envisage agriculture as a labour-absorbing sector for the economy. Most of the new technologies in agriculture are labour-saving and capital-intensive. Historically, productivity gains in agriculture have been associated with reductions—rather than increases—in farm employment. It remains to be seen whether a different path could emerge in view of the new constraints posed by climate change and land scarcity.

Combined with the manufacturing trends discussed earlier, it is difficult to avoid the conclusion that services will remain the main labour-absorbing sector in developing countries. This poses a significant challenge. Some countries, such as India and the Philippines, have been successful in creating productive, globally competitive, tradable services industries. However, these are typically activities—such as information technology and business process offshoring—that are skills intensive. Such services sectors face the same disadvantage from a developmental standpoint as today's GVC-oriented manufacturing firms—they have limited potential to create much employment for the typically low-educated, low-skilled workforce of a developing economy.

Moreover, today, jobs are being created in a very different segment of the economy—a hodgepodge of largely self-proprietorships or micro/small firms, typically non-tradable and often informal. The central question posed is whether productivity and demand can be increased in these labour-absorbing services activities. A three-pronged strategy is thus proposed for governments: (i) encourage lower-skilled job creation by larger firms that operate in non-tradable services, (ii) provide public inputs and access to productivity-enhancing investments for smaller enterprises, and (iii) invest in technologies that complement rather than replace low-skilled workers in services sectors.

The bulk of small, informal enterprises in developing countries will never become very productive. It is not realistic to aim for productivity increases for all of these firms. However, dualism can be reduced over time, both by encouraging the expansion of existing formal firms and by increasing productivity amongst some of the more dynamic, smaller, informal firms. Therefore, a strategy targeting the domestic services sector must be selective. The government would engage in a variety of programmes that have the potential to increase employment and productivity. It would then let the more entrepreneurial and dynamic amongst services-sector firms—including micro and small enterprises—select into and take advantage of these programmes.

The three elements of the strategy can be illustrated with concrete cases. As an example of the first component, the state government of Haryana, India, established a partnership in 2018 with the private cab aggregators Ola and Uber (Mugulur, 2019). The partnership was motivated by the government's objective to increase employment for young people. Based on an explicit *quid pro quo*, the government helped the firms identify and hire drivers by changing some of the regulations that hampered the expansion of ride-sharing services, sharing targeted databases of unemployed youth in the state, and holding exclusive job fairs for the companies. The firms, in turn, made soft commitments to expand the number of youth that they employed. It was understood that the promises, on each side, were not contractual obligations, but good-faith intentions subject to changing circumstances, meant to engender mutual trust over time. In less than 1 year, the partnership is said to have created more than 44,000 new jobs for youth.

An example of the second type of programme is provided by a Colombian initiative to reduce the time and financial costs of street fruit and vegetable vendors in Bogotá (McKenzie, 2019). Unlike large retail stores, these vendors have inefficient supply chains, requiring them to spend an inordinate amount of time looking for and buying the products that they eventually sell. These vendors in Bogotá get up at 4:30 a.m. and spend 2 hours in travel to purchase produce from a central wholesaler. A social enterprise, Agruppa, came up with the idea that it could group and consolidate orders from individual vendors, buy in bulk directly from the growers, and deliver the fruits and vegetables to the vendors. This would not only reduce the costs of the vendors but also lessen prices for customers, often poor themselves. Using seed money from the World Bank, the initiative was launched with just a few products initially and then expanded. A World Bank evaluation found that it held promise, although the experiment eventually folded due to Agruppa's inability to scale it up in a timely manner.

As both examples illustrate, local governments or entities will often be better placed than national governments to create jobs-centred partnerships with entrepreneurs or firms providing services. Given the multitude of services activities, variation in local circumstances, and heterogeneity in the size and shape of firms, local governments may also be better positioned to craft suitable arrangements. Significant experimentation with different types of initiatives is still needed, however, given the dearth of successful precedents to emulate. Moreover, social enterprises have often taken the lead in developing countries, as their approach is more conducive to experimentation.

There are some similarities between these programmes and what was needed to bring advances in technology to farmers in the United States in the 19th century, as both entailed many small enterprises scattered over the entire country. The Government of the United States created an agricultural extension service to engage in experimentation at the local level and to bring knowledge to local farmers. Similarly, governments in developing countries, both local and national, will have to become more entrepreneurial and more engaged with experimentation and focus on bringing innovation insights to small enterprises if the strategy is to make a significant difference beyond individual initiatives.

Finally, there is significant room to invest in and to deploy new technologies, especially for those employed in services. Automation and other innovations in manufacturing have been typically skills- and capital-biased, contributing to significant labour shedding in manufacturing globally. However, the direction of technological change is not exogenous and predestined; it responds to economic incentives, governmental policies, and prevailing social norms amongst the innovator community.[18] Explicit governmental efforts to stimulate the development of labour-friendly technologies can play an important role in services. There are already some prominent examples of how digital technologies and artificial intelligence (AI) can empower lower-skilled workers to expand the range of tasks that they can perform, taking over some of the responsibilities of more experienced and skilled professionals and becoming more productive in the process. AI cannot just replace labour; it can augment labour's productivity and thus even increase the demand for labour and wages (Korinek and Stiglitz, 2019).

In medicine and long-term care, digital tools enable the least-skilled caregivers to provide more advanced services to their patients. Specially designed software can assist community health workers in some countries by helping conduct timely visits and providing access to health and learning resources online. In education, similar digital tools can enable less experienced teachers to engage in pedagogy that is more closely tailored to the needs of different groups of students. In call services, conversational assistance by generative AI has been shown to significantly increase the productivity of the least experienced customer support employees.[19] Since such technologies already exist, developing countries could facilitate their dissemination and use amongst domestic firms.

Today, it is widely recognised that governments have a critical role in fostering green technologies. Given the importance of promoting green jobs, it could be argued that governments have an equally critical role in promoting labour-friendly technologies.[20] Since the bulk of innovation takes place in advanced economies, such nations could play a significant role in facilitating economic development. Rebuilding the middle class and overcoming labour market polarisation is a priority for them as well, so investing in labour-friendly technologies is a task that serves their own immediate interests. Still, the technologies that are appropriate for advanced countries may—and almost surely will—differ from those that are best for developing countries. There is scope for an international effort to develop all technologies; just like green innovation, labour-friendly innovation is a global public good.

Beyond the advanced economies, many middle-income countries—such as Brazil, India, South Africa, and Türkiye—are also becoming centres of innovation. There is some evidence that technologies and organisational forms that are more suited to the developing country context disseminate more rapidly amongst developing nations (Lerner et al., 2024). Hence, these larger economies amongst the developing world face significant opportunities but also bear significant responsibility in this area.

Even in the best-case scenario, a services-based model is unlikely to deliver growth rates approaching those experienced in East Asia in the past. Increasing productivity in labour-absorbing services is likely to prove more difficult than in manufacturing, even if the strategies outlined previously prove successful and a significant gap in productivity remains in the services sector between developed and developing countries. Manufacturing technologies are more standardised and are easier to copy despite large differences in developing countries.[21]

Yet there is another general equilibrium reason as well. Under manufacturing-led growth strategies, a succession of export-oriented sectors—such as toys, garments, automobiles, and steel—could take off, one after the other, without regard to domestic demand. In contrast, the expansion of non-tradable services—those that are most likely to absorb employment—is ultimately limited by the size of the domestic market. Individual services sectors cannot keep growing if other services sectors are not also expanding and increasing their productivity;

the growth of retail depends on the growth of personal services, hospitality, and the rest of the economy, for example. Otherwise, the profitability of the more rapidly expanding services would soon collapse. This complementarity on the demand side necessitates balanced growth and lowers the ceiling on the potential growth rate of the economy.[22]

The kind of growth strategy described is more inclusive and equitable. It delivers direct income gains for poorer segments of society through better jobs and builds a middle class, rather than waiting for a trickle-down phenomenon from the export champions and largest firms. The quality of growth is higher, even if its quantity is lower.

7.5 New Industrial Policies for the Green Transition and Labour-Absorbing Services

Governments have a significant role to play in the strategy outlined, both for investments in the green transition and for good jobs programmes in services. Markets left to their own devices do not foster the kind of structural changes needed on either front. In general, structural transformation is impeded by credit and risk market failures, coordination failures, externalities, and learning spillovers. That is why the most rapidly growing economies of the past all relied heavily on industrial policies promoting productive diversification and the growth of new industries. Such barriers will be even greater in the transition to green industries and productive, labour-absorbing services. Hence, private markets and entrepreneurship must be augmented by a public vision and a supporting set of public incentives, inputs, and services.

In theory, market failures that impede dynamic efficiency can sometimes be addressed through targeted tax/subsidy schemes that result in private agents internalising the full social consequences of their actions. Learning spillovers and climate-change externalities, for example, should be corrected through Pigouvian subsidies and taxes, respectively. The magnitude of these interventions should equal the difference between private and social costs/benefits (at the margin), subject to second-best considerations (e.g. the deadweight loss of raising taxes), which may call for smaller interventions.[23]

In practice, governments face uncertainty on multiple dimensions, undermining the practical applicability of the standard recipe.[24] Problems associated with imperfections of credit markets and the absence of insurance markets are not easily handled by the standard Pigouvian approach. The specific sources of market failures; their respective magnitudes; the behavioural responses of firms, investors, innovators, and consumers; range of possible technological trajectories; and efficacy of different types of policies can vary. In such contexts, learning and capacity building by the government must be built into policy design, rather than assumed. Moreover, the relationship between the government and firms has to be conceptualised as an inherently dynamic one. Although East Asian industrial policies are often portrayed as top-down policies implemented by autonomous, well-informed governments, the reality was quite different. Many of these governments started with little experience with and capacity to conduct extensive industrial policies. The requisite governmental capacity was not a precondition for their policies but was built over time. Successful industrial policies entail learning by society at large.[25]

The practice of industrial policy has five key interconnected elements: embeddedness, coordination, monitoring, conditionality, and institutional development. The first of these refers to the establishment of a strategic dialogue and collaboration with firms to elucidate the information on obstacles and opportunities for productive investments, including market failures. As the sociologist Peter Evans discussed, in successful cases, states' relative autonomy from private firms—and hence their ability to prevent regulatory capture—was combined with embeddedness, which Evans (1995) defined as 'institutionalized channels for the continual negotiation and re-negotiation of goals and policies'. These channels of communication enable governmental agencies to understand private firms' constraints and potential as well as reshape their understanding in light of new information and changing circumstances. The channels can be ad hoc and informal or formal (e.g. joint councils, commissions, or roundtables).[26]

The second element is policy coordination. Unlike in the standard model, there is no presumption that Pigouvian taxes/subsidies will be adequate or that they can be specified *ex ante*. The requisite remedies may range from alterations in certain governmental regulations to the provision of specific training or technologies to financial incentives (e.g. the Haryana cab employment scheme). In many cases, finance and risk absorption has been crucial.[27] The nature of the needed remedies become clear over time and cannot be determined at the outset. Appropriate responses may require actions across different parts of the government. Therefore, governmental agencies charged with industrial policies need the ability to coordinate and to mobilise these actions. If they lack the authority or capacity to do so effectively, they should be able to elevate the task to a higher level of governmental authority (e.g. governor or president's offices).

Third, a government's learning has to be systematised and reflected in its subsequent actions and decisions. This requires an explicit effort to monitor and to evaluate the outcomes of industrial policy decisions. Many of these decisions will inevitably lead to sub-optimal outcomes and mistakes. What matters for the success of industrial policies is not just the ability to 'pick winners'[28]—or equally importantly, to identify projects with large externalities—but also the ability to let the losers go, a less difficult but still demanding requirement. Often, the phasing in or partial implementation of programmes can allow rigorous evaluation of policies through RCTs or econometric tools (e.g. the Bogotá fruit and vegetable vendor scheme). Yet even if formal evaluation methods cannot be deployed, it is possible to learn from outcomes and to adjust policies appropriately. For example, in China's industrial policies, the willingness to experiment with new policies in designated zones or provinces was key as was its ability to adjust incentive schemes when they produced excess capacity or blatant inefficiency.

Fourth, and relatedly, successful industrial policies have typically provided strong incentives for compliance. In East Asia, the financial support was not a gift; continued support required sustained success on the part of the firm, often with objective indicators, like exports. Governments looked for enterprises with substantial net worth, so they would also suffer significant losses in the event of failure.[29]

Fifth, successful industrial policies require new institutions and institutional development as previously discussed. In many countries, development banks have played an important role. Institutional arrangements were created so that they were not captured but were sensitive to market failures and social needs.

These lessons derive largely from the experience with industrial policy in manufacturing but are also broadly applicable to new challenges in decarbonisation and the services sector. They entail building a new kind of cooperative relationship between the government and private firms, with mutual responsibilities and obligations.

7.6 Concluding Remarks

In some ways, the challenges facing developing countries have not changed. Broad capabilities such as skills, education, learning, and good governance remain fundamental determinants of long-term economic development. Although these are necessary, they are not sufficient. Sustained growth will require structural transformation, and structural transformation will, in general, not necessarily come about on its own—at least at the pace desired. Explicit governmental policies are needed to foster it. Where structural change and associated policies are concerned, the future of economic growth will look very different from its past. The climate challenge, new technologies and digitalisation, premature de-industrialisation, the changing global geopolitical landscape, and receding hyper-globalisation render the export-oriented industrialisation strategies of the past less viable and effective. This chapter argued for a strategy with two key prongs—investment in the green transition and productivity enhancement in labour-absorbing, mostly non-tradable services.

This does not mean that other sectors of the economy, and manufacturing and agriculture, in particular, are unimportant and should be neglected. In most low-income economies, agriculture will continue to employ considerable numbers of people. Improving their plight will require investments in agricultural productivity and making use of new technologies as well as diversification into non-traditional crops. However, as agriculture modernises, it will almost certainly continue to release labour to the rest of the economy, necessitating the creation of more productive jobs in urban areas.[30] In the past, manufacturing was the key sector that could absorb these new migrants as well as workers from unproductive informal activities. Productive manufacturing sectors can still make important contributions to the economy (e.g. generating exports, tax revenues, and demand spillovers for other domestic sectors). There are opportunities for strengthening links between manufacturing exporters, whether domestically or foreign-owned, and domestic suppliers and input providers to increase productive employment and to disseminate new technologies. Yet manufacturing's ability to absorb the bulk of jobseekers will be much more limited than in the past, hence the emphasis on labour-absorbing services.

Steering the requisite structural changes will require new modes of industrial policies, focussed on these new strategic priorities. Economists traditionally view industrial policy as top-down interventions by 'hard' states that keep business and other stakeholders at arms' length. This picture never accurately reflected how successful industrial policy was in East Asia. For green industries and services, it is even less useful. The significant uncertainties in technological evolution, heterogeneities amongst production units, and the highly dynamic settings in these new areas require a new model of iterative, strategic collaboration between firms and governmental agencies, both at the national and sub-national levels. The focus should be on experimentation and learning, with objectives, instruments, performance criteria, and institutions developed and shaped over time. Governmental capacity would be accumulated in the process, rather than presumed as given.

All governmental policies, either by commission or omission, shape the economy and affect economic growth. In that sense, every country has an industrial policy—some just do not recognise that. An awareness of how the rules of the game, public expenditures and taxes, and explicit industrial policies shape an economy is not only important to prevent capture but also to promote sustainable and inclusive growth.

Notes

1 A key issue, addressed later in greater detail, is structural transformation towards what? The early success of East Asia was due to structural transformation from agriculture to manufacturing. The thrust of this chapter is that that form of structural transformation will not work, however. Learning and structural transformation imply that past comparative advantages do not matter as much as the new comparative advantages that are created in this dynamic process. South Korea in 1960 obviously did not have a comparative advantage in chips. An essential part of the structural transformation, though, is 'learning to learn', converting a static economy into a dynamic one (Stiglitz, 1987).

2 For example, Kerala State in India has consistently emphasised investments in education and health, but the improvement of human development indicators has not been matched with strong economic growth, undermining the long-run sustainability of its development model. This is also one reason why many countries in Latin America and Africa that adopted Washington Consensus policies have had disappointing growth outcomes, despite significant improvements in education, governance, and macroeconomic stability indicators. The empirical literature on conditional convergence suggested that there are returns to improvements in these fundamentals, but the estimated rates of conditional convergence are generally too slow and cannot account for the kind of rapid growth seen in successful cases in East Asia and elsewhere. See Rodrik (2014).

3 Countries that are overly dependent on an inflow of foreign capital (and therefore face increasing indebtedness) are subject to sudden changes in market sentiment, engendering a crisis with significant consequences. Competitive exchange rates simultaneously reduce dependence on foreign capital inflows and are an instrument of industrial policy. See, for example, Guzman, Ocampo, Stiglitz (2018) and Rodrik (2008).

4 There is extensive theoretical literature on why the government must do this and why markets themselves cannot be relied upon, which focusses on market failures. Beginning with the work of Greenwald and Stiglitz (1986) and Stiglitz and Weiss (1981),

an understanding developed of the range and nature of these market failures, and what governments can do to overcome them or at least mitigate their consequences (Stiglitz, 1989). In the context of development and decisions about the structure of production, literature was generated on industrial policies for developing countries (Greenwald and Stiglitz, 2013) as discussions centred on the importance of innovation; these were dubbed learning, industrial, and technology policies (Noman and Stiglitz, 2011).

5 Trade barriers did not fall uniformly; there was a large gap between rhetoric and reality. New trade barriers also appeared, such as those associated with intellectual property.

6 In Africa, de-industrialisation had set in earlier. Its causes, consequences, and potential remedies are discussed in Noman and Stiglitz (2011).

7 Two countries seem to be exceptions to this trend—Bangladesh and Viet Nam. Bangladesh is more of an apparent exception than a real one. While the country has been highly successful with ready-made garments for export, Bangladesh's manufacturing sector remains heavily concentrated, and diversifying out of ready-made garments has proved difficult. Despite its export orientation, the share of informal employment in textiles and garments is above 90%. A shortage of skills and need for technological upgrading are common themes in discussions of Bangladesh's manufacturing sector, both of which obviate the country's fundamental comparative advantage in low-skilled labour (Rodrik, 2022b). Viet Nam has been much more successful, with a particularly sharp rise in manufacturing employment after the mid-2010s. Yet it has the singular advantage of geographical proximity to China and other East Asian exporters. It has been the leading beneficiary of the first rising wage costs in China, then the Trump tariffs on China, and eventually the US emphasis on 'friend-shoring'. In Viet Nam, too, integration into the world economy through inward direct investment has increased the demand for skills. Skills shortages—and consequent problems of 'job hopping' and 'employer poaching'—are reported to be amongst the most important constraints that export-oriented foreign investors, such as Samsung, face (Sheldon and Kwon, 2023).

8 Some natural resources-rich countries can manage periods of very rapid economic growth, but if the proceeds of the natural resources are not reinvested in structural transformation—which typically occurs—the growth is limited. When the resources run out or prices come down, growth stops and often reverses.

9 The concern is not with the overall quantity of jobs or with full employment but with the structure of jobs. Reasonable macroeconomic policies—along with 'flexible' labour markets—will ensure full employment, but the resulting structure can be sub-optimal from a developmental standpoint and not growth-promoting. The focus, therefore, is on the creation of more jobs in the more productive sectors of the economy as a vehicle of structural transformation and growth, analogous to the role that industrialisation has played historically.

10 This is not to say that a few smaller countries may be able to establish a niche in manufacturing and succeed through such a strategy. Thus, the contention that a few countries have been able to sustain growth so far through a manufacturing export-oriented strategy is not inconsistent with the overall thrust of this chapter.

11 Stiglitz (2021) deconstructed why the export-oriented industrialisation growth strategy was so successful and what a 21st-century replacement—a multi-pronged strategy—may look like.

12 The reasons for this are set forth more fully in Stern and Stiglitz (2023).

13 This discussion follows Songwe et al. (2022) and Stern and Stiglitz (2023).

14 This can be an especially important part of development strategies if arrangements can be established that would compensate developing countries for the global environmental services that they provide.

15 The traffic jams that mark large capitals of developing countries around the world are bad for the climate and living standards.

16 See also chapters by Ocampo (Chapter 10) and Songwe (Chapter 12) in this collection.

17 This is a transitory increase in output associated with the green investment drive. It is a simple supply-side calculation, assuming that all of the additional investment is incremental to the capital stock. In practice, some of it may go to replace dirty productive capacity, in which case the incremental supply-side effect would be lower. There may be, however, additional demand-side effects, arising from reductions in under-employment and movement of labour from low-productivity to higher-productivity modern activities. This demand-side bonus can boost the growth rate further.

18 See Acemoglu and Restrepo (2020a) and Acemoglu (2021). For a broader discussion of the direction of innovation and its implications for development, see Korinek, Schindler, Stiglitz (2021).

19 For these and other examples, see Acemoglu and Restrepo (2020b); Acemoglu (2021); Rodrik (2022b); Kremer et al. (2021); Ton (2017); and Brynjolfsson, Li, Raymond (2023).

20 Within the standard market failures paradigm, there are a host of failures related to the pace and direction of innovation (e.g. Stiglitz and Greenwald, 2014).

21 This fact is reflected in the finding that formal manufacturing sectors have long exhibited unconditional convergence in labour productivity. That is, these sectors tend to catch up to the global productivity frontier regardless of local conditions, such as the quality of institutions or human capital. This has not been a regular feature of the rest of the economy (i.e. traditional agriculture and most services) (Rodrik, 2013).

22 Moreover, Baumol's disease contends that the pace of innovation—the movement of the frontier itself—will be lower in services.

23 The implementation of such interventions faces important impediments in the presence of uncertainties and asymmetries of information. There is much literature on the design of optimal schemes in such circumstances. When there are multiple market failures, as is the case in practice, there cannot just be a reliance on Pigouvian subsidies. See the next footnote and Stiglitz (2019).

24 Economist Martin Weitzman showed that quantity targets may dominate Pigouvian price instruments in the presence of uncertainty about demand and supply elasticities. The price instrument may minimise the efficiency costs of the policy but risks undershooting and producing too small a behavioural response. Quantity targets may be superior when the social costs of missing the socially optimal target—reducing emissions, for example—are higher than the deadweight costs that may otherwise be created (Weitzman, 1974). More generally, non-linear interventions are preferable to either of the two extremes. In some contexts, governments actually implement such schemes.

25 See Greenwald and Stiglitz (2013). A recent overview of the evidence on industrial policy is provided in Juhász, Lane, Rodrik (2024).

26 Executive roundtables (*Mesas Ejecutivas*) in Peru were discussed in Ghezzi (2017). As summarised in Juhász, Lane, Rodrik (2024): 'The objective of the roundtables was to institutionalize public-private dialog aimed at addressing coordination failures among firms and between the firms and the government, and thereby encourage productivity-increasing investments. The roundtables started as open-ended conversations to share information on and uncover constraints. Instead of lengthy industry reports, the focus was on developing an initial list of blockages or obstacles to productivity and means of removing them, to be revised as needed as more knowledge was acquired in the process. The responsibilities for action were divided into separate categories of "my problems" and "your problems." The former category refers to government responsibilities (e.g., removing red tape for exports or establishing a national phytosanitary agency); the latter refers to firms' actions (e.g., making specific investments in quality upgrading)'.

27 In the context of the East Asian miracle, see Stiglitz (1996) and Stiglitz and Uy (1996). In advanced countries, venture capital firms often play a role in coordinating the provision of critical inputs for the firms in which they invest.

28 Under the old trade theory, picking winners was simple—identifying projects or sectors in which a country had a comparative advantage given its resources endowment (e.g. its capital, human capital, or natural capital). In more dynamic contexts, this approach is less helpful; with factor flows, comparative advantage relates only to immobile factors, and a country with a skills shortage may be able to obtain the requisite skills from abroad. More importantly, changing technologies; institutions; and more broadly, individual, organisational, and institutional learning mean that comparative advantages can change over time. Thus, a critical question facing any country as it embarks on structural change is what comparative advantages to acquire (Greenwald and Stiglitz, 2013).

29 For a discussion of conditionality, see Mazzucato and Rodrik (2023).

30 Changes in consumption patterns may ameliorate this tendency somewhat. For example, flowers and vegetables use more labour than wheat.

References

Acemoglu, Daron. 2021. "AI's Future Doesn't Have to Be Dystopian." *Boston Review*, May 20. https://www.bostonreview.net/forum/ais-future-doesnt-have-to-be-dystopian/.

Acemoglu, Daron, and Pascual Restrepo. 2020. "The Wrong Kind of AI? Artificial Intelligence and the Future of Labour Demand." *Cambridge Journal of Regions, Economy and Society* 13 (1): 25–35. https://doi.org/10.1093/cjres/rsz022.

Brynjolfsson, Erik, Danielle Li, and Lindsey R. Raymond. 2023. "Generative AI at Work." *Working Paper. Working Paper Series*. Washington, DC: National Bureau of Economic Research. https://doi.org/10.3386/w31161.

Diao, Xinshen, Mia Ellis, Margaret S. McMillan, and Dani Rodrik. 2021. "Africa's Manufacturing Puzzle: Evidence from Tanzanian and Ethiopian Firms." *Working Paper. Working Paper Series*. Washington, DC: National Bureau of Economic Research. https://doi.org/10.3386/w28344.

Evans, Peter B. 1995. *Embedded Autonomy: States and Industrial Transformation. Princeton Paperbacks*. Princeton, NJ: Princeton University Press.

Ghezzi, Piero. 2017. "Mesas Ejecutivas in Peru: Lessons for Productive Development Policies." *Global Policy* 8 (3): 369–80. https://doi.org/10.1111/1758-5899.12457.

Greenwald, Bruce, and Joseph E. Stiglitz. 2013. "Industrial Policies, the Creation of a Learning Society, and Economic Development." In *The Industrial Policy Revolution I: The Role of Government Beyond Ideology*, edited by Joseph E. Stiglitz and Justin Yifu Lin, 43–71. Basingstoke; New York: Palgrave Macmillan UK. https://doi.org/10.1057/9781137335173_4.

Greenwald, Bruce C., and Joseph E. Stiglitz. 1986. "Externalities in Economies with Imperfect Information and Incomplete Markets." *The Quarterly Journal of Economics* 101 (2): 229. https://doi.org/10.2307/1891114.

Guzman, Martin, José Antonio Ocampo, and Joseph E. Stiglitz. 2018. "Real Exchange Rate Policies for Economic Development." *World Development* 110 (October): 51–62. https://doi.org/10.1016/j.worlddev.2018.05.017.

Juhász, Réka, Nathan Lane, and Dani Rodrik. 2024. "The New Economics of Industrial Policy." *Annual Review of Economics* 16: 213–42. https://doi.org/10.1146/annurev-economics-081023-024638.

Korinek, Anton, Martin Schindler, and Joseph E. Stiglitz. 2021. "Technological Progress and Artificial Intelligence." In *How to Achieve Inclusive Growth*, edited by Valerie Cerra, Barry Eichengreen, Asmaa El-Ganainy, and Martin Schindler, 163–211. Oxford: Oxford University Press. https://doi.org/10.1093/oso/9780192846938.003.0005.

Korinek, Anton, and Joseph E. Stiglitz. 2019. "Artificial Intelligence and Its Implications for Income Distribution and Unemployment." In *The Economics of Artificial Intelligence: An Agenda*, edited by Ajay Agrawal, Joshua Gans, and Avi Goldfarb, 349–90. University of Chicago Press. https://www.nber.org/books-and-chapters/economics-artificial-intelligence-agenda/artificial-intelligence-and-its-implications-income-distribution-and-unemployment.

Kremer, Michael, Sasha Gallant, Olga Rostapshova, and Milan Thomas. 2021. "Is Development Economics a Good Investment? Evidence on Scaling Rate and Social Returns from USAID's Innovation Fund." *Working Paper*. https://cpb-us-w2.wpmucdn.com/voices.uchicago.edu/dist/0/2830/files/2021/09/SROR–21.03.12_clean–3.pdf.

Lankes, Hans Peter, Rob Macquarie, Éléonore Soubeyran, and Nicholas Stern. 2024. "The Relationship between Climate Action and Poverty Reduction." *The World Bank Research Observer* 39 (1): 1–46. https://doi.org/10.1093/wbro/lkad011.

Lerner, Josh, Junxi Liu, Jacob Moscona, and David Y Yang. 2024. "Appropriate Entrepreneurship? The Rise of China and the Developing World." *Harvard Business School Working Papers*, no. 24-061, February.

Mazzucato, Mariana, and Dani Rodrik. 2023. "Industrial Policy with Conditionalities: A Taxonomy and Sample Cases." *UCL Institute for Innovation and Public Purpose, Working Paper Series*, October. https://www.ucl.ac.uk/bartlett/public-purpose/publications/2023/oct/industrial-policy-conditionalities-taxonomy-and-sample-cases.

McKenzie, David. 2019. "Shortening Supply Chains for Fruit and Vegetable Vendors in Bogota." *Finance and PSD Impact*, no. 54, August. https://doi.org/10.1596/32297.

Mugulur, Aneesh. 2019. "How Haryana is Working with Cab Aggregators to Solve the Unemployment Puzzle." *Samagra, Transforming Governance*, July 5. https://samagragovernance.in/.

Noman, Akbar, and Joseph E. Stiglitz. 2011. "Strategies for African Development." In *Good Growth and Governance in Africa: Rethinking Development Strategies*, edited by Akbar Noman, Kwesi Botchwey, Howard Stein, and Joseph E. Stiglitz. Oxford: Oxford University Press. https://doi.org/10.1093/acprof:oso/9780199698561.001.0001.

Rodrik, Dani. 2008. "The Real Exchange Rate and Economic Growth." *Brookings Papers on Economic Activity*, no. 2. https://www.brookings.edu/articles/the-real-exchange-rate-and-economic-growth/.

Rodrik, Dani. 2013. "Unconditional Convergence in Manufacturing." *The Quarterly Journal of Economics* 128 (1): 165–204. https://doi.org/10.1093/qje/qjs047.

Rodrik, Dani. 2014. "The Past, Present, and Future of Economic Growth." In *Towards a Better Global Economy: Policy Implications for Citizens Worldwide in the 21st Century*, edited by Franklin Allen, Jere R. Behrman, Nancy Birdsall, Shahrokh Fardoust, Dani Rodrik, Andrew Steer, and Arvind Subramanian. Oxford: Oxford University Press. https://doi.org/10.1093/acprof:oso/9780198723455.003.0002.

Rodrik, Dani. 2016. "Premature Deindustrialization." *Journal of Economic Growth* 21 (1): 1–33. https://doi.org/10.1007/s10887-015-9122-3.

Rodrik, Dani. 2022a. "An Industrial Policy for Good Jobs." *Policy Proposal. The Hamilton Project*. https://www.hamiltonproject.org/wp-content/uploads/2023/03/20220928_THP_Proposal_Rodrik_GoodJobs.pdf.

Rodrik, Dani. 2022b. "Prospects for Global Economic Convergence Under New Technologies." In *An Inclusive Future? Technology, New Dynamics, and Policy Challenges*, edited by David Autor, Kaushik Basu, Zia Qureshi, and Dani Rodrik, 88. Washington, DC: Brookings Institution. https://www.brookings.edu/articles/an-inclusive-future-technology-new-dynamics-and-policy-challenges/.

Rodrik, Dani, and Ishac Diwan. 2023. "Bridging the Climate-Development Gap." *Project Syndicate*, September 26, 2023. https://www.project-syndicate.org/commentary/low-middle-income-countries-debt-development-climate-crisis-by-dani-rodrik-and-ishac-diwan-2023–09.

Sheldon, Peter, and Seung-Ho Kwon. 2023. "Samsung in Vietnam: FDI, Business–Government Relations, Industrial Parks, and Skills Shortages." *The Economic and Labour Relations Review* 34 (1): 66–85. https://doi.org/10.1017/elr.2022.3.

Songwe, Vera, Nicholas Stern, Amar Bhattacharya, and United Nations. Economic Commission for Africa. 2022. "Finance for Climate Action: Scaling up Investment for Climate and Development." *United Nations. Economic Commission for Africa*, November. https://repository.uneca.org/handle/10855/49154.

Stern, Nicholas, and Joseph E. Stiglitz. 2023. "Climate Change and Growth." *Industrial and Corporate Change* 32 (2): 277–303. https://doi.org/10.1093/icc/dtad008.

Stiglitz, Joseph E. 1987. "Learning to Learn, Localized Learning and Technological Progress." In *Economic Policy and Technological Performance*, edited by Partha Dasgupta and Paul Stoneman, 125–53. Cambridge: Cambridge University Press. https://doi.org/10.1017/CBO9780511559938.007.

Stiglitz, Joseph E. 1989. *The Economic Role of the State*. Edited by Arnold Heertje. Oxford, UK; Cambridge, MA, USA: Basil Blackwell.

Stiglitz, Joseph E. 1996. "Some Lessons from the East Asian Miracle." *The World Bank Research Observer* 11 (2): 151–77.

Stiglitz, Joseph E. 2019. "Addressing Climate Change Through Price and Non-Price Interventions." *European Economic Review* 119 (October): 594–612. https://doi.org/10.1016/j.euroecorev.2019.05.007.

Stiglitz, Joseph E. 2021. "From Manufacturing-Led Export Growth to a Twenty-First Century Inclusive Growth Strategy: Explaining the Demise of a Successful Growth Model and What to Do about It." In *Inequality in the Developing World*, edited by Carlos Gradín, Murray Leibbrandt, and Finn Tarp, 284–318. Oxford: Oxford University Press. https://doi.org/10.1093/oso/9780198863960.003.0012.

Stiglitz, Joseph E., and Bruce C. N. Greenwald. 2014. *Creating a Learning Society: A New Approach to Growth, Development, and Social Progress. Kenneth J. Arrow Lecture Series*. New York: Columbia University Press.

Stiglitz, Joseph E, and Marilou Uy. 1996. "Financial Markets, Public Policy, and the East Asian Miracle." *The World Bank Research Observer* 11 (2).

Stiglitz, Joseph E., and Andrew Weiss. 1981. "Credit Rationing in Markets with Imperfect Information." *The American Economic Review* 71 (3): 393–410. https://www.jstor.org/stable/1802787.

Ton, Zeynep. 2017. "The Case for Good Jobs." *Harvard Business Review*, November 30, 2017. https://hbr.org/2017/11/the-case-for-good-jobs.

University of Groningen. 2017. "Maddison Historical Statistics." https://www.rug.nl/ggdc/historicaldevelopment/maddison/.

Weitzman, Martin L. 1974. "Prices vs. Quantities." *The Review of Economic Studies* 41 (4): 477–91. https://scholar.harvard.edu/files/weitzman/files/prices_vs_quantities.pdf.

World Bank, dir. 2023. "Delivering Growth to People through Better Jobs in Africa." *World Bank Live*. https://live.worldbank.org/en/event/2023/africa-pulse-regional-economic-update-growth-people-better-jobs.

World Bank, dir. n.d. "World Development Indicators." https://databank.worldbank.org/source/world-development-indicators.

8 The Need for Multipolar Artificial Intelligence Governance

*Daron Acemoglu**

8.1 Introduction

Advances in artificial intelligence (AI), and the amount of financial resources invested in newer models, are increasing at a breathtaking pace. Even considering that many of the rumoured capabilities and promises of new AI models are only hype, there is no doubt that AI will impact lives and the global economy for decades to come.[1]

These breakthroughs—and the potential use of this rapidly changing technology for both positive and negative purposes—mean that the governance of AI (i.e. how these technologies should be developed, used, and regulated, and how consumers and workers should become more informed about them) has become a central topic of discussion amongst social scientists and AI experts.[2] AI governance is partly about technical issues, such as assigning liability for misuse or malfunction, addressing reliability issues (e.g. hallucinations), and tracking progress and potential damages from the technology especially when AI is used in consumer-facing ways.[3] Yet often ignored in the technocratic debates is that governance is also about politics. Who has a voice in the development and adoption of new technology? Who will control these new AI tools?

As many authoritarian governments and especially China's Communist Party understand, whoever controls information will gain disproportionate social and political power.[4] It is also true that whoever controls the use of new technologies in production will gain a significant amount of power. Tech leaders—hoping to shape both information and technology deployment—promise that AI will remake the division of labour around the world. Yet who will benefit from this upheaval?

Currently, there is a serious imbalance of power over the design and diffusion of AI. This imbalance is exacerbating the current socially detrimental trajectory, philosophy, and usage of AI technologies. It is also undermining any kind of organic guardrails that could emerge from greater competition or countervailing forces of worker voices and civil society. Despite growing concerns about what AI will mean for everyday lives, this nascent technology is still controlled only by a few companies and executives in Silicon Valley and a similarly small number of companies and government leaders in China, with a secondary role for US regulators and the European Union. Better rules must be constructed for AI

DOI: 10.4324/9781003571384-8

governance, and there have been some promising ideas. Yet ultimately, the politics of governance will matter. Political outcomes depend, at least in part, on whose voices will be heard and whose will be stifled.

On the current trajectory of AI, two groups will bear the brunt of the consequences, especially if events go poorly—(i) workers in the industrialised world and (ii) citizens in the developing world. Neither of those two groups currently has any voice or power over the future of AI, however.

This chapter examines problems with the current direction of AI and possible solutions. It then posits why multi-polarity is important and discusses how the current environment—in which the poles are the tech companies, Government of China, US regulators, and EU policymakers—is not sufficient to make AI work for everyone. The importance of worker voices is stressed, and that the developing world is completely absent from the debate is emphasised. These themes are united in the conclusion, which also offers concrete policy ideas.

8.2 Why AI Governance Is Central: Promise and Peril

AI is an information technology; it can collect, process, and deploy information. As an information technology, AI offers new possibilities. Today, information is abundant (i.e. most human knowledge—and a lot of misinformation—is available on the internet), but useful information (i.e. that needed to reliably and immediately perform complex decision-making and problem-solving tasks) is scarce. AI tools, especially recent generative AI technologies, could be deployed to provide real-time, reliable, and context-dependent information to human decision makers.

The potential of AI is not just for office workers, academics, and journalists, as modern craft workers (e.g. electricians, plumbers, carpenters, and maintenance workers) also routinely navigate a series of problem-solving tasks in their jobs. Yet there is a lack of accessible information to handle the complex problems that such workers repeatedly encounter. As an example, electricians may be trying to correct issues with new electrical equipment or addressing unanticipated challenges from a quickly evolving electricity grid. Access to better information can enable these workers to attain and to apply greater expertise in a range of activities and to take on new, more sophisticated tasks. Past literature has explored and emphasised this potential avenue for pro-worker AI.[5]

This promise is particularly attractive because it could also help reverse the concerning trends of occupational and wage polarisation that have pervaded the United States and other industrialised nations since the late 1970s. Middle-income jobs have become more scarce; thus, displaced workers have been pushed disproportionately into low-wage jobs.[6] One major driver of this labour market bifurcation has been the preponderance of industrial automation (i.e. the substitution of capital for labour, reducing the need for workers in the production process by deploying industrial robots).[7] This automation-substitution tends to increase inequality and lead to only slow—or sometimes even negative—wage growth. This downward pressure could be relieved if new, productive tasks are created for workers to help reduce inequality and boost wages.[8] It is possible—although not inevitable—that deploying new AI tools could increase the demand for middle-skilled labour, enabling such workers to perform more expert work and allowing them to attain better compensation in return for their enhanced productivity.

AI, like other information tools, can also be used to further accelerate automation (i.e. deploying information for finding ways of mimicking human performance in various tasks). If so, it is likely to deliver the same type of inequality-boosting growth experienced in the United States over the last 4 decades. AI has the capability to automate white-collar tasks, and, in the future, it could be integrated with other technologies, including robotics, to deepen the automation of blue-collar tasks.[9] Moreover, AI's information can also be manipulated and distorted—as experienced with social media over the last 2 decades. It could also increase the effectiveness of digital ads and filter bubbles at a steep social cost.

The information provision capabilities of AI can also be used in new, pro-democratic ways. AI that provides more reliable information; increases transparency about government activities; creates new pathways for citizen participation in public decision-making; and builds new public spheres for debate, deliberation, and information exchange can be a boon to democratic citizenship.[10] Taiwan, which has rolled out AI tools to increase governmental transparency, bolstering citizen voices and participation by democratising access to and control of information, illustrates one pathway for this achievement.[11]

AI embodies a way to rebuild shared prosperity and democratic citizenship along one path, or further reinforce inequality and deepen the damage to democracy and well-being along another.[12] Unfortunately, there is ample evidence that the latter path is much more likely. First, the business models of tech companies shepherding AI advances are very similar to those that led to prioritising automation and information manipulation in the past. It is notable that the two areas that have received the most attention from the industry are (i) automation of additional white-collar tasks using generative AI and (ii) internet search and related activities, where profits come from digital ads.[13]

Second, advances in AI have intensified notions of artificial general intelligence, and these ideas have played an important role in shaping the approach to generative AI that has emerged (e.g. based on very large foundation models that mimic human conversation).[14] If it is perceived that human-level cognition and capabilities are soon coming, then it becomes natural—or even inevitable—to automate more tasks, so that the 'more efficient' AI models perform them instead of inconsistent humans. Moreover, if it is believed that AI will soon be better than much of humankind, it becomes much less problematic to accept algorithmic dominance over humans so that algorithms guide human decisions and, when necessary, manipulate those decisions (and extract abundant data for use without the need for permission or recompense).

Third, early evidence suggests that the AI playing field may be much more oligopolistic (i.e. dominated by two or three leading companies with similar visions and business models) than previous digital technologies.[15] Such an oligopolistic structure entails higher prices and a slower spread of beneficial AI applications.

More ominously, it could lock in a future path of AI development that is more pernicious—more focussed on only automation and more manipulative—while simultaneously making it harder for alternative business models that could usher in greater human complementarity and more pro-democratic uses of AI to become competitive.

If this perilous direction is indeed on the horizon, what are the options? The simple answer is to redirect the trajectory of AI. This will require not only technocratic regulation but also a broader mobilisation of society and changes in norms. This motivates the importance of multi-polarity.

8.3 The Centrality of Multi-Polarity

A multipolar governance structure for AI is needed. There is an imperative to redirect AI in a more socially beneficial direction, but such a challenge cannot be accomplished by just attempting unsystematic, ad hoc solutions to social symptoms as they arise. It requires new norms and a different balance of power that guides AI priorities towards what is broadly beneficial for society, not just a few select technologists.

Multi-polarity does not mean sidelining AI expertise. Of course, tech executives' advice and visions need to be considered, as they know much about the technology and make significant decisions about where it will go. Equally, any regulation would fail if it were not partly designed and enforced by mission-driven (i.e. democracy-driven) governmental experts.

More poles and more voices are needed, in part, because—despite apparent differences—there is also congruence between the approaches of the two AI superpowers, the United States and China. Implicit acceptance of algorithmic dominance over humans is common both in the United States and China. Leading players in both countries are committed to the advancement of digital technologies and the use of AI as a tool for collecting information from humans.[16] Moreover, companies and policymakers in both countries view algorithmic automation as the engine of future economic growth. In the United States, algorithmic dominance takes the form of large platforms collecting data and manipulating people, while in China, tech companies are empowered if they follow the government's agenda.[17] This difference notwithstanding, neither the United States nor China is likely to strengthen the privacy and protection of citizens or consumers. Nor are they likely, without further pressure, to pour resources into redirecting the trajectory of AI research in a more human-complementary direction.

To counter algorithmic dominance over humans, small, regulatory fixes will not work. Even if the right types of regulations were adopted, they would not be wholly effective unless norms in the tech industry also evolve. Yet norm changes require politics.[18] In addition, giving a voice to so-far ignored stakeholders would be an important step towards favouring the human perspective.

The European Union has played a leading role in regulating AI to date. It has been at the forefront of privacy protection against tech companies and anti-trust activity.[19] Top-down regulation, without changing the norms and power imbalance of the tech industry, can only go so far, however. Moreover, Europe does not house any of the leading AI companies. Of the six digital services gatekeepers specified by the 2022 EU Digital Markets Act, five are US companies (i.e. Alphabet, Amazon, Apple, Meta, and Microsoft) and the sixth is Chinese (i.e. ByteDance). The European Union's comparative advantage in regulating originates exactly from this absence of big powerful players, who would otherwise lobby against regulations. This also limits what the European Union can achieve since it cannot effectively embed those policies and regulations into the normative fabric of a wide-ranging ecosystem to encourage a different AI research direction.

8.4 Worker Voices

Worker voices are important for two reasons. First, organised labour can be a valuable counterweight to the emphasis on automation and surveillance. Its role can be particularly important when managers have incentives to use new technologies for automation—either because they believe it is the most effective business strategy or they are motivated by desires to undercut the power of labour. Labour unions can resist excessive automation and encourage firms to introduce new tasks and training opportunities for their workers.

There have been instances in the past where organised labour in the United States has succeeded in influencing the rollout of new technology and creation of new tasks for workers.[20] Notable examples include the integration of new numerically controlled tools in the automotive industry in the 1950s and 1960s, and more recently, the 2023 Writers Guild of America negotiations over the use of generative AI tools for scriptwriting.[21] The approach of negotiating over the terms of technology instead of only downstream issues like wages has been more common in Scandinavia and Germany. Nordic unions have often worked with companies on worker compensation and on how work itself is organised, while work councils and labour representatives on corporate boards have often represented workers' viewpoints in the process of technology adoption.[22]

Moreover, the importance of labour voices is even more central when it comes to AI, because, as previously articulated, AI is an information tool with the promise of improving how workers engage in problem-solving tasks. Trying to improve how workers use information and engage in problem-solving without actually consulting workers would be like trying to solve the problem of child malnutrition in a village in Malawi without ever finding out anything about Malawi or the village.[23] The real promise of worker voices is that they can provide context, as well as insight, about what types of information would be most useful to workers, as well as the training that workers would need to incorporate emergent AI tech capabilities.

Part of the reason why the current direction of AI is prioritising automation and not increasing worker productivity is that there are currently no worker voices in AI development and adoption. Robust worker voices used expertly and correctly—not as a barrier to technology adoption but to steer the development of workplace technology in a more pro-worker direction—could determine which alternative becomes the future of AI and jobs.

Robust worker voices necessitate more powerful labour organisations as well. It is not clear whether existing labour unions can play this role or if new organisational forms must develop. More bottom-up participation from workers is needed. Furthermore, the labour movement itself may have to change, becoming both more invested in AI expertise and more flexible about how it approaches technology. In short, the labour movement must find the right posture that is both accommodating to new technologies and forceful in articulating ways of using these technologies in more pro-worker ways.

8.5 Developing Country Voices

AI is a global technology. If its adoption is significant in the industrialised world, it will almost surely spread to the developing world. A glimpse of this is already apparent in AI technologies used for surveillance. Existing evidence indicates that as the Government of China intensifies data collection and increases its demand for technologies that process these data and use them for surveillance and monitoring, this is having a first-order impact on the direction of AI research amongst Chinese startups. This effect is not confined to China; these surveillance technologies are spreading to other countries, especially authoritarian ones that have a greater demand for citizen-monitoring capabilities.[24] The Chinese telecom giant Huawei, for example, is reported to have exported surveillance technologies to at least 50 other countries (Feldstein, 2019). Many Western countries are also using sophisticated AI tools for surveillance of their citizens.[25]

The case of surveillance technologies illustrates not just the inevitable spread of new AI tools around the world but also the more extreme dangers that some of these tools pose in countries with weaker institutions. Courts, civil society pressure, and the democratic process generate—albeit imperfect—barriers against limitless use of these tools by governments. Such checks and balances are much less likely to be forthcoming in authoritarian countries around the world, exacerbating concerns of abuse.[26] The same concerns apply to data collection and how AI-based technologies could be abused in workplaces (e.g. to reduce breaks or to increase the speed of work).[27]

AI adoption in the industrialised world would impact developing countries even if firms in those places did not invest in this technology because AI uptake in Western countries will inevitably remake the global division of labour. This raises another set of major concerns. If AI goes in the direction of automation, it may encroach into the set of tasks that could have been profitably performed in middle-income economies, especially as the education level of the workforce in these countries continues to improve. This could significantly reduce the remaining opportunities for rapid economic growth in those places, in a similar pattern to the premature de-industrialisation driven by globalisation and industrial automation that has held many developing countries in lower income levels (Rodrik, 2015).

The most prominent examples of fast growth amongst emerging economies (e.g., China, Malaysia, South Korea, and Viet Nam) over the last 6 decades occurred when these countries found a niche in the global division of labour by exporting products or tasks where their abundant labour supply created a comparative advantage, then upgrading their skills and competencies to move to the next rung of the value chain. If the goods in which these countries initially specialised (e.g. textiles, apparel, or toys) were automated cheaply at the time, then these growth opportunities would not have existed. Thus, AI focussing predominantly on automation may have similar effects for the next group of potential first-growers.

Currently, most of those who will be impacted by AI (around 6 billion people) are outside of the United States, Canada, China, and Western Europe. If the direction of AI is likely to have major consequences on their livelihoods and freedoms, it is worrisome that these many people have no voices in the trajectory of global AI technology. Establishing sufficient guardrails for AI rollout in their countries is thus especially important to avoid importing AI as an inappropriate technology. It is thus crucial to ensure that developing nations' voices are heard in the direction of global AI research.

It is unclear who will speak for these 6 billion people in the developing world. In an ideal world, governments or a consortia of governments could be candidates, but a large fraction of this population lives under authoritarian governments where leaders do not often defend regular people's interests.

8.6 Concluding Remarks

Including robust worker voices and developing country perspectives in the debates shaping the future of AI is not just a matter of fairness. The true promise of AI is its potential to empower workers and citizens, even if this promise is far from being realised. Such a promise necessitates detailed information about the needs, competencies, and perspectives of the people who will actually use the technologies. Yet whether key decision makers decide to listen to those who will be affected—and exactly whose voices are heard—is a political choice. At present, both the current ideology of the AI sector that sees data, computational capacity, and the genius of tech leaders as the most important inputs for the advancement of AI, as well as the financial interests of leading companies and their executives, do not favour broadening the set of voices and power centres influencing the future of this promising technology.

Broadening the set of stakeholders heard, although imperative, will not be easy. The challenge ahead is made more difficult by the fact that neither workers in the industrialised world nor workers and citizens around the developing world are particularly well organised. The labour movement has been in decline in much of the West for at least 5 decades, and this decline has accelerated in many countries, with a few attempts to unionise new sectors notwithstanding.[28] The developing world has rarely spoken with a common voice on any topic, especially one that runs counter to the interests of the United States and China. China's success in co-opting the BRICS grouping by expanding it to include its allies does not bode well for the hope that independent developing nations will be able to come together and forge a unified message on how AI can be best used and developed to help their citizens.[29]

There is a way forward, however. Attempts to change the current equilibrium in the field of AI and the current dominance of a few tech companies and executives are likely to be synergistic with other changes. For example, if democratic control over some of the AI functions occurs in the United States (e.g. if lawmakers pass legislation that limits the ability of tech companies to collect and to monetise data), then this can also pave the way for international regulation as tech companies would be weaker to resist reasonable demands from the developing world. Likewise, if worker voices become more robust, this could also facilitate the formation of a block of developing nations to articulate a common perspective on AI.

It would also be useful to develop several common perspectives that can make the voices of both workers and developing nations more effective. Centring the discussion on having a pro-worker and pro-citizen direction for AI or an anti-worker, anti-democracy one is a useful starting point. Once different parties in the conversation—including tech companies—accept that there is such a choice and that the pro-worker, pro-democracy direction is both technically feasible and socially desirable, it becomes much harder to pursue the current direction of research that has already caused harm for workers, equality, democracy, and well-being.

These debates could also broaden the scope of the discussion. For example, absent in current discussions is the question of whether foundation models (i.e. where resources are being spent to develop human-sounding communication capabilities in general interactions) are the best architecture for pro-worker AI tools that provide useful information to human decision makers. Any success by workers from industrialised nations in pushing tech companies to develop more tools that can be useful to human workers, and any brakes on excessive automation, would also help the developing world.

AI governance is about politics, and if the power to shape the direction of AI remains askew, the fruits of this new technological platform are unlikely to benefit most people. The antidote is multipolar AI governance that aims to produce a more inclusive political process. This will allow a richer set of voices to shape the future of AI in a way that is consistent with a broader set of objectives and interests.

Notes

* The author is grateful to Austin Lentsch and Julia Regier for help with references and editorial assistance. This chapter draws on joint research with David Autor, Pascual Restrepo, and especially Simon Johnson. All remaining errors are those of the author.

1 For example, an evaluation of the medium-term microeconomic effects of recent AI advances and examination of many forecasts that exaggerate the potential of AI are provided in Acemoglu (2024).

2 One famous contribution to the discourse from AI experts, which led to the departure of two notable Google researchers, is Bender et al. (2021). For an overview of more recent developments, see Capraro et al. (2024).

3 For example, see Huttenlocher, Ozdaglar, Goldston (2023) and Alam et al. (2024).

4 See as follows for more discussion of the Communist Party's control over direction of AI, as well as Chapter 10 on Chinese digital surveillance in Acemoglu and Johnson (2023b).

5 See Acemoglu and Johnson (2023a) and Acemoglu, Autor, Johnson (2023).

6 See Acemoglu and Autor (2011), Autor and Dorn (2013), and Autor (2019).

7 About 50%–70% of changes in the US wage structure since 1980 can be explained by the decline of work involving routine tasks in rapidly automating industries (Acemoglu and Restrepo, 2020, 2022).
8 See Acemoglu and Restrepo (2018, 2019).
9 Current AI–robotics integration research challenges include improving robot control, perception, decision-making, path planning, simultaneous localisation and mapping (SLAM), reinforcement learning, sensor fusion methods, and other topics. For an overview of large language models for robotics, see Zeng et al. (2023). For more on autonomous navigation, see Nahavandi et al. (2022). For additional AI-driven research questions related to multi-goal reinforcement learning, see Plappert et al. (2018).
10 In Acemoglu and Johnson (2023a), Jürgen Habermas's notion that 'the public sphere, defined as forums where individuals form new associations and discuss social issues and policy, is pivotal for democratic politics . . . [by allowing] people to freely participate in debates on issues of general interest without a strict hierarchy based on preexisting status' was noted (p. 372). In the early 2000s, social media held the promise of creating a new public sphere, but filter bubbles, content moderation failures, and other missteps largely squandered the opportunity. See also Habermas (1991).
11 See Acemoglu and Johnson (2023a: Chapter 10) and Weyl and Tang (2024).
12 For more discussion of the damages to democracy and mental health, see Acemoglu (2023a).
13 See Acemoglu and Johnson (2023a: Chapter 9); Acemoglu (2021); and Acemoglu and Restrepo (2019).
14 See Acemoglu and Johnson (2023a: Chapter 9) and Acemoglu, Jordan, Weyl (2021).
15 For more discussion on AI's tendency towards oligopoly, see Acemoglu and Johnson (2023b).
16 For more on the US perspective, see Zuboff (2019). For the China perspective, see Lei (2023).
17 For example, consider the challenges that Jack Ma has faced with Alibaba and the Ant Group after criticising China's regulatory system, or the scrutiny of DiDi Global's ride-hailing platform under China's national security and cybersecurity laws (Mulrenan, 2021). For more on China's comparative advantage in surveillance AI technology driven by governmental interests, see Beraja et al. (2023).
18 For more ideas on accomplishing changes in norms, see Acemoglu and Robinson (2023).
19 Amongst the more notable pieces of legislation protecting consumer data, privacy, and competition, the European Union paved the way with the General Data Protection Regulation in 2018 and Digital Markets Act and Digital Services Act in 2022.
20 This has not been the standard practice of labour unions in the United States; it is far more common to negotiate on the terms of work schedules, compensation, and benefits.
21 For more on the accomplishments of organised labour in the automotive industry of the 1950s and 1960s, see Noble (1984). For more discussion on the implications of the 2023 Writers Guild of America (WGA) strike, see Acemoglu, Johnson, Lentsch (2023). See also an overview of the AI provisions in the ratified WGA-Alliance of Motion Picture and Television Producers agreement (WGA West, 2024).
22 See Acemoglu and Johnson (2023a: Chapter 7) for further discussion of the US and Swedish cases of organised labour and their sway over the broader issues of work arrangements. Germany's case is outlined in Jäger, Noy, Schoefer (2022).
23 It is not an uncommon—nor recent—problem for the international aid community. See, for example, Gibson et al. (2005).
24 See Beraja et al. (2023). For an interactive map showing the global partnerships and relationships between Chinese AI and surveillance companies and various governments, companies, and universities, see ASPI. "Mapping China's Tech Giants." https://chinatechmap.aspi.org.au/#/map/

25 While Chinese companies supply surveillance technology to 63 countries, US companies also provide AI surveillance tech to 32 countries, with IBM (11 countries), Palantir (9 countries), and Cisco (6 countries) leading the way (Feldstein, 2019). The AI Global Surveillance (AIGS) index used in Feldstein (2019) suggested that the United States uses smart/safe city tech, facial recognition, and smart policing tools, including some from China. For more discussion on the use of surveillance and monitoring tools by the United States and the European Union, see Sahin (2020).

26 For example, the snooping technology Pegasus, developed in Israel and made available as a 'zero-click' Trojan horse virus, has been used extensively in India and Mexico. See Acemoglu and Johnson (2023a: Chapter 10) for more discussion. On the use of Pegasus in India, see Singh (2021); Priest, Timberg, Mekhennet (2021); and Bergman and Mazzetti (2021).

27 For more on the rise of worker tracking in firms like Amazon, JP Morgan Chase, McDonald's, and UnitedHealth, see Kantor et al. (2022).

28 For more discussion on the current state of unions and the collective action problem that precludes greater unionisation rates—even while pro-union sentiment is relatively high—see Naidu (2022). For further analysis of de-unionisation, see Farber et al. (2021).

29 See Acemoglu (2023b).

References

Acemoglu, Daron. 2021. "AI's Future Doesn't Have to Be Dystopian." *Boston Review*, May 20, 2021. https://www.bostonreview.net/forum/ais-future-doesnt-have-to-be-dystopian/.

Acemoglu, Daron. 2023a. "The Wrong BRICS Expansion." *Project Syndicate*, August 31, 2023. https://www.project-syndicate.org/commentary/brics-expansion-wrong-for-emerging-economies-by-daron-acemoglu-2023–08.

Acemoglu, Daron. 2023b. "Written Testimony: Hearing on 'The Philosophy of AI: Learning from History, Shaping Our Future.'" *Written Testimony for the Senate Committee on Homeland Security and Governmental Affairs*. https://www.hsgac.senate.gov/wp-content/uploads/Testimony-Acemoglu-2023-11-08.pdf.

Acemoglu, Daron. 2024. "The Simple Macroeconomics of AI." *National Bureau of Economic Research (NBER) Working Paper Series*, no. 32847, May. https://doi.org/10.3386/w32487.

Acemoglu, Daron, and David Autor. 2011. "Skills, Tasks and Technologies: Implications for Employment and Earnings." In *Handbook of Labor Economics*, edited by Orley Ashenfelter and David Card, 1st ed., Vol. 4B: 1043–171. Amsterdam: Elsevier. https://doi.org/10.1016/S0169–7218(11)02410–5.

Acemoglu, Daron, David Autor, and Simon Johnson. 2023. "Can We Have Pro-Worker AI? Choosing a Path of Machines in Service of Minds." *MIT Shaping the Future of Work Initiative, Policy Memo*. https://shapingwork.mit.edu/wp-content/uploads/2023/09/Pro-Worker-AI-Policy-Memo.pdf.

Acemoglu, Daron, and Simon Johnson. 2023a. "Big Tech is Bad. Big A.I. Will Be Worse." *The New York Times*, June 9, sec. Opinion. https://www.nytimes.com/2023/06/09/opinion/ai-big-tech-microsoft-google-duopoly.html.

Acemoglu, Daron, and Simon Johnson. 2023b. *Power and Progress: Our 1000-Years Struggle Over Technology and Prosperity*. New York: Hachette. https://shapingwork.mit.edu/power-and-progress/.

Acemoglu, Daron, Simon Johnson, and Austin Lentsch. 2023. "The Hollywood Writers' AI Fight is Everyone's Fight | by Daron Acemoglu, Simon Johnson and Austin Lentsch." *Project Syndicate*, August 2. https://www.project-syndicate.org/commentary/ai-wga-writers-strike-future-of-knowledge-work-by-daron-acemoglu-et-al-2023–08.

Acemoglu, Daron, Michael I. Jordan, and E. Glen Weyl. 2021. "The Turing Test is Bad for Business." *Wired*, November 8. https://www.wired.com/story/artificial-intelligence-turing-test-economics-business/.

Acemoglu, Daron, and Pascual Restrepo. 2018. "The Race between Man and Machine: Implications of Technology for Growth, Factor Shares, and Employment." *American Economic Review* 108 (6): 1488–542. https://doi.org/10.1257/aer.20160696.

Acemoglu, Daron, and Pascual Restrepo. 2019. "Automation and New Tasks: How Technology Displaces and Reinstates Labor." *Journal of Economic Perspectives* 33 (2): 3–30. https://doi.org/10.1257/jep.33.2.3.

Acemoglu, Daron, and Pascual Restrepo. 2020. "Robots and Jobs: Evidence from US Labor Markets." *Journal of Political Economy* 128 (6): 2188–244. https://doi.org/10.1086/705716.

Acemoglu, Daron, and Pascual Restrepo. 2022. "Tasks, Automation, and the Rise in U.S. Wage Inequality." *Econometrica* 90 (5): 1973–2016. https://doi.org/10.3982/ECTA19815.

Acemoglu, Daron, and James Robinson. 2023. "Culture, Institutions and Social Equilibria: A Framework." *National Bureau of Economic Research (NBER) Working Paper Series*, no. 28832. https://doi.org/10.3386/w28832.

Alam, Md. Ferdous, Austin Lentsch, Nomi Yu, Sylvia Barmack, Suhin Kim, Daron Acemoglu, John Hart, Simon Johnson, and Faez Ahmed. 2024. "From Automation to Augmentation: Redefining Engineering Design and Manufacturing in the Age of NextGen-AI." In *An MIT Exploration of Generative AI: From Novel Chemicals to Opera*, edited by Massachusetts Institute of Technology. https://mit-genai.pubpub.org/pub/9s6690gd.

Australian Strategic Policy Institute. n.d. "Mapping China's Tech Giants." Accessed December 26, 2024. https://chinatechmap.aspi.org.au/.

Autor, David H. 2019. "Work of the Past, Work of the Future." *AEA Papers and Proceedings* 109 (May): 1–32. https://doi.org/10.1257/pandp.20191110.

Autor, David H., and David Dorn. 2013. "The Growth of Low-Skill Service Jobs and the Polarization of the US Labor Market." *American Economic Review* 103 (5): 1553–97. https://doi.org/10.1257/aer.103.5.1553.

Bender, Emily M., Timnit Gebru, Angelina McMillan-Major, and Shmargaret Shmitchell. 2021. "On the Dangers of Stochastic Parrots: Can Language Models Be Too Big?" In *Proceedings of the 2021 ACM Conference on Fairness, Accountability, and Transparency*, 610–23. Virtual Event Canada; ACM. https://doi.org/10.1145/3442188.3445922.

Beraja, Martin, Andrew Kao, David Y. Yang, and Noam Yuchtman. 2023. "AI-Tocracy." *The Quarterly Journal of Economics* 138 (3): 1349–402. https://doi.org/10.1093/qje/qjad012.

Bergman, Ronen, and Mark Mazzetti. 2021. "Israeli Companies Aided Saudi Spying Despite Khashoggi Killing." *The New York Times*, July 17, 2021, sec. World. https://www.nytimes.com/2021/07/17/world/middleeast/israel-saudi-khashoggi-hacking-nso.html.

Capraro, Valerio, Austin Lentsch, Daron Acemoglu, Selin Akgun, Aisel Akhmedova, Ennio Bilancini, Jean-Francois Bonnefon, et al. 2024. "The Impact of Generative Artificial Intelligence on Socioeconomic Inequalities and Policy Making." *PNAS Nexus*, January, 71. https://doi.org/10.2139/ssrn.4666103.

Farber, Henry S, Daniel Herbst, Ilyana Kuziemko, and Suresh Naidu. 2021. "Unions and Inequality over the Twentieth Century: New Evidence from Survey Data." *The Quarterly Journal of Economics* 136 (3): 1325–85. https://doi.org/10.1093/qje/qjab012.

Feldstein, Steven. 2019. "The Global Expansion of AI Surveillance." *Carnegie Endowment for International Peace, Working Paper Series*, September. https://carnegieendowment.org/research/2019/09/the-global-expansion-of-ai-surveillance?lang=en.

Gibson, Clark C., Krister Andersson, Elinor Ostrom, and Sujai Shivakumar. 2005. *The Samaritan's Dilemma: The Political Economy of Development Aid*, 1st ed. Oxford University Press. https://doi.org/10.1093/0199278857.001.0001.

Habermas, Jürgen. 1991. *The Structural Transformation of the Public Sphere: An Inquiry Into a Category of Burgeois Society*. Translated by Thomas Burger. Cambridge, MA: MIT Press. Accessed December 26, 2024. https://mitpress.mit.edu/9780262581080/the-structural-transformation-of-the-public-sphere/.

Huttenlocher, Dan, Asu Ozdaglar, and David Goldston. 2023. "A Framework for U.S. AI Governance: Creating a Safe and Thriving AI Sector." *MIT Schwarzman College of Computing Policy Briefs*, November.

Jäger, Simon, Shakked Noy, and Benjamin Schoefer. 2022. "The German Model of Industrial Relations: Balancing Flexibility and Collective Action." *Journal of Economic Perspectives* 36 (4): 53–80. https://doi.org/10.1257/jep.36.4.53.

Kantor, Jodi, Arya Sundaram, Aliza Aufrichtig, and Rumsey Taylor. 2022. "The Rise of the Worker Productivity Score." *The New York Times*, August 15, 2022, sec. Business. https://www.nytimes.com/interactive/2022/08/14/business/worker-productivity-tracking.html.

Lei, Ya-Wen. 2023. *The Gilded Cage: Technology, Development, and State Capitalism in China*. Princeton, NJ: Princeton University Press.

Mulrenan, Stephen. 2021. "Tech Companies and Investors Respond to China's Regulatory Crackdown." *International Bar Association*, November 22, 2021. https://www.ibanet.org/Tech-companies-and-investors-respond-to-Chinas-regulatory-crackdown.

Nahavandi, Saeid, Roohallah Alizadehsani, Darius Nahavandi, Shady Mohamed, Navid Mohajer, Mohammad Rokonuzzaman, and Ibrahim Hossain. 2022. "A Comprehensive Review on Autonomous Navigation." *Working Paper*. Ithaca, NY: arXiv. https://doi.org/10.48550/arXiv.2212.12808.

Naidu, Suresh. 2022. "Is There Any Future for a US Labor Movement?" *Journal of Economic Perspectives* 36 (4): 3–28. https://doi.org/10.1257/jep.36.4.3.

Noble, David F. 1984. *Forces of Production: A Social History of Industrial Automation*, 1st ed. New York: Alfred A. Knopf.

Plappert, Matthias, Marcin Andrychowicz, Alex Ray, Bob McGrew, Bowen Baker, Glenn Powell, Jonas Schneider, et al. 2018. "Multi-Goal Reinforcement Learning: Challenging Robotics Environments and Request for Research." *arXiv*. https://doi.org/10.48550/arXiv.1802.09464.

Priest, Dana, Craig Timberg, and Souad Mekhennet. 2021. "Private Israeli Spyware Used to Hack Cellphones of Journalists, Activists Worldwide." *Washington Post*, July 18, 2021. https://www.washingtonpost.com/investigations/interactive/2021/nso-spyware-pegasus-cellphones/.

Rodrik, Dani. 2015. "Premature Deindustrialization." *National Bureau of Economic Research (NBER) Working Paper Series*, no. w20935, February. https://doi.org/10.3386/w20935.

Sahin, Kaan. 2020. "The West, China, and AI Surveillance." *Atlantic Council (blog)*, December 18, 2020. https://www.atlanticcouncil.org/blogs/geotech-cues/the-west-china-and-ai-surveillance/.

Singh, Sushant. 2021. "India's Watergate Moment." *Foreign Policy (blog)*, July 21, 2021. https://foreignpolicy.com/2021/07/21/india-israel-nso-pegasus-spyware-hack-modi-bjp-democracy-watergate/.

Weyl, E. Glen, and Audrey Tang. 2024. *Plurality: The Future of Collaborative Technology and Democracy*. RadicalxChange. https://www.plurality.net/.

Writers Guild of America West. 2024. "Know Your Rights: Artificial Intelligence." https://www.wga.org/contracts/know-your-rights/artificial-intelligence.

Zeng, Fanlong, Wensheng Gan, Yongheng Wang, Ning Liu, and Philip S. Yu. 2023. "Large Language Models for Robotics: A Survey." *arXiv*. https://doi.org/10.48550/arXiv.2311.07226.

Zuboff, Shoshana. 2019. *The Age of Surveillance Capitalism: The Fight for a Human Future at the New Frontier of Power*. New York: Hachette PublicAffairs. Accessed December 26, 2024. https://www.hbs.edu/faculty/Pages/item.aspx?num=56791.

9 The Green Industrial Revolution

Consequences and Policies

*Alessio Terzi**

9.1 Introduction

Climate change is upon us. The year 2023 was the warmest since records began in the late 1800s, at roughly 1.2°Celsius (C) above pre-industrial levels (Bardan, 2024). On the current path, surface temperatures are expected to breach the 1.5°C threshold before 2030, and 2.0°C in the 2040s (Lamboll et al., 2023). As this is an unacceptable risk to human lives and livelihoods, in 2015, global leaders signed an agreement to strive towards keeping temperature increases well below 2.0°C above pre-industrial levels. To do so, climate modelling suggests that the world economy needs to reach net-zero emissions, or climate neutrality, by mid-century (IPCC, 2021).

It is important to realise that, effectively, we currently live in a fossil fuel-based civilisation, meaning that practically every economic activity—directly or indirectly—relies on fossil fuels or emissions (Terzi, 2022c). As a consequence, reaching net-zero emissions will require reinventing production and consumption—energy generation, agriculture, transport, housing, clothing, and more. Such a radical transformation of the economic system is not without precedents in history, as this echoes past industrial revolutions (Terzi and Fouquet, 2023). If history never repeats itself, it often rhymes; the impact of this green transition is likely to resemble what happened during past comparable seismic economic transformations.

Following Donald Trump's re-election in 2025, and his administration's pushback against climate action, it might feel like the global decarbonisation effort has been derailed. It is, however, important to appreciate that the green transition is inevitable. First, the current economic model, based on fossil fuels and emissions, is unsustainable. Stein's law suggests that something unsustainable cannot be continued and will therefore eventually need to change (Coyle, 2011; Helm, 2023). Second, it has been shown how exposure to extreme weather events increases the belief in climate change (Myers et al., 2013), boosts voting for environmentally-conscious parties (Hoffmann et al., 2022), and prods many towards green investments (Fisman et al., 2023). At some point, the pressure of climate-induced disasters on human society will jolt all to action, making the green transition eventually happen.

DOI: 10.4324/9781003571384-9

It seems like humanity is therefore approaching an inevitable green transition that has commonalities with previous industrial revolutions, paving the way to abundance, green growth, and employment creation. This will be true for some countries and regions but will require careful policy-making, particularly to manage the adjustment in the short and medium term. Expanding on this point is the objective of the remainder of this chapter, which is organised as follows. Section 9.2 posits that the green transition will resemble an industrial revolution. Section 9.3 outlines the economic consequences of a green industrial revolution, which will set in motion a host of broad political economy dynamics that are illustrated in Section 9.4. Section 9.5 offers five credible policy recommendations, and brief concluding remarks are provided in Section 9.6.

9.2 A New Industrial Revolution

As noted by economic historian Roger Fouquet, 'Each technology revolution has created and will create a new period of abundance, a new phase of wealth' (Fouquet, 2008: 364). This occurs if the new technology (i) offers characteristics that are considered superior at the time of adoption and (ii) has scope for efficiency improvements and price reductions beyond the point of price parity with the incumbent technology. Without these characteristics, the new technology will fail to replace the incumbent altogether (Fouquet, 2010).

Renewables—and green technologies more broadly—seem to be well placed to display both key characteristics. They are perceived as superior, meaning that a subset of consumers is initially willing to pay a 'green premium' for them (Gates, 2021), including electric vehicles (EVs), heat pumps, or second-hand clothes. As associated production has expanded, aimed at satisfying the demand of early adopters, green technologies have reliably experienced cost reductions in line with Wright's law. Some of them have reached price parity, such as utility-scale solar energy or onshore wind, which is now cheaper in many jurisdictions than the fossil fuel alternative (IRENA, 2020; Terzi, 2023a). Similarly, following a set of price wars between producers, some EVs now have comparable prices to standard cars. As prices further drop, preferences will shift in favour of green technologies, accelerating the transition further (Besley and Persson, 2023). Moreover, a vast set of green goods is entering into an accelerating growth phase and challenging incumbent technologies, including solar photovoltaic cells, wind rotors, EVs, batteries, electrolysers, and heat pumps, which will also result in falling costs.

In the early stages of an industrial revolution—and the introduction of a general-purpose technology more broadly—the productivity-enhancing effects are not immediately apparent. Only once secondary innovations are rolled out will the full benefits become apparent. For the First Industrial Revolution, Juhász, Squicciarini, Voigtländer (2020) showed this quantitatively, arguing that mechanised cotton spinning required the invention of the factory and extensive trial and error before showing strong productivity-enhancing effects. The Second Industrial Revolution displayed similar characteristics. Although it appeared that one existing energy source (i.e. steam) was swapped for another (i.e. electricity), thanks to secondary innovation, the introduction of electricity allowed the move away from the line shaft organisation of factories. This paved the way for the assembly line and its huge productivity boost (David, 1990; Aghion, Antonin, Bunel, 2023).[1]

In light of these considerations, one should not consider the green transition as simply a switch from one polluting energy source to a climate-neutral alternative. Instead, the fundamental question is whether green technologies today display scope for further secondary innovation. Here, the evidence is quite clear. Electric engines are much more efficient than thermal ones at converting energy into motion (i.e. 89% versus 20%), suggesting a reduction in transport costs will occur. New waves of core technologies are associated with large initial returns to scale, fostering productivity growth (Freeman and Louçã, 2002), while those related to fossil fuels have entered into diminishing returns after 150 years of experimentation (Stern, Stiglitz and Taylor, 2022). Renewables are now widely expected to become the cheapest electricity source in human history (IEA, 2020), boosting productivity across the economy.

Like past industrial revolutions, and based on the best available evidence at the moment, the green transition is expected to boost growth over the longer term because it will be efficiency-enhancing, solving several externality problems (Stern and Stiglitz, 2023). It will improve overall well-being, going beyond a narrow focus on gross domestic product, contributing to improved air quality and decreased mortality related to respiratory diseases. It will also create millions of jobs at the global level (Kruse, Dellink, Chateau, 2017; ILO, 2018)—specifically jobs less prone to automation or delocalisation, requiring less repetitive tasks and more interpersonal skills (Consoli et al., 2016; Bowen, Kuralbayeva, Tipoe, 2018; Vona et al., 2018).

While today's parallel with industrial revolutions is becoming more accepted (Pisani-Ferry and Mahfouz, 2023; Tagliapietra and Veugelers, 2023), some reasons for scepticism remain, including (i) the potential role of stranded assets, and (ii) the fact that if this were truly an industrial revolution, then private sector forces should unleash it on its own, without the need for governmental support and intervention (Claeys, Tagliapietra, Zachmann, 2019; Jakob et al., 2020; Pisani-Ferry, 2021; Semieniuk et al., 2022).

9.2.1 Stranded Assets

Stranded assets are assets that have suffered from unanticipated or premature write-downs. The concern with the green transition is a reminder that much of the current infrastructure supporting the existing economy will need to be shut down ahead of schedule to achieve climate neutrality. As such, stranded assets feel like a peculiarity of the green transition.

Fouquet (2010) examined over 14 energy transitions that took place over the last 1,000 years, including the switch from residential wood-fuel to coal, residential coal to gas, ox to horse, animals to steam, and others. In the cases considered—with the exception of ox to horse—the method of supplying the energy source had to be changed. 'This generally involved new producers, distributors and retailers—often (and particularly since the Industrial Revolution) requiring major infrastructure investments, such as the gas, railway or electricity networks' (Fouquet, 2010: 6, 591). This suggests that stranded assets were likely created in each energy transition and are not a peculiar feature of the green transition.

Stranded assets today are concentrated in a specific sector, notably oil and gas, and are simply a manifestation of structural change rather than a concern for the aggregate economy. Recent estimates put the total net present value of global fossil fuel stranded assets at around US$1.4 trillion (Semieniuk et al., 2022). By means of comparison, the 'Magnificent Seven' (i.e. Alphabet, Amazon, Apple, Meta, Microsoft, Nvidia, and Tesla) added over US$2.0 trillion in market value—in just 3 weeks—in 2023. Preliminary empirical evidence suggests that the economic system is flexible enough to minimise the risk of stranded assets becoming a major systemic concern (Hong, Kubik, Shore, 2023).

9.2.2 Markets Not Governments

The argument is frequently made that the green transition is not an investment opportunity, let alone an industrial revolution, because if it were, businesses would be pushing ahead with it on their own. From this standpoint, the green transition has been imposed by governments through taxation and regulation—as part of the Inflation Reduction Act or the European Green Deal—and is therefore a sort of ideological project.

First, the mechanism previously described—at the intersection of shifting consumer preferences, technological adoption, and falling costs of green technology—would be sufficient on its own to make a green transition happen. In other words, the fact that the transition will eventually happen is certain. However, policies and governmental action are needed to undertake an industrial revolution against a deadline (Tagliapietra and Veugelers, 2020). Climate scientists have posited that the impact of biodiversity collapse, extreme weather events, droughts, sea-level rise, and wildfires will have cascading effects and exponential negative effects on humanity. Time is of the essence, which is what ambitious governmental action is targeting.

The narrative of markets back then versus present-day governments is based on caricatural and erroneous premises. It has been established that governments paved the way for past industrial revolutions in their early phases (Juhász and Steinwender, 2023). As argued by Beckert (2014), untrammelled free enterprise alone powering the First Industrial Revolution is just a myth. Rather, governments from Denmark to Mexico to Russia, but also including those of the United States and Britain, fuelled the early stages of this industrial revolution through policies, including by building and financing the infrastructure required or lending money to early manufacturers. Similarities can be noted with respect to policy measures currently being undertaken, such as investments in EV-charging stations as part of the US Bipartisan Infrastructure Law, or green loans granted by public banks such as the European Investment Bank. Both aim to break technological lock-ins and to kickstart the transition to a point at which it will be self-sustaining.

The argument can be made also at the sectoral level. As an example, when cars were first introduced in the early 20th century, it was not clear that they were more efficient than horse carriages, as they were expensive, prone to technical failure, and had a reduced travel range. Nonetheless, some early adopters started using them, given that maintaining horses was becoming difficult in crowded cities. Costs began to fall, also thanks to secondary innovations such as the assembly line and the famous Ford Model T. Eventually, bans were progressively used to accelerate the transition from horse carriages to cars in cities (Standage, 2021; Terzi and Fouquet, 2023). Recent climate regulations, such as those introduced in California, the United Kingdom, and the European Union, banning the sale of cars with internal combustion engines after a certain date—typically 2035—follows the same logic.

That governments are facilitating the green transition today does not disprove the growth-enhancing potential of carbon-neutral technologies; it echoes the early steps taken during past industrial revolutions.

9.3 Economic Consequences

In light of the aforementioned considerations, what will the economic consequences of the green transition be beyond the positive long-term impact on growth? A large structural transformation by historical standards should be expected. In addition, new policy measures will also be taken to accelerate its pace. Significant skills and job relocation can therefore be expected, and for some sectors and people, the change will proceed faster than re-training and education can follow. Historically, when this has occurred, protest movements have ensued, such as the famous Luddite movement in reaction to mechanised cotton spinning, or England's Swing Riots of 1830s against new threshing machines (Caprettini and Voth, 2020). Similar localised events cannot be excluded from happening during the green transition, and recent farmers' protests in Europe follow this pattern.

Within an environment of significant and fast structural change, some companies will experience turbo-charged growth, as they secure their niche in technologies that are key to decarbonised societies. Others will remain stuck in paradigms of the past, experiencing long-term decline and eventual demise. If left unattended, this process is likely to aggravate inequalities within countries, similar to what was observed at the onset of past industrial revolutions (Perez, 2010) and with known episodes such as the Gilded Age in the United States.

More broadly, a sharp shift in comparative advantages and clusters of key technologies will be observed. That a country or company was an innovation leader in technologies that were central in a specific era hardly secures its leadership in a subsequent one (Freeman and Louçã, 2002). A classic example is how Britain, albeit the leading country in the First Industrial Revolution, was not the central locus of economic supremacy less than one century later during the Second Industrial Revolution.

Even if net-zero emissions are reached by mid-century, some extreme weather events will still materialise with increased frequency, leading to economic losses across the whole planet—and in some areas more than others (Carleton et al., 2022; Cruz and Rossi-Hansberg, 2024). Some will be able to cushion the shocks, respond, and adapt. Others will progressively degrade and experience falling economic complexity, emigration, conflict, and decline (Pearson and Pearson, 2012). Where technological and societal adaptation fail, the only adaptation mechanism left will be to relocate (Butzer and Endfield, 2012). Migration can thus be expected to increase significantly in the coming decades (Vince, 2022), reaching up to 300 million displaced people over the century (Burzyńskia, Deuster, and Docquier2019). While most of this migration is expected to be within countries, some of it will be international, with potentially cascading negative effects at the regional level. Countries particularly affected will be those where weak institutions and limited financial resources will complicate successful migrant integration.

All of these effects combined imply that a generalised increase in economic divergence will occur in the first half of the 21st century, after decades of broad income convergence across the globe (Terzi, 2023b; Rodrik and Stiglitz, 2025).

9.4 Policies in the New Global Economic Order

These economic developments, as well as some political economy considerations and an evaluation of incentive structures, set the scene for policy-making. In this section, broad policy trends expected over the coming years are examined (positive statement), before expanding on where policy action is desirable and achievable in the next section (normative statement). Before doing so, the logical framework underlying this approach is detailed.

The damning predictions made by climate science, combined with recent advances in understanding the history of humankind with climate and environmental shocks (Brooke, 2014; Frankopan, 2023), have led some to embrace radical climate determinism, which risks sliding towards fatalism (i.e. there is nothing humanity can do to save itself) (Terzi, 2020). On the other side of the spectrum are those who choose to ignore humankind's experience with past climate and environmental challenges—and history more broadly—to proclaim that this time is different and that anything is possible as long as climate science is embraced, differences are set aside, and the right policy advice is heeded. The approach presented in this chapter takes a pragmatic, narrow path between climate fatalism and this utopianism.

Economic and climate megatrends can be combined to generate a policy possibility set or universe of policy outcomes that is politically feasible. Specific circumstances, as well as politics broadly defined, will eventually lead to specific policy actions within the set. The broad contours of the policy possibility are as follows.

First, in knowing that the present is witnessing a technological turning point and that winners and losers will emerge, one can expect governments to do everything they can to increase the chance that their countries and companies end up as winners. Indeed, both the US's Inflation Reduction Act and China's green industrial policy were launched as strategies to secure dominance of the critical technologies of the 21st century, along with artificial intelligence, chips, aerospace innovations, quantum computing, and others with military applications (Terzi, Sherwood, Singh, 2023). In the shadow of this Great Power competition, other countries are following suit. This dynamic is why a progressive shift in the economic paradigm is happening, away from the *laissez-faire* nature of the Washington Consensus towards more governmental intervention. The increasing use of industrial policy across the world was thus predictable and, to an extent, inevitable (Cherif and Hasanov, 2019; Juhász, Lane, Rodrik, 2024).

Second, activist policy tools will generate defensive policy tools (Terzi, 2023b). Take, for instance, large-scale green industrial policy, where a sizeable use of subsidies is laying the foundation for domestic content requirements, as seen in the Inflation Reduction Act. However, this is also true for high levels of carbon pricing, the optimal solution to climate change according to textbook economics (Stern, 2007). The European Union has heeded this lesson, and the price of carbon in its cap-and-trade system now hovers around US$100 per tonne. Such a high price level inevitably led to domestic calls for a carbon tax at the border to avoid competitiveness losses; this is being implemented as through the Carbon Border Adjustment Mechanism. The implication is that, irrespective of the path chosen to accelerate the green transition, an economic paradigm will follow that edges inexorably towards greater trade fragmentation after decades of hyper-globalisation (Rodrik, 2011).

Third, if mastering specific technologies is key—and national prosperity will depend on it for decades perhaps after significant taxpayer funding has gone into subsidising them—it is highly unlikely that significant voluntary technology transfers to other nations will occur. Broad appeals that this would be in the long-term interest of humanity because it would accelerate decarbonisation will hardly change this incentive structure.

Fourth, as climate-change mitigation demands large investments and extreme weather events require spending on climate-change adaptation, all countries will have difficulty spreading increasingly limited financial resources amongst competing needs. This is particularly true at a time of high public debt and rising interest payments. Moreover, significant scores of the population will be demanding protection from technological change as well as re-training. Voluntary financial transfers from developed to developing countries will probably remain subdued and far from that necessary to finance climate-change mitigation and adaptation (Bhattacharya et al., 2023). Once again, one can make the case for it from a climate justice perspective, but this is unlikely to translate into policy action.

A decarbonisation strategy planned at the global level would be much more efficient, cheaper, and faster. The trade-off between national interest and fast-tracked decarbonisation should be evident. From a strict efficiency perspective, if China has a comparative advantage in making solar panels or extracting and processing critical green minerals, it would be cheaper for the rest of the world to import the totality of them. Trying to foster local production (e.g. through the Inflation Reduction Act or the EU's Net-Zero Industry Act) and raising trade barriers will cost more and slow down decarbonisation in the short term. However, cascading political economy dynamics and geopolitical considerations will most likely push the deep global cooperation option out of the policy feasibility set.

The future economic order can be expected to be marked by (i) activist governments, (ii) trade fragmentation, (iii) limited voluntary technological transfers amongst countries, and (iv) subdued financial transfers between countries. Any credible policy recommendation that goes beyond general aspirations must therefore factor these considerations into account. Sensible policy recommendations should go beyond appeals for the greater good and consider individual national policy-making incentives instead.

It is important to note that a decarbonisation strategy based on national policies can lead the world towards net-zero emissions. Developing nations with limited financial resources will be underserved by this solution—but only in the very short term. This is because pioneering countries will be investing vast financial resources in—while competing to secure leadership in—green technologies. As these new production methods scale up, they will become cheaper and eventually breach through price parity vis-à-vis the incumbent technology. At that point, developing nations will no longer face the current trade-off between economic development and decarbonisation, as the cheap option and green option will coincide. This will represent an implicit and unintended technology-driven financial subsidy to decarbonisation in developing nations, as it will significantly lower the costs of the transition for latecomers. It will also significantly increase access to financing, as international capital seeking returns will naturally find green investments profitable in developing nations.

9.5 Policy Recommendations

While the policy possibility set above may seem stringent, several policy decisions are still possible that will have first-order repercussions on the speed of climate action, economic growth, and human lives and livelihoods, within and amongst countries. Broad policy recommendations are listed as follows that apply to decision makers both in developed and developing countries.

9.5.1 Avoid Trying to Obstruct Structural Transformation

The green transition is inevitable, and trying to obstruct it will fail, resulting only in a waste of financial resources. Decisions to double-down on oil and gas infrastructure fall into this category, as in the case of Argentina's Vaca Muerta Formation of largely unexploited shale gas fields. Likewise, embracing isolationism through high tariff or non-tariff barriers in the hope of banning a country from technological developments happening elsewhere will secure only poverty vis-à-vis other nations (Terzi, 2022c). Accompanying structural change with mitigating short-term social and technological challenges represent a much better use of the limited fiscal resources available (Terzi, Sherwood, Singh, 2023).

9.5.2 Aim to Be a Pioneer in Green Technology

For a long time, it seemed better to adopt a wait-and-see stance on climate-change mitigation and adaptation actions; other countries or companies could start and should they succeed, their technologies and policies could be easily imitated. Yet this narrative has inevitably led to a tragedy of the commons on climate-change actions (Bowen and Fankhauser, 2011). It has failed to realise that trial and error develop a high degree of tacit knowledge (Hausmann and Rodrik, 2003) and that catching up cannot occur by simply importing blueprints from market leaders at a later stage. The very direction of technological development should be seen as endogenous, allowing pioneers to create an innovation frontier and technical standards closer to their existing comparative advantages and economic characteristics (Rodrik, 2014). Followers are left struggling to adopt a technology that is poorly adapted to their national characteristics. As a result, it is good economics to try to be a pioneer in green technologies.

Because much of technological development takes place in developed nations, this recommendation may seem addressed only to them. However, it is true for poorer nations as well. There is scope for all countries to enter the green value chain at various stages of development; it does not necessarily have to be high-tech immediately (Terzi, 2022b; Rodrik and Stiglitz, 2024). For example, countries can become pioneers in the extraction and processing of green minerals or the production and export of green energy (e.g. hydrogen), batteries, or two-wheel electric mobility or EV components—all of which are currently experiencing exponential growth. Many countries are already exploiting this trend, such as Indonesia with its large extraction and processing of copper. Green development no longer needs to be an oxymoron (Hausmann, 2021). In the 21st century, the wealth of nations will be defined by whether they develop comparative advantages in key technologies underpinning a carbon-neutral economy.

9.5.3 Mitigate Inequalities Within Countries

The point that policies are needed to mitigate inequalities is often made from a moral perspective. In *Innovation and Its Enemies*, the late Harvard professor Calestous Juma analysed the conditions of acceptance or resistance to innovation across geographies and 6 centuries of technology history (Juma, 2016). He concluded that when an innovation is perceived as benefiting only a few, resistance will follow. Unless inequalities within countries are contained as structural transformation accelerates, protest movements will flare, slowing down the green transition and effectively eroding a country's long-term chances of prosperity. Thus, it follows that the benefits of green growth must be spread out or they will not occur. Climate policies must be mirrored by social policies, as is the case in the European Union with the Just Transition Mechanism, which aims to alleviate the socio-economic impact of the transition in the most affected European regions.

9.5.4 Safeguard an Open Society and Scientific Collaborations

Given that the new global order will be characterised by increasing trade fragmentation and economic and technological competition, some are in favour of policies aimed at containing cross-national scientific collaboration in an effort to prevent industrial/scientific espionage. Yet while national security considerations can be introduced in science policy, they should be kept to an absolute minimum in terms of sectoral and geographical coverage. The risk is undermining the very process of innovation creation, which rests on the free exchange of ideas (Rees, 2022) and is central to any successful national climate-change mitigation and adaptation scenario. Technology is the greatest asset against climate change (Terzi and Fouquet, 2023). The extension of the EU's flagship research funding programme Horizon Europe to like-minded countries, such as the United Kingdom and Canada, represents a good blueprint in this respect.

Likewise, it will be important to retain, as much as possible, an open society that champions liberal values, as this is the environment that is most conducive to scientific discovery, entrepreneurial spirit, and talent attraction from abroad (Terzi, 2022a).

9.5.5 Build International Alliances Bridging Rich and Poor Countries

The policy feasibility set rules out deep global cooperation on climate policy or voluntary donation of money and technology on a large scale between developed and developing countries. It does not exclude win-win collaborations and exchanges, however. Such international economic alliances should be encouraged, as no single national economy will be strong enough on its own to deal with climate change and all other challenges in the new global economic order. Bilateral or regional partnerships can be easily envisaged whereby developing nations can provide green minerals, high-quality renewable energy, and market access to green products in exchange for foreign direct investment (which carries technology transfers) and aid aimed at building green infrastructure (e.g. under the current Just Energy Transition Partnerships). In addition, developing nations that are considered partners and allies could gain exemptions from domestic content requirements of green industrial policies in the developed world (Terzi, 2023b). This argument is in favour of friend-shoring, aimed at minimising the economic damage originating from deglobalisation in the new world order.

9.6 Concluding Remarks

The climate reality is hardly positive. This leads some—in particular, younger generations—to 'eco-anxiety'. Others are drawn to denialism often as a coping strategy. Structural change needed to avoid the worst of climate change and the political difficulties that this will entail should instead make policymakers anxious. However, for the countries that manage to navigate this narrow path in mastering climate-change mitigation, adaptation, and green technologies, prosperity awaits in the era of the Green Industrial Revolution. As such, treading between climate fatalism and utopianism, climate action can be reconciled with the belief in progress, as defined in Mokyr (2018)—the idea that the future can be better than the past—but this depends on human actions.

Notes

* The views expressed here are those of the author and do not necessarily reflect those of the institution to which he is affiliated. The author would like to thank Diane Coyle and Cecilia Trasi for comments on a previous version of this essay. All errors and omissions remain the sole responsibility of the author.

1 The same dynamic can be seen also within specific sectors. During the First Industrial Revolution, it seems obvious today that steam ships must have been much more efficient than sailing, fostering commerce. Yet early steamers had highly inefficient engines, requiring huge amounts of coal that needed to be carried onboard due to the lack of port infrastructure for re-fuelling, taking away precious cargo space. Only major improvements in fuel efficiency, coupled with more widespread coal infrastructure in the second half of the 19th century, made the productivity gains evident (Fouquet, 2010; Smil, 2017).

References

Aghion, Philippe, Céline Antonin, and Simon Bunel. 2023. *The Power of Creative Destruction: Economic Upheaval and the Wealth of Nations*. Translated by Jodie Cohen-Tanugi, 1st Harvard University Press Paperback ed. Cambridge, MA; London, England: The Belknap Press of Harvard University Press.

Bardan, Roxana. 2024. "NASA Analysis Confirms 2023 as Warmest Year on Record—NASA." *NASA (blog)*, January 12, 2024. https://www.nasa.gov/news-release/nasa-analysis-confirms-2023-as-warmest-year-on-record/.

Beckert, Sven. 2014. *Empire of Cotton: A Global History*. New York: Alfred A. Knopf.

Besley, Timothy, and Torsten Persson. 2023. "The Political Economics of Green Transitions." *The Quarterly Journal of Economics* 138 (3): 1863–906. https://doi.org/10.1093/qje/qjad006.

Bhattacharya, Amar, Vera Songwe, Éléonore Soubeyran, and Nicholas Stern. 2023. *A Climate Finance Framework: Decisive Action to Deliver on the Paris Agreement*. London: Grantham Research Institute on Climate Change and the Environment, London School of Economics and Political Science.

Bowen, Alex, and Samuel Fankhauser. 2011. "The Green Growth Narrative: Paradigm Shift or Just Spin?" *Global Environmental Change* 21 (4): 1157–59. https://doi.org/10.1016/j.gloenvcha.2011.07.007.

Bowen, Alex, Karlygash Kuralbayeva, and Eileen L. Tipoe. 2018. "Characterising Green Employment: The Impacts of 'Greening' on Workforce Composition." *Energy Economics* 72 (May): 263–75. https://doi.org/10.1016/j.eneco.2018.03.015.

Brooke, John L. 2014. *Climate Change and the Course of Global History: A Rough Journey. Studies in Environment and History*. New York: Cambridge University Press.

Burzyńskia, Michał, Christoph Deuster, and Frédéric Docquier. 2019. "Climate Change, Inequality, and Human Migration." *IZA—Institute of Labor Economics, Discussion Paper*, no. 12623, September. www.iza.org.

Butzer, Karl W., and Georgina H. Endfield. 2012. "Critical Perspectives on Historical Collapse." *Proceedings of the National Academy of Sciences* 109 (10): 3628–31. https://doi.org/10.1073/pnas.1114772109.

Caprettini, Bruno, and Hans-Joachim Voth. 2020. "Rage against the Machines: Labor-Saving Technology and Unrest in Industrializing England." *American Economic Review: Insights* 2 (3): 305–20. https://doi.org/10.1257/aeri.20190385.

Carleton, Tamma, Amir Jina, Michael Delgado, Michael Greenstone, Trevor Houser, Solomon Hsiang, Andrew Hultgren, et al. 2022. "Valuing the Global Mortality Consequences of Climate Change Accounting for Adaptation Costs and Benefits." *The Quarterly Journal of Economics* 137 (4): 2037–105. https://doi.org/10.1093/qje/qjac020.

Cherif, Reda, and Fuad Hasanov. 2019. "The Return of the Policy that Shall Not Be Named: Principles of Industrial Policy." *IMF Working Paper*, no. WP/19/74. Washington, DC: International Monetary Fund.

Claeys, Gregory, Simone Tagliapietra, and Georg Zachmann. 2019. "How to Make the European Green Deal Work." *Research Report 2019/13. Bruegel Policy Contribution.* https://www.econstor.eu/handle/10419/237632.

Consoli, Davide, Giovanni Marin, Alberto Marzucchi, and Francesco Vona. 2016. "Do Green Jobs Differ from Non-Green Jobs in Terms of Skills and Human Capital?" *Research Policy* 45 (5): 1046–60. https://doi.org/10.1016/j.respol.2016.02.007.

Coyle, Diane. 2011. *The Economics of Enough: How to Run the Economy as If the Future Matters*. Princeton, NJ: Princeton University Press. https://press.princeton.edu/books/hardcover/9780691145181/the-economics-of-enough?srsltid=AfmBOoqOtQcE3EEOdRrlBnnXxoo928uoJKLo8fcVcg8PUahbk-Z-_Izm.

Cruz, José-Luis, and Esteban Rossi-Hansberg. 2024. "The Economic Geography of Global Warming." *Review of Economic Studies* 91 (2): 899–939. https://doi.org/10.1093/restud/rdad042.

David, Paul A. 1990. "The Dynamo and the Computer: An Historical Perspective on the Modern Productivity Paradox." *The American Economic Review* 80 (2): 355–61. https://www.jstor.org/stable/2006600.

Fisman, Raymond, Pulak Ghosh, Arkodipta Sarkar, and Jian Zhang. 2023. "Dirty Air and Green Investments: The Impact of Pollution Information on Portfolio Allocations." *National Bureau of Economic Research (NBER) Working Paper Series*, no. w31813, October. https://doi.org/10.3386/w31813.

Fouquet, Roger. 2008. *Heat, Power and Light: Revolutions in Energy Services*. Cheltenham; Northampton, MA: Edward Elgar. https://www.e-elgar.com/shop/gbp/heat-power-and-light–9781849800075.html?srsltid=AfmBOoqPabxN0RH66LsE1MIpfUeFEj4GtzRKLlGFFj0FBvn7xO4pqDEw.

Fouquet, Roger. 2010. "The Slow Search for Solutions: Lessons from Historical Energy Transitions by Sector and Service." *Energy Policy* 38 (11): 6586–96. https://doi.org/10.1016/j.enpol.2010.06.029.

Frankopan, Peter. 2023. *The Earth Transformed: An Untold History*. New York: Alfred A. Knopf.

Freeman, Christopher, and Francisco Louçã. 2002. *As Time Goes by: From the Industrial Revolutions to the Information Revolution*. Oxford: Oxford University Press. https://doi.org/10.1093/0199251053.001.0001.

Gates, Bill. 2021. *How to Avoid a Climate Disaster: The Solutions We Have and the Breakthroughs We Need*, 1st ed. New York: Alfred A. Knopf.

Hausmann, Ricardo. 2021. "Is Green Development an Oxymoron?" *Project Syndicate*, June 1. https://www.project-syndicate.org/commentary/decarbonization-green-technologies-developing-countries-growth-by-ricardo-hausmann-2021–06.

Hausmann, Ricardo, and Dani Rodrik. 2003. "Economic Development as Self-Discovery." *Journal of Development Economics, 14th Inter-American Seminar on Economics*, 72 (2): 603–33. https://doi.org/10.1016/S0304–3878(03)00124-X.

Helm, Dieter. 2023. *Legacy: How to Build the Sustainable Economy*, 1st ed. Cambridge University Press. https://doi.org/10.1017/9781009449212.

Hoffmann, Roman, Raya Muttarak, Jonas Peisker, and Piero Stanig. 2022. "Climate Change Experiences Raise Environmental Concerns and Promote Green Voting." *Nature Climate Change* 12 (2): 148–55. https://doi.org/10.1038/s41558-021-01263-8.

Hong, Harrison, Jeffrey D Kubik, and Edward P Shore. 2023. "The Cost of Climate Policy to Capital: Evidence from Renewable Portfolio Standards'." *National Bureau of Economic Research (NBER) Working Paper Series*, no. w31960, December.

Intergovernmental Panel on Climate Change (IPCC). 2021. *Climate Change 2021: The Physical Science Basis. Contribution of Working Group I to the Sixth Assessment Report of the Intergovernmental Panel on Climate Change*. Cambridge, UK; New York, NY, USA: Cambridge University Press. https://doi.org/10.1017/9781009157896.

International Energy Agency. 2020. "Renewables 2020." Paris. https://www.iea.org/reports/renewables–2020.

International Labor Organization (ILO), ed. 2018. *World Employment Social Outlook 2018: Greening with Jobs*. Geneva: International labour office. https://www.ilo.org/publications/world-employment-and-social-outlook-2018-greening-jobs.

International Renewable Energy Agency (IRENA). 2020. *Renewable Power Generation Costs in 2019*. Abu Dhabi: International Renewable Energy Agency. https://www.irena.org/publications/2020/Jun/Renewable-Power-Costs-in–2019.

Jakob, Michael, William F. Lamb, Jan Christoph Steckel, Christian Flachsland, and Ottmar Edenhofer. 2020. "Understanding Different Perspectives on Economic Growth and Climate Policy." *WIREs Climate Change* 11 (6): e677. https://doi.org/10.1002/wcc.677.

Juhász, Réka, Nathan Lane, and Dani Rodrik. 2024. "The New Economics of Industrial Policy." *Annual Review of Economics* 16 (1): 213–42. https://doi.org/10.1146/annurev-economics-081023–024638.

Juhász, Réka, Mara Squicciarini, and Nico Voigtländer. 2020. "Technology Adoption and Productivity Growth: Evidence from Industrialization in France." *National Bureau of Economic Research (NBER) Working Paper Series*, no. w27503, July. https://doi.org/10.3386/w27503.

Juhász, Réka, and Claudia Steinwender. 2023. "Industrial Policy and the Great Divergence." *National Bureau of Economic Research (NBER) Working Paper Series*, no. w31736, September. https://doi.org/10.3386/w31736.

Juma, Calestous. 2016. *Innovation and Its Enemies: Why People Resist New Technologies*, 1st ed. Oxford, UK: Oxford University Press.

Kruse, Tobias, Rob Dellink, and Jean Chateau. 2017. "Employment Implications of Green Growth: Linking Jobs, Growth, and Green Policies." *OECD Report for the G7 Environment Ministers*. Paris: OECD.

Lamboll, Robin D., Zebedee R. J. Nicholls, Christopher J. Smith, Jarmo S. Kikstra, Edward Byers, and Joeri Rogelj. 2023. "Assessing the Size and Uncertainty of Remaining Carbon Budgets." *Nature Climate Change* 13 (12): 1360–67. https://doi.org/10.1038/s41558-023-01848-5.

Mokyr, Joel. 2018. *A Culture of Growth: The Origins of the Modern Economy. First Paperback Printing. The Graz Schumpeter Lectures*. Princeton, NJ: Princeton University Press.

Myers, Teresa A., Edward W. Maibach, Connie Roser-Renouf, Karen Akerlof, and Anthony A. Leiserowitz. 2013. "The Relationship Between Personal Experience and Belief in the Reality of Global Warming." *Nature Climate Change* 3 (4): 343–47. https://doi.org/10.1038/nclimate1754.

Pearson, Leonie J., and Craig J. Pearson. 2012. "Societal Collapse or Transformation, and Resilience." *Proceedings of the National Academy of Sciences* 109 (30): 2030–31. https://doi.org/10.1073/pnas.1207552109.

Perez, Carlota. 2010. "Technological Revolutions and Techno-Economic Paradigms." *Cambridge Journal of Economics* 34 (1): 185–202. https://www.jstor.org/stable/24232030.

Pisani-Ferry, Jean. 2021. "Climate Policy is Macroeconomic Policy, and the Implications Will Be Significant." In *Policy Briefs*, 20–21. Peterson Institute for International Economics (PIIE).

Pisani-Ferry, Jean, and Selma Mahfouz. 2023. *Les Incidences Économiques de L'action Pour Le Climat*. Paris: France Strategie. https://www.strategie.gouv.fr/publications/incidences-economiques-de-laction-climat.

Rees, Martin J. 2022. *If Science is to Save Us*. Cambridge, UK: Polity Press.

Rodrik, Dani. 2011. *The Globalization Paradox: Democracy and the Future of the World Economy*. New York; London: W.W. Norton.

Rodrik, Dani. 2014. "Green Industrial Policy." *Oxford Review of Economic Policy* 30 (3): 469–91. https://www.jstor.org/stable/43664659.
Rodrik, Dani, and Joseph E. Stiglitz. 2025. "A New Growth Strategy for Developing Nations." Chapter 7 in *The New Global Economic Order*, edited by Lili Yan Ing and Dani Rodrik. New York: Routledge.
Semieniuk, Gregor, Philip B. Holden, Jean-Francois Mercure, Pablo Salas, Hector Pollitt, Katharine Jobson, Pim Vercoulen, Unnada Chewpreecha, Neil R. Edwards, and Jorge E. Viñuales. 2022. "Stranded Fossil-Fuel Assets Translate to Major Losses for Investors in Advanced Economies." *Nature Climate Change* 12 (6): 532–38. https://doi.org/10.1038/s41558-022-01356-y.
Smil, Vaclav. 2017. *Energy and Civilization: A History*. Cambridge, MA: The MIT Press.
Standage, Tom. 2021. *A Brief History of Motion: From the Wheel, to the Car, to What Comes Next*. New York: Bloomsbury Publishing.
Stern, N. H., ed. 2007. *The Economics of Climate Change: The Stern Review*. London: Cambridge University Press.
Stern, Nicholas, Joseph E. Stiglitz, and Charlotte Taylor. Journal version of 2022 from the Journal of Economic Methodology: https://www.tandfonline.com/doi/full/10.1080/1350178X.2022.2040740#abstract.
Tagliapietra, Simone, and Reinhilde Veugelers. 2020. *A Green Industrial Policy for Europe*, Vol. 31. Brussels: Bruegel Blueprint.
Tagliapietra, Simone, and Reinhilde Veugelers, eds. 2023. *Sparking Europe's New Industrial Revolution: A Policy for Net Zero, Growth and Resilience. Bruegel Blueprint Series*, Vol. 33. Brussels, Belgium: Bruegel. https://www.bruegel.org/book/sparking-europes-new-industrial-revolution-policy-net-zero-growth-and-resilience.
Terzi, Alessio. 2020. "Crafting an Effective Narrative on the Green Transition." *Energy Policy* 147 (December): 111883. https://doi.org/10.1016/j.enpol.2020.111883.
Terzi, Alessio. 2022a. "Climate Political Economy." *Project Syndicate*, September 12, 2022. https://www.project-syndicate.org/magazine/climate-change-democracy-vs-eco-authoritarianism-by-alessio-terzi-2022–08.
Terzi, Alessio. 2022b. "Green Development is Now the Only Option." *Project Syndicate*, September 8. https://www.project-syndicate.org/commentary/developing-countries-must-go-green-fossil-fuels-are-a-dead-end-by-alessio-terzi-2022–09.
Terzi, Alessio. 2022c. *Growth for Good: Reshaping Capitalism to Save Humanity from Climate Catastrophe*. Cambridge, MA: Harvard University Press.
Terzi, Alessio. 2023a. "Enrolling Capitalism in the Fight Against Climate Change." *ProMarket (blog)*, March 3. https://www.promarket.org/2023/03/03/enrolling-capitalism-in-the-fight-against-climate-change/.
Terzi, Alessio. 2023b. "Green Industrial Policy: The Necessary Evil to Avoid a Climate Catastrophe." In *Sparking Europe's New Industrial Revolution a Policy for Net Zero, Growth and Resilience*, Vol. 33, edited by Simone Tagliapietra and Reinhilde Veugelers, 107–22. Brussels, Belgium: Bruegel. https://www.bruegel.org/book/sparking-europes-new-industrial-revolution-policy-net-zero-growth-and-resilience.
Terzi, Alessio, and Roger Fouquet. 2023. "The Green Industrial Revolution: Lessons from the History of Past Energy Transitions." *EconPol Forum* 24 (6): 16–22. https://hdl.handle.net/10419/281154.
Terzi, Alessio, Monika Sherwood, and Aneil Singh. 2023. "European Industrial Policy for the Green and Digital Revolution." *Science and Public Policy* 50 (5): 842–57. https://doi.org/10.1093/scipol/scad018.
Vince, Gaia. 2022. *Nomad Century: How to Survive the Climate Upheaval*. London: Allen Lane an imprint of Penguin Books.
Vona, Francesco, Giovanni Marin, Davide Consoli, and David Popp. 2018. "Environmental Regulation and Green Skills: An Empirical Exploration." *Journal of the Association of Environmental and Resource Economists* 5 (4): 713–53. https://doi.org/10.1086/698859.

10 International Financial and Tax Reforms

*José Antonio Ocampo**

10.1 Introduction

Strengthening the international financial and tax systems has been at the centre of recent global debates. The United Nations has proposed various associated policies and offered a forum for discussions towards global agreements in these areas (UN, 2023b, 2023c). Several proposals were also endorsed by the UN High-Level Political Forum on Sustainable Development held in September 2023 (UN, 2023a). In addition, the Group of 20 (G20) convened an independent expert group that provided recommendations on enhancing the role of multilateral development banks (MDBs) (G20, 2023b), and its Leaders' Summit endorsed an agreement to strengthen development financing (G20, 2023a). This was complemented by the proposed Evolution Roadmap of the World Bank Group (World Bank, 2022b, 2024). Recurring institutional recommendations include equitable participation of developing countries[1] in international financial institutions, an issue that has been underscored in various UN Conferences on Financing for Development from 2002 to 2015.

This chapter outlines five elements of this global reform agenda. Section 10.2 analyses development financing. Section 10.3 looks at international monetary reform. Section 10.4 considers proposals on how to mitigate the over-indebtedness of several developing countries. Section 10.5 looks at international tax cooperation, and Section 10.6 looks at the institutional dimensions of global cooperation in all these areas.

10.2 Development Financing

In 1944, at Bretton Woods, the International Bank for Reconstruction and Development was created, which is now part of the World Bank Group. This was followed by the development of several regional and inter-regional institutions; their financing goes to both the public and private sectors and has evolved from project financing to the support of development programmes. They offer preferential lines for the poorest countries through institutions like the International Development Association (IDA) of the World Bank Group or special credit facilities within their general programmes. They also play a countercyclical role, compensating for the pro-cyclical pattern of international private financing that developing

DOI: 10.4324/9781003571384-10

countries face. In addition, they analyse national, regional, and global economic conditions and recommend appropriate policies to manage them, essentially acting as knowledge banks (Ocampo and Ortega, 2022).

As Figure 10.1 indicates, traditional regional banks—excluding the European Investment Bank—have grown faster than the World Bank Group in recent decades, even surpassing it in terms of financing since the mid-2010s. Nevertheless, the World Bank continues to play the strongest countercyclical role, as reflected in the sharp increase in its financing during the North Atlantic financial crisis[2] and recent adverse global economic conditions, such as the COVID-19 pandemic and the global slowdown with inflation in 2022–2023. This recent countercyclical function was performed more strongly by IDA than by the International Bank for Reconstruction and Development (part of the World Bank), thus supporting, in particular, low-income countries.

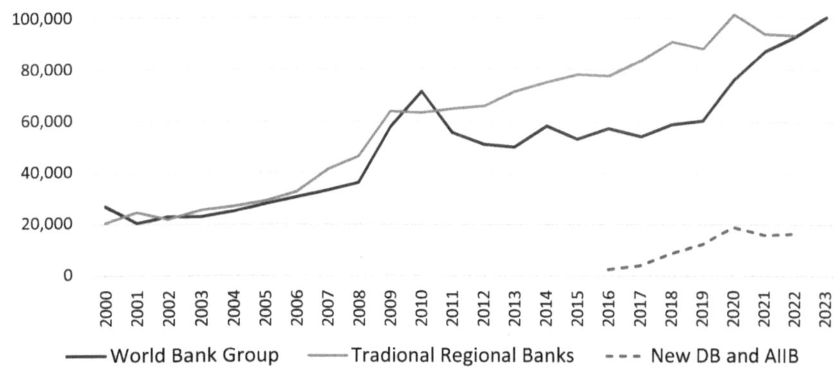

Figure 10.1 Loan Commitments for Developing Countries From Multilateral Development Banks (US$ Million)

Notes: Traditional regional banks include the African Development Bank, Asian Development Bank, Development Bank of Latin America and the Caribbean, European Bank for Reconstruction and Development, Inter-American Development Bank, and Islamic Development Bank. New banks include the New Development Bank (New DB) and Asian Infrastructure Investment Bank (AIIB). The data from the World Bank Group refer to fiscal years.

Sources: Annual reports of each institution.

In terms of relative support to different regions, the World Bank Group provides the most funding to Sub-Saharan Africa and South Asia—the world's poorest regions. Financing by regional banks is dominant in Europe, due to role of the European Investment Bank, followed by Latin America and the Caribbean (Ocampo and Ortega, 2022).

The UN, G20, and World Bank reports mentioned in the introduction proposed three key recommendations on development financing.[3] First, besides fostering equitable and sustainable development, MDBs must finance the contributions of developing countries for the provision of global public goods, especially the prevention of pandemics and fight against climate change. Second, they called for contingency clauses on the vulnerability of developing countries to climate and health issues as well as on the effects of international economic crises on them. These clauses would allow the temporary suspension of debt service with these institutions and, if necessary, a reduction in associated liabilities. Lastly, they emphasised the need for closer collaboration with the private sector, including supporting its possible contribution to the provision of global public goods.

In relation to the first issue, MDBs substantially increased their financing to global public health after the outbreak of the COVID-19 pandemic, from US$2.6 billion to US$11.1 billion between 2019 and 2020. Commitments to climate finance have been larger and have grown over a longer period. In 2022, they provided US$60.3 billion to low- and middle-income countries, which is more than double the financing that they had provided in the mid-2010s, and have mobilised private finance concurrently (Ocampo and González, 2024).

An essential part of these proposals is the need for concessional credits or donations to be channelled through MDBs. These benefits should be extended to support the contribution of middle-income countries to global public goods and include mechanisms for partially subsidising private sector credits to leverage their investments in those goods. Achieving this requires a significant increase in official development assistance (ODA), a challenging issue given the current limitation of aid resources. Beyond the concessional character of the resources needed, these proposals advocated for longer-term MDB loans (e.g. 30–50 years) with extended grace periods and lower interest rates. Furthermore, to manage exchange rate volatility, they suggested more lending in the countries' national currencies.

In addition, these included various proposals for leveraging the capital of MDBs, thus allowing expanded lending by these institutions, maintaining their investment grades.[4] Innovations must also be developed in financial mechanisms that support private investments, including guarantees and public-private partnerships.

To fulfil these functions—and their more traditional ones—it is critical to adequately capitalise MDBs. The capitalisations of the World Bank Group in 2018, and of all MDBs after the North Atlantic financial crisis, responded to this demand. It is remarkable that the 2023 G20 agreements were much weaker than those of 2009, which called for capitalising all MDBs (G20, 2009).

The magnitude of the funding proposals from MDBs differed significantly. The G20 Independent Experts Group proposed increasing the annual financing of these institutions to US$500 billion by 2030—approximately tripling the value of their loans—one-third of which would be in ODA or concessional credits (G20, 2023b). The proposals of the UN were much more ambitious; they called for a return to the 1960 ratio financing by MDBs and the size of the world economy, which implied increasing those loans to nearly US$2 trillion, a figure closer to the estimate of the Sustainable Development Goal financing gap (UN, 2023c).

Finally, the reports posited that MDBs should be strengthened as a service network. For the World Bank, this entails participating in regional projects alongside regional partners. Furthermore, all MDBs should collaborate with national development banks and other public institutions (Griffith-Jones and Ocampo, 2018). This collaboration would allow national development banks to execute global public goods programmes and to serve as information conduits on the financing needs of their respective countries.

10.3 International Monetary Reform

Unlike development financing, international monetary reform has not been central to recent global debates. In November 2023, the International Monetary Fund (IMF) Executive Board proposed to its Board of Governors a 50% increase in quotas, maintaining member countries' shares but opening the discussion for quota realignments. This should lead to a decision in 2025.

In terms of credit lines, major reforms were adopted in 2009–2010, including (i) the duplication of all existing lines; (ii) the creation of contingency (or precautionary) instruments, comprising a flexible credit line with no conditionality for countries with solid macroeconomic fundamentals, and a precautionary and liquidity line, to which a broader set of countries have access but with conditionality; and (iii) more flexible lines for low-income countries, for whom interest payments were also eliminated in 2015.

During the COVID-19 pandemic, emergency credit lines were widely used, offering financing with no conditionality for 80 countries, although in limited amounts up to each country's quota. A limited short-term liquidity line was also created for up to 145% of the quota. In October 2023, the IMF Executive Board allowed eligible members to concurrently use the flexible and short-term liquidity lines, with certain limits (IMF, 2023a). Improvements in the contingency credit lines must continue, as they are essential crisis prevention tools and efficient alternatives to reserve accumulation.

The magnitude of IMF financing since its origin, estimated as a proportion of the world's gross domestic product (GDP), is in Figure 10.2. Until the 1970s,

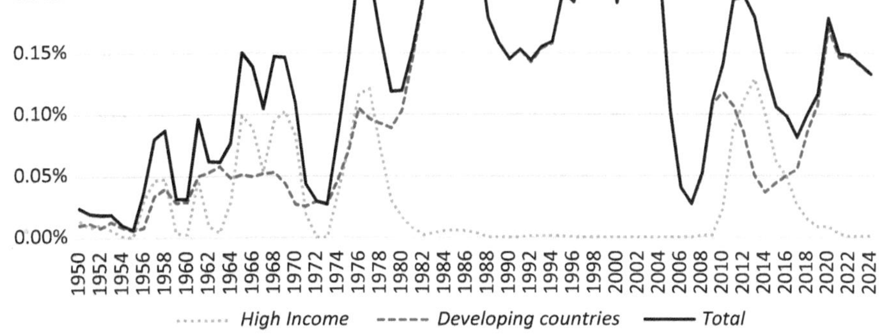

Figure 10.2 International Monetary Fund Lending Relative to Gross Domestic Product, 1950–2022 (%)

Source: Author's estimates based on IMF data, using World Bank classification of countries by income in 2000.

high-income countries were the most active users of IMF lending. The situation changed radically in the 1980s, when developing countries became the major borrowers. They have remained so, except temporarily during the Eurozone crisis. Although IMF financing increased during the North Atlantic and recent crises, it was much smaller than during the Latin American and Asian crises.

Conditionality continues to be regarded as IMF's stigma in global debates. In 2002, it was agreed to return to the principle of macroeconomic conditionality, thus eliminating the complementary focus on structural conditionality that had been in place since the 1980s. In 2009, it was further determined that failure to meet structural goals would not prevent credit disbursements. Conditionality was strengthened in 2018, when IMF was allowed to determine conditionality grounded in governance standards and anti-corruption efforts.

The inclusion of governance is part of a broader set of agreements reached since 2012 that have also comprised standards on social spending, gender equality, climate change, and digital money in surveillance and lending programmes to the extent that they have macroeconomic effects (i.e. on the balance of payments or economic and financial stability). The Independent Evaluation Office has analysed the extent to which this has implied an excessive expansion of the IMF mandate (Rustomjee et al., 2023).

The management of capital account shocks is a critical issue for developing countries that have access to international private financing but on a pro-cyclical basis. In this regard, an important decision, adopted in 2012, was the approval of an 'institutional view' on capital account management, which indicates that the liberalisation of the capital account is not always positive[5] and that regulations of capital flows may thus be convenient in certain circumstances—although temporarily so, according to this vision (IMF, 2012). This institutional view remains in place today.

An additional issue is the more active use of Special Drawing Rights (SDR). Two funds have been created that are financed by countries willing to deposit their unused SDR: (i) the Poverty Reduction and Growth Trust, for balance-of-payments problems of low-income countries; and (ii) Resilience and Sustainability Trust, which supports prospective balance-of-payments stability for low-income and vulnerable middle-income countries, including managing risks associated with climate change and pandemics (IMF, n.d.). These mechanisms ensuring the liquidity of SDR have been essential to maintain their reserve currency status.

SDR should be the focus of more ambitious reforms, however. There have only been four historical allocations. The initial allocation was in the early 1970s, and then another occurred in 1980. The last two, which were in 2009 and 2021, happened in response to international crises, with the latter after a 1-year lag, as the United States did not support it in 2020. Analyses on this matter—e.g. IMF (2011), Kenen (2010), Ocampo (2017), and Williamson (2009)—indicated that SDR releases could be much higher, at least US$200 billion and even up to US$400 billion per year, with a countercyclical character. For more active use, a main reform would be to eliminate IMF's dual accounting, which currently separates SDR from its current operations. Once this duality is eliminated, the unused SDR could be considered deposits of IMF countries, which could be used to finance its credit programmes (Ocampo, 2017). There have also been proposals to change the criteria for allocating SDR to include—beyond IMF quotas—criteria that would increase the share of developing countries.

A notable distinction of MDBs is the weakness of regional institutions in the international monetary system. They include the European Stability Mechanism, created in 2012 during the Eurozone crisis; Chiang Mai Initiative, amongst the countries of the Association of Southeast Asian Nations (ASEAN), China, Hong Kong, and South Korea, launched in 2000 and significantly expanded in 2009; and Latin American Reserve Fund, created in 1991 as a successor to the Andean Fund from 1978, which comprises nine countries. It is essential, therefore, to expand the role of regional monetary institutions and to encourage IMF to engage more actively with them during crises. One incentivising mechanism could be considering contributions to these institutions as an additional criterion in SDR allocation.

In addition to IMF and regional arrangements, swap facilities also play a role as short-term financing mechanisms, including the US Federal Reserve, but these basically benefit only other developed countries. The Central Bank of China has also been increasingly active in these facilities.

10.4 Sovereign Debt Restructuring

The restructuring of sovereign debts is an absent element of international financial cooperation. The only traditional mechanism is the Paris Club, but this focusses on bilateral official debts with Organisation for Economic Co-operation and Development (OECD) countries.

Ad hoc mechanisms have been adopted in the past to manage sovereign debt crises. After the Latin American debt crisis, the Brady Plan was launched in 1989, which helped reduce debts and catalysed the development of a sovereign bond market for developing countries. For low-income nations, the Heavily Indebted Poor Countries Initiative was adopted in 1996. It was complemented in 2005 with the Multi-Lateral Debt Relief Initiative, which cancelled the debts of eligible countries with IMF, World Bank Group, and African Development Fund. A similar mechanism was adopted by the Inter-American Development Bank in 2007. Following the 1994 Mexican peso crisis, OECD's G10 proposed introducing collective action clauses in US bond contracts, resembling the system already used in London bond contracts. These provide a mechanism by which a qualified majority of holders can agree on changes in the bonds' contracts.

The only attempt to create a stable institutional framework for debt restructuring took place during 2001–2003 at IMF. The objective was to create a mechanism that would allow unsustainable international debts to be restructured through a rapid, orderly, and predictable process while protecting the rights of creditors (Krueger, 2002). The proposal excluded domestic public debts from these renegotiations. In the final versions of the proposal, it was agreed that the body to be created would be independent of IMF's Executive Board and Board of Governors.[6] However, the final proposal was rejected by the United States as well as some developing countries, such as Brazil and Mexico. As an alternative, Mexico spearheaded in

2004 the use of collective action clauses in US-issued bonds. Additionally, in 2013, the Eurozone mandated the inclusion of aggregation clauses in its members' bond contracts, which would allow the joint renegotiation of several bond issues.

Argentina's defeat in 2013–2014 US court litigation showed the problems associated with the interpretation of the *pari-passu* clause, which forced the country to fully repay creditors that had not participated in two previous renegotiations, known as the holdouts. The solution adopted by most countries was the introduction of both a revised *pari-passu* clause[7] and the European aggregation mechanisms. Mexico led the way in November 2014 and also replaced the fiscal agent with a trustee to represent bondholders in negotiations, a system already in use in London. Nevertheless, these changes did not exclude the possibility of blocking majorities and coherence between bonds and other debt contracts. Also, the revised collective action clauses do not solve the problem that about half of the sovereign bonds of emerging and developing countries lack expanded collective action clauses (World Bank, 2022a).

The COVID-19 pandemic helped expose the high interest rates that the global economy has faced in recent years. Figure 10.3 shows that the share of highly indebted low-income nations had declined significantly after the 2005 Multi-Lateral Debt Relief Initiative but has surged back since the mid-2010s to almost 30% (Chuku et al., 2023; Volz et al., 2021). Similarly, the proportion of middle-income countries with high debt decreased in the first decade of the 21st century but increased later, reaching a new peak in 2020.

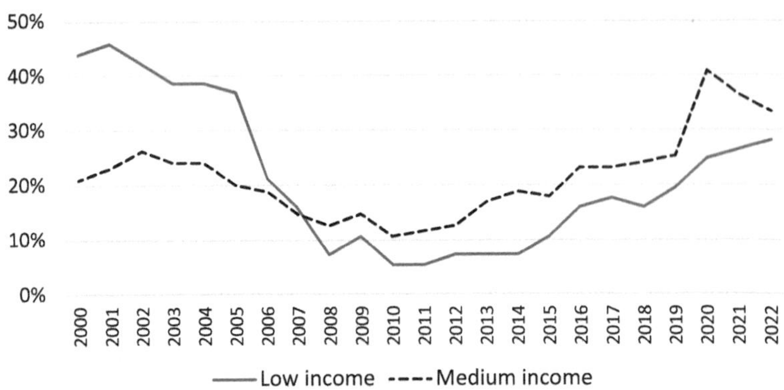

Figure 10.3 Developing Countries With High Debt Levels (%)

Note: More than 70% of national income.

Source: IMF, World Economic Outlook Databases, https://www.imf.org/en/Publications/SPROLLs/world-economic-outlook-databases [accessed August 2024].

The high interest rates and low availability of financing for developing countries in private international financial markets have generated further problems, including the illiquidity of several solvent countries. IMF projections indicated that all groups of developing countries will continue to have higher debt levels than those in 2019, portraying persistent debt stress even for countries that do not face default risks (IMF, 2023b).

During the pandemic, the G20 and Paris Club created the Debt Service Suspension Initiative for low-income countries, which helped suspend payments of US$12.9 billion from 48 out of 73 eligible countries between May 2020 and December 2021 (World Bank, 2022a). At the end of 2020, the G20 and Paris Club also launched a debt-restructuring mechanism, the Common Framework for Debt Treatment for Debt Service Suspension Initiative-eligible countries. However, only Chad, Ethiopia, Ghana, and Zambia have requested debt relief under this agreement. For these reasons, it is essential to establish a permanent institutional mechanism for sovereign debt restructuring (UN, 2023b, 2023c). This mechanism should preferably operate within the UN but also in IMF if decisions by the appropriate dispute settlement body remain independent of IMF's Executive Board and Board of Governors. The renegotiations framework should follow a three-stage process, each with a fixed deadline—voluntary renegotiation, mediation, and arbitration.

However, since these negotiations would be a long and complex process, it is essential to adopt a complementary ad hoc instrument to help avoid total deadlock and lack of progress. One possibly is the expansion of a revised Common Framework for Debt Restructuring, as proposed by the UN and other institutions. In that case, it should include a clear and shorter time frame, suspend debt payments during negotiations, establish clear processes and precise rules, guarantee the participation of private creditors, and expand eligibility to middle-income countries.

An alternative to the framework could be a mechanism supported by IMF and/or MDBs. The institution in charge would provide the renegotiation framework and could provide some financing—which would facilitate the restructuring process (Ocampo, 2022). This and additional financing for developing countries should consider long-term needs, including those associated with climate change as suggested in Baqir, Diwan, Rodrik (2023).

A complex problem is whether debts owed to MDBs and IMF should be included in the restructuring processes, as occurred in 2005 for low-income countries. As argued by Zucker-Marques, Volz, Gallagher (2023), this could be necessary, as a significant proportion of the debts of highly indebted countries lies with MDBs. It should be added that the traditional separation between official and private creditors has become more complex due to new official lenders—notably China—but also various debt contracts that are different from bonds. Future aggregations must encompass all obligations. A global debt registry is therefore necessary, encompassing all types of private and official credits and both external and domestic debts. This mechanism is essential for equitable creditor treatment and to enhance the transparency of debt-restructuring processes.

Finally, to reduce the risk of future debt crises, World Bank (2022a) and other analyses suggested a broad adoption of debt instruments like state-contingent bonds, offering variable returns linked to economic conditions or commodity prices. These instruments alleviate pressure on sovereign balance sheets during economic downturns and hold potential advantages for investors. It is worth noting that, unlike the positive proposals for development financing, the 2023 G20 Summit showed little progress in addressing the over-indebtedness of many developing countries, except in supporting the existing but relatively ineffective Common Framework (G20, 2023a: para. 54). Since then, proposals in this area have continued to be absent.

10.5 International Tax Cooperation

International tax cooperation has been historically managed through a large network of bilateral tax treaties. The Committee of Experts on International Cooperation in Tax Matters, a subsidiary body of the UN Economic and Social Council, became a regular committee in 2004 and was upgraded in the UN Conference on Financing for Development in 2015. The bilateral treaties follow two basic models, designed by OECD and the UN, which are generally viewed as favouring countries where the headquarters of multi-national corporations (MNCs) are located and where they have investments, respectively.

In recent decades, the convergence of tax reforms in developed countries and OECD's soft-law standards has created a landscape where MNCs take advantage of tax benefits, preferential regimes, and tax havens. To respond to these challenges, in 2013 base erosion and profit shifting (BEPS) negotiations were launched in OECD, resulting in a multilateral convention signed in 2017. It was followed by an inclusive framework on BEPS, now encompassing 145 countries. The Global Forum on Transparency and Exchange of Information for Tax Purposes had been previously launched, in 2000, and now includes 169 countries.

The outcome of the inclusive framework negotiations was an agreement in October 2021, comprising two elements. Under Pillar I, parts of the global profits of MNCs would be apportioned to countries in which their customers are located. However, this only applies to very large and profitable firms—those with annual global turnovers exceeding €20 billion and profit margins of at least 10% of revenue—and only for 25% of their residual profits, defined as exceeding a 10% profit margin. Pillar II established a minimum effective tax rate of 15%.[8]

Although the agreement represented progress in tax cooperation, it has faced several criticisms. On Pillar I, developing countries consistently advocated for a meaningful reallocation of taxing rights to countries where MNCs conduct their business. In turn, the tax rate adopted under Pillar II has been deemed as too low by many analysts; it is below the 21% proposed by the United States and well below the current corporate tax rates of African and Latin American countries, which are around 25%. Although it was intended as an effective rate, several carveouts imply that it will be significantly below 15%.

Another problem is that signatories are required to remove unilateral measures like digital services taxes, a condition that is unsatisfactory for many developing economies as it would limit their ability to tax digital MNCs in the future. Despite its weaknesses, most OECD Inclusive Framework members accepted the agreement, except Kenya, Nigeria, and Sri Lanka. Pillar I still needs a convention to be effective, and its approval by all parliaments, particularly by the US Congress, is an additional uncertainty.

According to a recent analysis by the European Union Tax Observatory, exchange of information has been effective in reducing untaxed offshore financial wealth. However, the global tax revenue loss due to shifting of profits from MNCs to tax havens continues to be high—close to 10%—and the effective tax rates for billionaires are very low (Alstadsæter et al., 2023). Indeed, the greatest benefits of these tax reforms are expected to go to high-income countries, where the headquarters of the main MNCs are located (Alstadsæter et al., 2023).

In response to the marginal benefits for the developing world, African countries proposed negotiating a UN tax convention. In November 2023, the UN approved—by a wide margin[9]—the establishment of an intergovernmental committee to draft the terms of reference for a convention aimed at an effective and inclusive international tax cooperation system. This committee started its negotiations in 2024.

The future UN convention must build upon—but go beyond—the reallocation of taxing rights provided by the OECD agreement. This entails developing an effective mechanism to tax MNCs operating in all markets—including those that use digital services—which should be based on the principle of 'significant economic presence'. A higher effective minimum tax rate should also be adopted as well as clear criteria for taxing activities associated with the exploitation of natural resources. Minimum standards for income taxes for richer people should also be drawn up, including a wealth tax (i.e. taxing billionaires at least 2% of their wealth). It should also include an agreement to create a global asset registry that identifies the final beneficial ownership of all assets.[10]

The challenges of these negotiations must not be underestimated, as most developed countries voted against the OECD agreement. The hope is that they will realise that it is in their own best interests to join and to support this inclusive process.

There are two additional issues in international tax cooperation that must be considered. The first relates to the transformation of the UN Committee of Experts on International Cooperation in Tax Matters into an intergovernmental organ. This proposal has been defeated twice: (i) in 2004, when the committee was given permanent status; and (ii) in 2015, when the Group of 77 presented a similar proposal at the Addis Ababa Financing for Development Summit. The alternative would be to create a new UN institution—the International Tax Authority. The second is the weakness of regional tax cooperation processes. OECD has its own system of cooperation amongst its members. The African Tax Administration Forum is also one of those mechanisms. In turn, the Latin American and Caribbean Taxation Platform was created in July 2023 under the leadership of Brazil, Chile, and Colombia. Both mechanisms must expand tax cooperation activities amongst their members.

10.6 Concluding Remarks: Critical Institutional Issues

In institutional terms, the reform of the international financial and tax system must address four key issues. The first is to continue with the reform of Bretton Woods institutions, especially enhancing the voices and participation of developing countries. This requires updating capital shares based on the relative size of economies, continuing the reforms adopted in 2008–2010. Additionally, increasing the weight of the basic votes[11] and expanding the use of double-majority decisions would favour developing countries, given that they have a larger number of members. The possibility of veto power for decisions requiring 85% of votes should also be eliminated.

To ensure a transparent and equitable system for electing the heads of IMF and World Bank, it is crucial to uphold the principle of equal treatment of all member countries in their aspiration to lead these international organisations, which are part of the UN system. For IMF, there is at least competition amongst European countries for the appointment of its managing director. For the World Bank, the only semi-competitive process for the election of its president was in 2012, in which there were two candidates from developing countries.

There are also proposals to alter the power of the different decision-making bodies. This is related to the fact that the agreements made in the ministerial meetings—the IMF International Monetary and Financial Committee and World Bank Development Committee—are not binding but only recommendations to the executive boards and boards of governors. Due to information asymmetries and coordination costs, management is powerful in both institutions and limits the executive boards' ability to modify proposals prepared by staff and cleared by management.

The second key institutional issue involves creating a representative committee at the top of the international economic cooperation system. This recommendation is essential to overcome the elite multilateralism constituted by the OECD's G10, G7, and G20 and aligns with a longstanding history of proposals advocating the creation of an economic security council or an L27 based on the current Economic and Social Council of the United Nations (Derviş and Özer, 2005; Rosenthal, 2007). The Global Economic Coordination Council is the most interesting, proposed by the Commission of Experts on Reforms of the International Financial and Monetary System (known as the Stiglitz Commission), convened by the UN General Assembly after the North Atlantic financial crisis (UN, 2009). According to this proposal, this council would coordinate the activities of the UN system; IMF, World Bank, and the World Trade Organization would also be integrated into the system. It would adopt a representation regime based on constituencies and weighted voting, mirroring the structure of the Bretton Woods institutions, and operate as a council at the level of heads of government that could convene ministerial meetings. Although this would not follow the UN principle of 'one country, one vote', it would recognise that a global economic governmental system cannot function if the most powerful countries are not sitting at the negotiating table. It should be noted that, if a new apex body is created, the Economic and Social Council should continue to function as coordinator of the economic, social, and environmental activities of the UN Secretariat, funds, and programmes.

The third reform is, as discussed in previous sections, to create global institutions in the areas of debt and tax reform. In the first of these areas, a permanent institutional mechanism should be established for sovereign debt restructuring. In international tax cooperation, the UN Committee of Experts on International Cooperation in Tax Matters could be transformed into an intergovernmental organ, or the new UN International Tax Authority could be formed. In both cases, it would be essential to determine the complementary roles of the UN and OECD in this area.

The fourth key institutional issue is the development of multi-level architecture in which regional institutions play a crucial role. Such a scheme acknowledges that globalisation is also a world of open regionalism, which implies that there is synergy between regional and global entities and that competition between them can be constructive. Additionally, that architecture would benefit from the sense of ownership of regional institutions by small and medium-sized countries, as they have very limited voices in global ones.

An architecture of this type already exists in MDBs, which should also continue to improve. It should also be extended to the international monetary system, where this network is a half-empty set, and to international tax cooperation, where it is almost non-existent.

Notes

* The author is grateful to Juan Sebastián Betancur, Tommaso Faccio, Karla Daniela González, and Natalia Quiñonez for their support while drafting this chapter.

1 These countries include ‘emerging’ economies.

2 This term refers to the 2007–2009 crisis, generally called the global financial crisis. Since its axes were the United States and Western Europe, this is a more appropriate term.

3 The need for additional financing includes official development assistance, which is not discussed in this chapter, except in relation to supporting MDB programmes.

4 See, in particular, G20 (2023a) and World Bank (2022b).

5 On the analysis of the associated risks by IMF staff, see Ostry et al. (2012), amongst many others.

6 Hagan (2005) provided an authoritative account of these negotiations.

7 This clause generally means ‘of equal rank’, but the US courts interpreted it as equal to pro-rata payments. A change was introduced in the new contracts that eliminates any possibility of interpreting the clause as pro-rata.

8 OECD. “Base Erosion and Profit Shifting.” https://www.oecd.org/en/topics/policy-issues/base-erosion-and-profit-shifting-beps.html

9 125 votes in favour, 48 against, and 9 abstentions.

10 See the proposals made by ICRICT (2022a, 2022b). The proposal for minimum taxation of the billionaires comes from the EU Tax Observatory (2023).

11 In the case of IMF, returning to the levels agreed in 1944 would mean increasing them from 5.5% to one-ninth of total votes.

References

Alstadsæter, Annette, Sarah Godar, Panayiotis Nicolaides, and Gabriel Zucman. 2023. *Global Tax Evasion Report 2024*. Paris: European Union Tax Observatory. https://www.taxobservatory.eu//www-site/uploads/2023/10/global_tax_evasion_report_24.pdf.

Baqir, Reza, Ishac Diwan, and Dani Rodrik. 2023. “A Framework to Evaluate Economic Adjustment-Cum-Debt Restructuring Packages.” *Paris School of Economics, Finance for Development Lab Working Papers*, no. 2, January. https://www.hks.harvard.edu/publications/framework-evaluate-economic-adjustment-cum-debt-restructuring-packages.

Chuku, Chuku, Prateek Samal, Joyce Saito, Dalia Hakura, Marcos Chamon, Martin Cerisola, and Guillaume Chabert. 2023. *Are We Heading for Another Debt Crisis in Low-Income Countries? Debt Vulnerabilities: Today vs the Pre-HIPC Era. IMF Working Papers*, 2023/079. Washington, DC: International Monetary Fund. https://doi.org/10.5089/9798400236709.001.

Derviş, Kemal, and Ceren Özer. 2005. *A Better Globalization: Legitimacy, Governance, and Reform*. Washington, DC: Brookings Institution Press. https://www.cgdev.org/sites/default/files/9780815717638-Dervis-better-globalization.pdf.

G20. 2009. "Declaration on Delivering Resources through the International Financial Institution." https://g7g20-documents.org/fileadmin/G7G20_documents/2009/G20/United%20Kingdom/Leaders/2%20Leaders'%20Annexes/Annex%20to%20Leaders'%20Statement%20-%20Declaration%20on%20Delivering%20Resources%20through%20the%20International%20Financial%20Institutions_0204-2009.pdf.

G20. 2023a. "G20 New Delhi Leaders' Declaration." https://www.mea.gov.in/Images/CPV/G20-New-Delhi-Leaders-Declaration.pdf.

G20. 2023b. *Strengthening Multilateral Development Banks: The Triple Agenda—Report of the Independent Experts Group*. India: Independent Expert Group (IEG), G20. https://www.cgdev.org/sites/default/files/The_Triple_Agenda_G20-IEG_Report_Volume1_2023.pdf.

Griffith-Jones, Stephany, and José Antonio Ocampo, eds. 2018. *The Future of National Development Banks. The Initiative for Policy Dialogue Series*. Oxford, UK: Oxford University Press. https://doi.org/10.1093/oso/9780198827948.001.0001.

Hagan, Sean. 2005. "Designing a Legal Framework to Restructure Sovereign Debt." *Georgetown Journal of International Law* 36 (2): 299–402.

Independent Commission for the Reform of International Corporate Taxation (ICRICT). 2022a. *An Emergency Tax Plan to Confront the Inflation Crisis*. ICRICT. https://www.icrict.com/presse/2022-9-16-icrict-declaration-an-emergency-tax-plan-to-confront-the-inflation-crisis/.

Independent Commission for the Reform of International Corporate Taxation (ICRICT). 2022b. *It is Time for a Global Asset Registry to Tackle Hidden Wealth*. ICRICT. https://www.icrict.com/wp-content/uploads/2022/04/ICRICTGARreportEN.pdf.

International Monetary Fund. 2011. "Enhancing International Monetary Stability—a Role for the SDR?" *Policy Papers*, no. 47. https://doi.org/10.5089/9781498339483.007.

International Monetary Fund. 2012. "The Liberalization and Management of Capital Flows—an Institutional View." *IMF, Policy Papers*. https://www.imf.org/en/Publications/Policy-Papers/Issues/2016/12/31/The-Liberalization-and-Management-of-Capital-Flows-An-Institutional-View-PP4720.

International Monetary Fund. 2023a. "Review of the Flexible Credit Line, The Short Term Liquidity Line and the Precautionary and Liquidity Line, and Proposals for Reform." *Policy Papers*, no. 2023/039. Washington, DC: International Monetary Fund. https://doi.org/10.5089/9798400254703.007.

International Monetary Fund. 2023b. *World Economic Outlook: A Rocky Recovery*. World Economic Outlook/International Monetary Fund, April. Washington, DC: International Monetary Fund. https://www.imf.org/en/Publications/WEO/Issues/2023/04/11/world-economic-outlook-april–2023.

International Monetary Fund. n.d.-a. "2023 Review of Resource Adequacy of the Poverty Reduction and Growth Trust, Resilience and Sustainability Trust, and Debt Relief Trusts." In *IMF, Policy Papers*, 85. Accessed December 24, 2024. https://www.imf.org/en/Publications/Policy-Papers/Issues/2023/04/25/2023-Review-of-Resource-Adequacy-of-the-Poverty-Reduction-and-Growth-Trust-Resilience-and-532788.

International Monetary Fund. n.d.-b. *World Economic Outlook Databases*. International Monetary Fund. Accessed December 24, 2024. https://www.imf.org/en/Publications/SPROLLs/world-economic-outlook-databases.

Kenen, Peter. 2010. "An SDR Based Reserve System." *Journal of Globalization and Development* 1 (2): 13. https://doi.org/10.2202/1948–1837.1111.

Krueger, Anne O. 2002. *A New Approach to Sovereign Debt Restructuring*. Washington, DC: International Monetary Fund. https://www.imf.org/external/pubs/ft/exrp/sdrm/eng/sdrm.pdf.

Ocampo, José Antonio. 2017. *Resetting The International Monetary (Non)System*, 1st ed. Oxford, UK: Oxford University Press. https://academic.oup.com/book/9072.

Ocampo, José Antonio. 2022. "A Pandemic of Debt." *Project Syndicate*, December 12, 2022. https://www.project-syndicate.org/magazine/debt-crisis-default-relief-world-bank-imf-by-jose-antonio-ocampo-2022–12.

Ocampo, José Antonio, and Karla Daniela González. 2024. "The Role of Multilateral Development Banks and Development Assistance in the Provision of Global Public Goods." *Human Development Reports*. New York: United Nations. https://hdr.undp.org/content/role-multilateral-development-banks-and-development-assistance-provision-global-public.

Ocampo, José Antonio, and Victor Ortega. 2022. "The Global Development Banks' Architecture." *Review of Political Economy* 34 (2): 224–48. https://doi.org/10.1080/09538259.2021.1977543.

OECD. n.d. "Base Erosion and Profit Shifting (BEPS)." Accessed December 24, 2024. https://www.oecd.org/en/topics/base-erosion-and-profit-shifting-beps.html.

Ostry, Jonathan D., Atish R. Ghosh, Marcos Chamon, and Mahvash S. Qureshi. 2012. "Tools for Managing Financial-Stability Risks from Capital Inflows." *Journal of International Economics, NBER Global*, 88 (2): 407–21. https://doi.org/10.1016/j.jinteco.2012.02.002.

Rosenthal, Gert. 2007. "Economic and Social Council." In *The Oxford Handbook on the United Nations*, edited by Sam Daws and Thomas G. Weiss, 1st ed., 136–48. New York: Oxford University Press.

Rustomjee, Cyrus, Anthony De Lannoy, Joshua Wojnilower, Andrea Arevalo Arroyo, and Lukasz Jannils. 2023. *The Evolving Application of the IMF's Mandate*. Washington, DC: IMF Independent Evaluation Office. https://ieo.imf.org/en/Evaluations/Completed/2024#x2013;0618-evolving-application-of-the-imfs-mandate&.

United Nations. 2009. *Report of the Commission of Experts of the President of the United Nations General Assembly on Reforms of the International Monetary and Financial System*. New York: United Nations. https://digitallibrary.un.org/record/657634.

United Nations. 2023a. *Political Declaration of the High-Level Political Forum on Sustainable Development Convened under the Auspices of the General Assembly*. UN. https://digitallibrary.un.org/record/4025276.

United Nations. 2023b. "Reforms to the International Financial Architecture." *6. Our Common Agenda Policy Briefs*. New York: United Nations. https://digitallibrary.un.org/record/4012531.

United Nations. 2023c. *United Nations Secretary-General's SDG Stimulus to Deliver Agenda 2030*. New York: United Nations. https://digitallibrary.un.org/record/4005810.

United Nations, and UN Ad Hoc Committee to Draft Terms of Reference for a United Nations Framework Convention on International Tax Cooperation. 2024. *Promotion of Inclusive and Effective International Tax Cooperation at the United Nations*. New York: United Nations. https://digitallibrary.un.org/record/4062430.

Volz, Ulrich, Shamshad Akhtar, Kevin P Gallagher, Stephany Griffith-Jones, Jörg Haas, and Moritz Kraemer. 2021. *Debt Relief for a Green and Inclusive Recovery: Securing Private-Sector Participation and Creating Policy Space for Sustainable Development*. Berlin; London; Boston, MA: Heinrich-Böll-Stiftung; SOAS, University of London; Boston University. https://www.bu.edu/gdp/files/2021/06/DRGR-Report-2021-FIN.pdf.

Williamson, John. 2009. "Understanding Special Drawing Rights (SDRs)." *Peterson Institute for International Economics*. https://elischolar.library.yale.edu/ypfs-documents2/4851.

World Bank. 2022a. *Evolving the World Bank Group's Mission, Operations, and Resources: A Roadmap*. Washington, DC. https://documents1.worldbank.org/curated/en/099845101112322078/pdf/SECBOS0f51975e0e809b7605d7b690ebd20.pdf.

World Bank. 2022b. *World Development Report 2022: Finance for an Equitable Recovery*. Washington, DC: World Bank. https://doi.org/10.1596/978-1-4648-1730-4.

World Bank. 2024. "From Vision to Impact: Implementing the World Bank Group Evolution—Update to Governors." In *Board Report*, 188790. Washington, DC: World Bank. https://doi.org/10/BOSIB11b64b67b0511a66d139b76c4235f6.

Zucker-Marques, Marina, Ulrich Volz, and Kevin P. Gallagher. 2023. *Debt Relief by Multilateral Lenders: Why, How and How Much?* Boston; London; Berlin: Boston University Global Development Policy Center; Centre for Sustainable Finance, SOAS, University of London; Heinrich-Böll-Stiftung. https://www.bu.edu/gdp/files/2023/09/DRGR-MDBs-Report-FIN.pdf.

11 Global Resource Mobilisation

Health and Economic Recovery

Jayati Ghosh

11.1 Global Health Challenges

Health has always been a global concern, but the cross-border implications of drivers of ill health and their spread have more recently come to the fore. Events such as the COVID-19 pandemic have shown how unwise it can be to consider health concerns only in terms of their local and national impacts since both prevention and treatment of many forms of morbidity require a supra-national approach. Unfortunately, the lessons from that experience seem to have been rapidly forgotten by policymakers, especially those based in developed countries.

In the 20th century, the approach to health policies was inherently national—even local—in scope and orientation. Policies and spending varied with per capita income and levels of health infrastructure and services. The spread of infectious diseases was mostly viewed as an attribute of lack of economic development, associated with poor nutrition, sanitation, and housing conditions. It was believed that as countries moved up the per capita income scale, morbidity would be concentrated in 'lifestyle' diseases and disorders, rather than in diseases contracted through transmission.

However, this approach was outdated even before the COVID-19 pandemic, as other epidemics such as severe acute respiratory syndrome (SARS), Ebola, and H1N1 indicated new potential for infectious disease spread. Some new health challenges also emerged from the very processes of health delivery, such as the increasing dangers posed by antimicrobial resistance, which renders many existing disease treatments ineffective and can be spread through human mobility.

Pollution, climate change, and the degradation of nature pose a host of new challenges to health and are already undermining progress in health indicators in some of the poorest and most vulnerable populations. Pollution generates clear, well-known health risks. Climate change threatens some basic human requirements, such as clean air, safe drinking water, nutritious food supply, and safe shelter, and is creating heat conditions that are impossible to live and work in. According to the World Health Organization (WHO), between 2030 and 2050, climate change is expected to cause around 250,000 additional deaths per year, from undernutrition, malaria, diarrhea, and heat stress.[1] Heat-driven morbidity is particularly acute for workers who are forced to continue to labour under extreme conditions. Many are informal workers in low- and middle-income countries (LMICs) with little or no legal or social protection and poor access to affordable health care.

DOI: 10.4324/9781003571384-11

Even these numbers are underestimates; they exclude the mortality and morbidity associated with major climate shocks as well as the more gradual but nevertheless significant increase in communicable diseases due to various impacts of global warming, such as the increased incidence of typhoid in Nepal[2] or spread of flood-related diseases like cholera in Uganda.[3] In addition, various zoonotic diseases are emerging, which are strongly associated with economic activity, along with changes in the natural environment and rising temperatures. The areas and regions where health infrastructure is already weak—as in the majority of developing countries—are the least able to cope with these threats without assistance, both technical and financial.

Even during the COVID-19 pandemic, short-term national interests triumphed over what could have been a much more effective and efficient multilateral approach, especially with regard to the appropriation of vaccines and treatment drugs. Recently, addressing health concerns multi-laterally has been confined to a few halting and inadequate measures.[4] The failure to come to an agreement on a pandemic accord at the World Health Assembly in May 2024—just 2 years after a global pandemic led everyone to say 'never again'—is another reminder of the perilous state of multilateral processes today.

The absence of an international approach to health is only one concern. Another is the prevailing international economic architecture that reduces the ability of nation-states, especially in lower-income countries, to develop and to finance health systems and policies that can confront these challenges. Moreover, the fiscal space of governments is reduced through high sovereign debt servicing requirements that often become the first charge on public resources; an outdated global tax system that makes it difficult to raise revenues by adequately taxing both corporate and individual high-income earners; and limits on public spending and on running deficits, even in situations of extreme need, due to fear of flight of highly mobile capital. The global intellectual property regime also constrains the transmission of essential knowledge and technology that can counter existing and emerging health threats.

11.2 Constraints Posed by the International Economic Architecture and the Limited Fiscal Space of Developing Countries

The international economic system generates balance-of-payments deficits or dollar shortages in the poorest nations and concentrates surpluses in a few countries. Such surpluses must be recycled to ensure the stability of the global system and progress in developing countries. The standard recycling mechanisms are grants, concessional aid, foreign direct investment, and debt. In practice, debt has dominated, and it must be serviced. Yet global inequality and inadequate economic diversification in LMICs provide structural reasons for continued deficits, which then generate continued borrowing to meet amortisation and interest.

The role of private creditors in international debt markets has recently increased. Between 2000 and 2021, the share of public and publicly guaranteed external debt of low- and lower-middle-income countries owed to bondholders jumped from

10% to 50% (UNCTAD, 2024a). Meanwhile, 'aid fatigue' has led to declines in the volume of bilateral flows and concessional credit from Paris Club official creditors, just as China's bilateral lending significantly increased. Indeed, China is now the most important bilateral lender for many countries.

The multiplicity of creditors has made debt crisis resolution difficult. There are differences between the major bilateral creditors, and no effective pressure exists on private creditors to force them to participate in debt relief. Multilateral development banks (MDBs) have refused to take 'haircuts' (i.e. a reduction of the amounts that must be repaid), arguing that these would affect their credit ratings and therefore their ability to borrow at low interest rates. As a result, the burden of whatever restructuring has occurred has fallen on bilateral creditors, which, in practice, mainly impacts China.[5]

In late 2023, more than half of low-income countries were at high risk of debt distress or in debt distress (World Bank, 2022). Middle-income countries were also affected, with explicit defaults (e.g. Sri Lanka) or severe debt stress (e.g. Egypt and Pakistan). The general presumption is that dramatically increased external debt stress resulted from the COVID-19 pandemic, which caused public revenues to fall due to the lockdowns and impact of the disease, even as public spending increased for the same reasons. However, this interpretation is incorrect for several reasons.

The current explosion of debt distress across a range of LMICs is the culmination of a medium-term process, beginning with increased access to credit that was enabled after the massive liquidity expansions by central banks in developed countries after the 2008 global financial crisis. This began yet another boom-bust cycle of capital flows to developing countries' markets since the 1970s. Low interest rates and increased access to funds generated a greater appetite for risky investment. Even countries that were previously not attractive for financial markets—so-called 'frontier markets'—became recipients of credit and bond market access. Many LMICs took advantage of this and received capital inflows much greater than in the past from a wider variety of sources, including private lenders and new bilateral lenders like China. In some of the recipient countries, these funds were not always used for productive investment that could generate foreign exchange but were spent on imports of non-essential consumption goods or vanity projects of leaders.

When economies are lower down in the pecking order of international finance, periods of capital inflows tend to be followed by periods of outflow, driven by concerns about growing current account deficits or—more often—by global factors such as changes in rates of return in 'core' countries. The COVID-19 pandemic, inflationary pressures activated by Russia's invasion of Ukraine, and the subsequent tightening of monetary policies in developed economies ended the period of easy access to international finance for most LMICs. Meanwhile, the impact of the pandemic and rise in global food and fuel prices meant that many countries were less able to generate foreign exchange for debt services. Several countries effectively resorted to Ponzi financing, taking on fresh debt to service existing debt. They were thus especially vulnerable to shifts in capital markets.

Current debt problems have had little to do with actual increases in the public debt of LMICs during and after the pandemic. Indeed, many LMICs face sovereign debt crises although they were much more fiscally prudent than developed economies throughout the pandemic and after. The increase in public spending by these countries as a group has been relatively modest—even negligible—especially when compared to the massive increases in public expenditure (and consequent deficits) in developed economies (Table 11.1). LMICs largely controlled their discretionary spending and primary deficit–gross domestic product (GDP) ratios despite sharp decreases in revenue, which meant not spending adequately for social protection or countercyclical attempts at recovery. Such fiscal rectitude on the part of LMICs meant that the burden of the pandemic was even greater on the populations in these countries.

Table 11.1 Fiscal Indicators (% of GDP)

	2018	*2019*	*2020*	*2021*	*2022*	*2023*
Advanced economies						
General government revenue	36.0	35.7	36.1	37.0	37.4	36.9
General government expenditure	38.4	38.7	46.4	44.5	41.7	41.3
Primary balance	–0.9	–1.5	–9.0	–6.2	–2.8	–2.8
Middle-income countries						
General government revenue	27.9	27.4	25.6	26.5	26.5	26.0
General government expenditure	31.4	32.0	34.4	31.8	31.8	31.8
Primary balance	–1.8	–2.7	–7.1	–3.4	–3.4	–3.7
Low-income countries						
General government revenue	14.8	14.5	13.8	14.3	14.7	14.9
General government expenditure	18.0	18.0	18.7	19.0	18.9	19.1
Primary balance	–1.7	–1.9	–3.2	–2.8	–2.3	–2.4

GDP = gross domestic product, IMF = International Monetary Fund.

Note: Numbers for 2023 are IMF projections.

Source: IMF (2023b).

Such fiscal discipline did not result in lower levels of the debt–GDP ratio for LMICs, however. Figure 11.1 shows that Developed economies already had significantly higher levels of public debt in 2018, greater than their GDPs on average; this further increased to 123% of their total GDP in 2020. Their public debt–GDP levels fell in 2021, however, and continued to decline in subsequent years. There was no such decline in public debt–GDP levels for LMICs; rather, these continued to increase slightly, although the ratios remained well below those of developed economies.

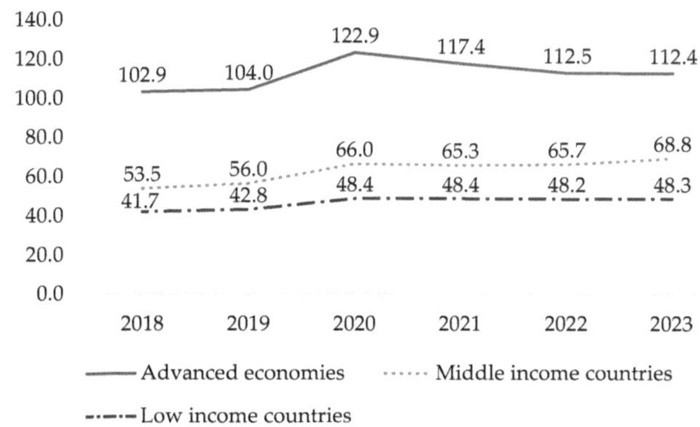

Figure 11.1 General Government Gross Debt (% of GDP)

GDP = gross domestic product, IMF = International Monetary Fund.

Source: IMF (2023a).

This highlights two anomalies that capture the inequality and injustice embedded in global financial markets. First, public debt–GDP ratios continued to increase for LMICs, although they spent relatively less and contained their primary deficits over the pandemic period. Second, despite significantly lower debt–GDP ratios than developed countries, sovereign debt crises have been concentrated in these countries rather than in developed economies that started the period with higher public debt levels and were, in fact, more profligate with spending. Clearly, private capital flows are not determined by macroeconomic fundamentals but rather by investor behaviour driven by currency hierarchies and perceptions of power in the global economy.

Far from being rewarded for this excessive fiscal prudence, LMICs have been further punished by financial markets, as the average spread on their sovereign debt (above the United States [US] Federal Reserve rate) ballooned from the start of 2020. This has been unlike the experience of developed economies, where average spreads on sovereign debt have remained low—generally well below 1 basis point—despite sharply increased public debt in those countries. Figures 11.2 and 11.3 illustrate this point.

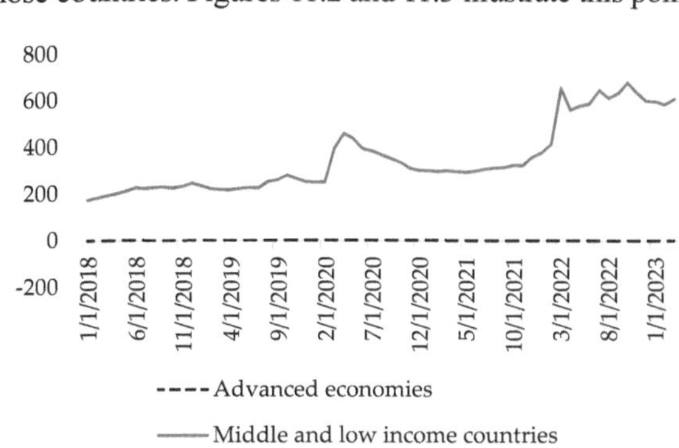

Figure 11.2 Spreads on Sovereign Debt (Basis Points)

Source: IMF (2023a).

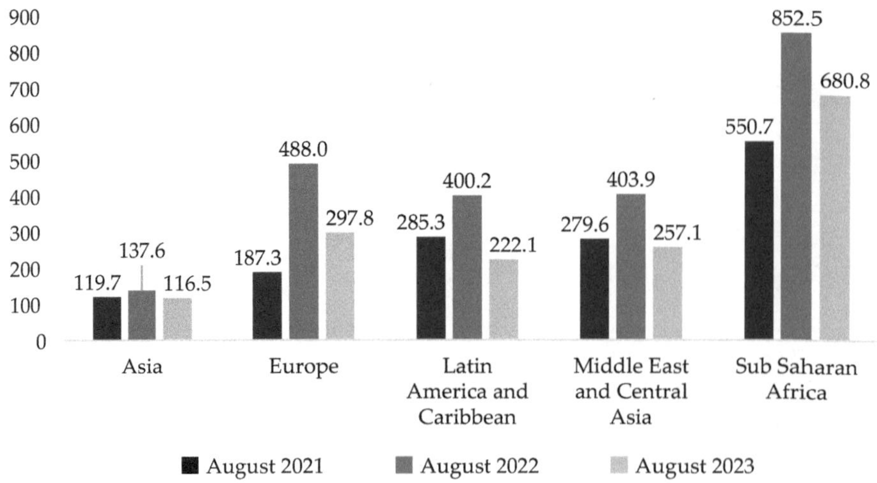

Figure 11.3 Median Sovereign Spreads in Lower-Middle-Income Countries (Basis Points)
Source: IMF (2023b).

These increasing spreads on sovereign bonds issued by LMICs have little to do with economic fundamentals. Rather, monetary tightening in the major developed economies created a 'flight to safety' to wealthy economies that do not have to play by the conservative fiscal rules imposed on poorer countries. Ironically, such capital outflows make adverse expectations become self-fulfilling for LMICs, creating new difficulties in repayment as the costs of borrowing keep rising. By 2023, the debt–GDP ratio for middle-income countries had ballooned to 68%, mostly because of new fiscal spending, while the ratio for low-income countries increased to an even higher 73%, mainly because of legacy debt and compounding higher interest payments.

The rising cost of debt servicing has put pressure on government budgets. A study by Debt Relief International found that in all developing regions in 2021, debt service represented more than two-thirds of total core social expenditures (i.e. education, health, and social protection taken together) (Martin and Waddock, 2022). In relation to total public health spending in 2021, debt service numbers were even worse—nearly 10.0 times across all developing countries, nearly 6.0 times in the Middle East and North Africa, 7.5 times in Asia, 8.6 times in Sub-Saharan Africa, 9.6 times in Latin America and the Caribbean, and 10.0 times in Europe. Effectively, debt repayment has become the first charge on public resources, forcing spending on the social and economic rights of citizens to be curtailed, affecting health spending during and after the pandemic. Even countries that were not experiencing external debt difficulties or large debt service outflows restricted fiscal expansion because of fears of possible capital outflows.

Meanwhile, the outdated global taxation architecture has ensured that wealthy people and global companies can avoid paying the same tax rates on their income as those less favoured. International cooperation can play a major role in curtailing this—even through the simple sharing of information across countries.

The US Foreign Account Tax Compliance Act implemented in 2014 requires all banks everywhere to report on the account holdings of US taxpayers under the threat of penalties. Moreover, the automatic exchange of banking information through the Common Reporting Standard of the Organisation for Economic Cooperation and Development (OECD) began in 2017 and now involves more than 110 jurisdictions. While offshore tax evasion by individuals has not disappeared, it has been significantly reduced (Alstadsæter et al., 2023).

However, the loopholes for tax evasion within countries remain strong. Global billionaires have effective tax rates equivalent to as little as 0%–0.5% of their wealth, largely because they use opaque trusts that do not declare the beneficial owners and 'shell companies' to avoid income taxation. The obvious remedy for this is to institute a wealth tax on billionaires. Even a relatively low tax rate of 2% would generate significant tax revenues—close to US$250 billion annually from less than 3,000 people (Alstadsæter et al., 2023).

Another international tax initiative, the OECD base erosion and profit shifting (BEPS) process to control tax avoidance by multi-national companies (MNCs) shifting their profits to low-tax or no-tax jurisdictions, has been less successful. Prolonged negotiations led to an agreement in 2021 to enforce a minimum corporate tax rate, but the compromise rate was only 15%—much lower than 25%, which is the median of global corporate tax rates. Carveouts introduced subsequently (e.g. showing 'economic substance') further reduced revenue gains from this tax. Profit shifting has continued unabated, as about 35% of foreign profits of MNCs—around US$1 trillion—were shifted to tax havens in 2022, about the same amount as before the BEPS (Alstadsæter et al., 2023). A proper implementation of a 20% minimum corporate tax rate without loopholes would generate an estimated US$250 billion per year.

The lack of proper global tax reform combined with decelerating economic activity has put further pressure on fiscal space in LMICs, to the point that it has been estimated that 85% of the world's population was likely living in the grip of austerity measures in 2023 (Ortiz and Cummings, 2022). This adds to inequality between and within countries, economic insecurity, and worsening health conditions, especially for women and girls.

Increased poverty and hunger can also be directly related to the constraints posed by the international financial architecture. Around 122 million more people faced hunger in 2022 than in 2019 (i.e. before the global COVID-19 pandemic), while an estimated 42% of the world's population—more than 3.1 billion people—were unable to afford a healthy diet in 2021 (FAO et al., 2023). As always, women and girls are the worst affected in terms of nutrition indicators, as gender inequalities in food access continue to be pervasive, especially in the poorest parts of the world. The countries experiencing the biggest increases in food insecurity are also those reeling under debt crises and facing severe climate-change impacts.

Growing hunger and undernutrition reflect the interplay between lack of access to physical supplies of food, purchasing power (and therefore livelihoods), and prices of food items. Prices are driven by national and international trade patterns—and therefore by the local, national, and global concentration of agribusinesses

(Ghosh, 2023). There is also the effect of speculative activity in commodity futures markets and their impact on spot markets for global trade prices of food items. Indeed,

> Corporate profits from financial operations appear to be strongly linked to periods of excessive speculation in commodities markets and to the growth of shadow banking . . . During the period of heightened price volatility since 2020, certain major food trading companies have earned record profits in the financial markets, even as food prices have soared globally, and millions of people faced a cost-of-living crisis.
>
> (UNCTAD, 2024b)

Speculative activity, however, tends to be short-lived. The sharp spike in food prices from the run-up to Russia's invasion of Ukraine in 2022 peaked in June 2023; thereafter, food prices (especially of wheat) fell equally sharply. By August 2023, data showed that wheat prices were well below their levels of 2 years previously (FAO, 2023). This should have made life easier for food-importing countries; indeed, several analysts concluded that such temporary spikes in food prices can be ignored because they come down again relatively quickly. Yet for many countries, domestic food prices have stayed very high or continued to rise even as global prices fell.

This phenomenon can be traced to the ability to import food and exchange rate devaluations. The period from early 2022 onwards was marked by cascading shocks impacting several food-importing countries—the end of the moratorium on sovereign debt repayments; a shift to tighter monetary policies and higher interest rates in rich countries, which led to capital flight out of these countries; and pressure on import bills coming from higher energy prices. Most of all, the rigidity of debt repayments created a severe constraint on other essential imports. These forces also led to substantial currency devaluations, further increasing the local prices of imported food. This is yet another mechanism through which international economic relations affect nutrition and therefore health across the world.

Another concern is that there is still no adequately funded mechanism to enable the prevention of and preparation for future global health threats like pandemics. Even as a global pandemic accord continues to be negotiated without result thus far (WHO, 2024b), there are concerns that essential principles (e.g. an emphasis on equity and not allowing private profits to be privileged over public welfare) are not being adequately foregrounded.

The Pandemic Fund was established in September 2022 and formally launched under Indonesia's G20 Presidency at the G20 meetings in Bali in November 2022. Its mandate is to finance critical investments to strengthen pandemic prevention, preparedness, and response capacities, with a focus on LMICs. However, it has thus far remained significantly underfunded, having mobilised less than US$2.0 billion of the initially assessed requirement of around US$10.6 billion.[6] Similarly, the Global Fund to combat HIV, tuberculosis, and malaria is underfunded relative to its aims (Green, 2024), while WHO itself remains considerably underfunded as well (WHO, 2024a). Moreover, its functioning is constrained by increasing dependence on voluntary contributions that are earmarked for donor-specified programmes and projects (Iwunna, Kennedy, Harmer, 2023).

There are more current failures of the international financial system. For example, there is no global financial safety net to provide liquidity during crises. The system is also unable to address the central challenges of financing development and global public goods to meet climate and health challenges. International financial institutions—particularly the International Monetary Fund (IMF)—continue to impose conditions on borrower countries that undermine a nation-state's ability to ensure the socio-economic rights of its citizens and to provide necessary public health infrastructure and services (Kentikelenis and Stubbs, 2023). Further, the legal system underpinning the financial architecture—in particular that associated with intellectual property rights—allows the profitability of private investors to take precedence over human rights. This has very direct and strong public health implications because of the ability of pharmaceutical companies to take advantage of monopolies over knowledge to restrict production and to raise prices of essential medicines, diagnostics, and instruments. This was already a major concern in advanced economies (Baker, 2016)—and even more so in LMICs (Azam, 2016)—but became sharply evident during the COVID-19 pandemic (Ghosh, 2021). All of this has immediate and sustained impacts on health and other socio-economic conditions throughout the world.

11.3 Current Reform Proposals

Since the COVID-19 pandemic, several important proposals for reform and for multilateral initiatives to address some of these concerns have emerged. The Independent Panel for Pandemic Preparedness and Response, chaired by Helen Clark and Ellen Johnson Sirleaf, argued for stronger leadership and better coordination regarding health at national, regional, and international levels, including a more focussed and independent WHO, a pandemic treaty, and a senior Global Health Threats Council (IPPPR, 2021). It also proposed a pre-negotiated platform to produce vaccines, diagnostics, therapeutics, and supplies and to secure their rapid and equitable delivery as essential global common goods. This requires greater access to financial resources, both for investments in preparedness and to be able to inject funds immediately at the onset of a potential pandemic.

The WHO Council on the Economics of Health for All, chaired by Mariana Mazzucato, noted that delivering health for all will require more and better finance suited to the particular demands of health investments (WHO, 2023). Therefore, it proposed long-term financing, with more fiscal space for lower-income countries to make critical investments in health; a redesign of the international financial architecture to fund health equitably and proactively; and a properly resourced and governed WHO to play a key global coordination role. With regard to the quality of finance, the council emphasised the need to coordinate private investment activity with public spending using a combination of incentives, regulations, and controls. It also called for an international fund to stabilise low-income countries' emergencies, supplemented by a longer-term borrowing facility.

The Global Preparedness Monitoring Board noted that global financing of pandemic preparedness remains woefully inadequate, inefficient, uncoordinated, and insufficiently aligned to country needs and processes (GPMB, 2023).

Like others, the board has argued that the international financial system requires comprehensive reform to make it fit-for-purpose; address urgent funding gaps with predictability and timeliness; align it with national priorities and needs; enable new ways to bolster national and international financing; generate the fiscal space for domestic resource mobilisation; and align the modalities for grants, loans, and debt relief with long-term prevention and preparedness.

There have been broader proposals for reform of the international financial system, which would also impact health financing. The Bridgetown Initiative proposed reforming the governance of international financial institutions; increasing global liquidity through further issues of IMF Special Drawing Rights (SDR); increasing multilateral lending, primarily through MDBs; and increasing private sector investment for green transformation (Gold, 2023). It called for the inclusion of disaster and pandemic clauses in all loans issued by major lenders to ensure automatic debt suspension in the event of a climate or other major disruption. The United Nations High-level Advisory Board on Effective Multilateralism[7] similarly recommended reform of international financial institutions; strengthening and improving the global debt architecture to enable more rapid and effective debt relief; repurposing the MDB system to provide more stable long-term finance; improving the regulatory frameworks governing financial flows, both within and across borders; and pursuing reforms in global taxation.

Two proposals from the United Nations High-Level Advisory Board on Effective Multilateralism are of special significance—a global financial safety net and enabling greater automaticity and fairness in the issuance and allocation system of SDR. To give all countries access to foreign currencies during global and regional crises, it recommends an IMF multilateral SDR-swap facility to overcome the selectivity and fragmentation of today's bilateral central bank swap arrangements, which are led by a few major central banks. It also proposed regular annual allocations of SDR as well as selective SDR allocation so that only those countries that face weak external positions or external/natural shocks would receive SDR in a general allocation. The conditions under which these SDR allocations are triggered would be pre-specified to ensure a swifter global response.

Given this plethora of sensible proposals, what prevents any movement forwards towards real change in the system? Clearly, both national and international politics are currently impacting the potential for multilateral reform initiatives. Ongoing wars and conflicts create obvious political barriers to cooperation. Within countries, the continuing reliance on a neoliberal economic policy paradigm by many governments and international institutions creates even more inequality and breeds popular distrust and a lack of legitimacy. Hyper-nationalism and domestic political polarisation are socio-political responses to various threats, but they also add to them. They generate and accentuate the increasingly inward and nationalist orientation of major players, such as the United States and many European countries, constraining the need to empower WHO and to provide it with the necessary financial resources. Meanwhile, the idea of more global funds seems valid in principle but is unlikely to have much traction—not only because of less enthusiastic donors, concerns about governance of such funds, and unclear principles on which the resources would be allocated—but also due to a lack of legitimacy and trust amongst potential recipients. The less-than-impressive experience of the few funds that are currently in operation or have been recently created adds to the scepticism.

11.4 What Can Be Done

In this context, what are the realistic proposals for a new international economic order that would enable both better conditions of health and sustained economic recovery in the world, especially in the Global Majority? Some of the proposals noted previously bear repetition since they could well be the minimum conditions for achieving any real change in the international economic order, specifically for ensuring better health for all.

The first relates to the reform of international financial institutions, which must affect not only the governance structure but their approach and manner of functioning. The need for reform of the management and governance structure of IMF and World Bank has been reiterated often in the recent past since the current institutions are outdated and too slow and meagre in their responses to have any meaningful impact. Their policy orientation must be shifted. They must recognise flaws in previous functioning and be better aligned with current needs for global public investment to cope with global challenges to the environment and health. SDR issuance must become a regular annual process, in line with the expansion of the global economy, and the focus should be on selective issuance to countries in need, with new SDR automatically provided according to predefined criteria such as climate events and disasters, health crises, terms of trade and interest rate shocks, and other shocks outside of the control of the country concerned. In addition, lending by international financial institutions—especially IMF—must not contain policy conditionalities that worsen current or future health challenges. This means abandoning the principle of fiscal austerity as a device for dealing with all imbalances, regardless of the conditions of the economy, and following a process of social pre-audit of loan-related conditions to meet health, human rights, and other requirements.

The second requirement, in light of the debt distress and heavy debt servicing needs noted earlier, is speedy and effective sovereign debt resolution. An example is the 1953 London Agreement on German External Debts, which wrote off fully half of Germany's debt and converted the remainder into long-term loans repayable at extremely low interest rates, with interest payments capped at 3% of export earnings (Galofré-Vilà et al., 2019). It has been noted that—apart from other benefits (including the contribution to the subsequent Wirtschaftswunder)—this debt relief was associated with a substantial and statistically significant increase in real per capita social spending, with obvious positive effects on health. By contrast, the Common Framework for debt relief developed by the G20 has thus far proved to be ineffectual, sluggish, and rife with conflicts amongst official creditors; it also features a lack of participation from private creditors. It must be dramatically revised or replaced with a new approach.

Major revisions in the Debt Sustainability Analysis currently provided by IMF are also necessary, with a macro model that recognises the adverse impacts of fiscal compression on GDP and is more realistic and responsive to the specific conditions faced by debtor countries. An effective debt resolution process requires a standstill—not just a pause—on all debt payments during the process, which also incentivises speed on the part of creditors. Private creditors' involvement must be compulsory, as in most national bankruptcy laws. This would require legal changes in the major jurisdictions of debt contracts (e.g. London and New York) or global agreements that override such legal barriers.

The problems created by the need for significant amounts of debt servicing are not confined to countries in immediate debt distress or on the verge of it. Indeed, as noted previously, many countries are expending large amounts on external debt service, thereby reducing their ability to make necessary outlays on health and other essential social spending, as well as climate-related investments. To deal with such problems of illiquidity rather than insolvency, a bridging programme has been proposed to postpone payment of debt obligations through rescheduling, along with increased funding from multilateral institutions, to enable future repayments coming out of economic recovery rather than squeezing an already strained population (Rodrik and Diwan, 2023).

Currently, currency hierarchies in the global economy make it difficult for most LMICs to benefit from open capital accounts. In addition to increased volatility and associated financial fragility, there are seigniorage costs associated with the higher returns on financial assets in recipient LMICs compared with much lower rates of return on their own capital (and central bank reserves) invested in wealthy countries. Capital controls, internal financial regulation, and reduced reliance on external debt are now essential for LMICs, given the vulnerability and volatility created by financial markets reacting to forces not of their own making. In addition, there needs to be wider and tighter regulations of international financial markets, particularly commodity futures markets that affect the prices of essential traded commodities like food and fuel.

The overwhelming need for greater fiscal space in LMICs also points to the need to ensure that the international taxation system does not prevent governments from raising revenues in an equitable and just manner. To change the structure of taxation by emphasising more progressive taxation, it is especially important to ensure the equitable taxation of MNCs using unitary taxation with formulary apportionment, impose taxes on extreme wealth utilising cross-country information sharing, and enact taxes on financial transactions. Negotiations at the United Nations will be critical in this regard.

The tight intellectual property regimes that prevent greater access to essential knowledge for health need urgent reform and rehaul as well. Both the Agreement on Trade-Related Aspects of Intellectual Property Rights (TRIPS) and the various intellectual property rights restrictions in assorted international economic agreements need to be reconsidered, renegotiated, and made more compatible with the demands of economic justice and global health and environmental needs.

A critical concern relates to the quality of finance for health investments. Current incentives for governmental and private financing for health are still oriented towards short-term results, whether in response to particular health crises, in terms of generating improved health outcomes, or (in the case of private investment) pecuniary returns. However, health is a sector that requires patient finance and needs significant spending that will never generate profits or be commercially viable. Health for all further requires investments in a wide range of economic and social sectors that may not always appear to be directly related to health. This, in turn, calls for a whole-of-government approach within countries and more coordination across international agencies, neither of which is evident at present. Ensuring the quality of health financing necessitates substantial reform in the functioning of international organisations and national governments, moving away from silos and turf battles to a more systematic and coordinated approach. More sustained and better financing for WHO is also essential, since it plays a critical role in coordinating health delivery, supporting public health systems, and ensuring health conditions in ways that individual countries or even groups of countries cannot.

Of course, the constraints and power imbalances that have prevented such changes at the global level still persist, so what can be done to nudge the multilateral system towards such changes in strategy and institutional reform? One possible route could be through issue-based coalitions of countries to promote or to implement particular approaches. For example, debtor countries could cooperate and coordinate their strategies to assess debt sustainability, monitor negotiations on debt restructuring, and approach negotiations as a group to become 'systemically important'. Regional groups of countries could coordinate tax reforms (e.g. as already occurring in Latin America), which could, in turn, generate pressure for wider adoption of sensible and cooperative tax strategies in multilateral spaces. There is also scope for regional coordination of financial regulation efforts. All of these could become catalysts for broader changes at the multilateral level. Specifically on health, the need for coordination is evident; the issue now is to ensure that such coordination occurs on a context of greater trust and legitimacy amongst various governments, and between governments and their countries' populations.

Notes

1 WHO. "Climate Change." https://www.who.int/health-topics/climate-change#tab=tab_1
2 BBC. "How Vaccinating Children Could Prevent Disease during Extreme Weather." *Storyworks*. https://www.bbc.com/storyworks/the-climate-and-us/gsk-nepal-typhoid
3 BBC. "The Vet Increasing the Awareness of Climate-triggered Human–Animal Diseases." *Storyworks*. https://www.bbc.com/storyworks/the-climate-and-us/path-zoonotics
4 For example, most countries identify health as a priority sector vulnerable to climate change, and there was a day of discussions on the issue at the 2023 United Nations Climate Change Conference in Dubai. The direct damage costs to health (excluding costs in health-determining sectors such as agriculture and water and sanitation) have been estimated at US$2 billion–US$4 billion per year by 2030. Despite this, less than 2% of multi-lateral climate finance goes to health projects. See WHO. "Fast Facts on Climate and Health." https://cdn.who.int/media/docs/default-source/climate-change/fast-facts-on-climate-and-health.pdf?sfvrsn=157ecd81_5&download=true

5 China has actually provided substantial debt relief in the form of debt rescheduling to many of its debtor countries.
6 The Pandemic Fund. "Frequently Asked Questions." https://www.worldbank.org/en/topic/pandemics/brief/factsheet-financial-intermediary-fund-for-pandemic-prevention-preparedness-and-response
7 "High-level Advisory Board on Effective Multilateralism, A Breakthrough for People and Planet." https://highleveladvisoryboard.org/breakthrough/

References

Alstadsæter, Annette, Sarah Godar, Panayiotis Nicolaides, and Gabriel Zucman. 2023. *Global Tax Evasion Report 2024*. Paris: European Union Tax Observatory. https://www.taxobservatory.eu//www-site/uploads/2023/10/global_tax_evasion_report_24.pdf.

Azam, Monirul. 2016. *Intellectual Property and Public Health in the Developing World*, 1st ed. Open Book Publishers. https://www.jstor.org/stable/j.ctt1d41dm1.

Baker, Dean. 2016. *Rigged: How Globalization and the Rules of the Modern Economy Were Structured to Make the Rich Richer*. Washington, DC: Center for Economic and Policy Research. https://deanbaker.net/images/stories/documents/Rigged.pdf.

BBC. n.d.-a. "How Vaccinating Children Could Prevent Disease during Extreme Weather." *Storyworks*. Accessed December 24, 2024. http://www.bbc.com/storyworks/the-climate-and-us/gsk-nepal-typhoid.

BBC. n.d.-b. "The Vet Increasing the Awareness of Climate-Triggered Human–Animal Diseases." *Storyworks*. Accessed December 24, 2024. https://www.bbc.com/storyworks/the-climate-and-us/path-zoonotics.

FAO, IFAD, UNICEF, WFP, and WHO. 2023. *The State of Food Security and Nutrition in the World 2023*. Rome, Italy: FAO; IFAD; UNICEF; WFP; WHO; https://doi.org/10.4060/cc3017en.

Food and Agriculture Organization of the United Nations (FAO). 2023. "Monthly Report on Food Price Trends." #7. *Food Price and Monitoring and Analysis Bulletin. FAO of the UN*. https://www.fao.org/3/cc7752en/cc7752en.pdf.

Galofré-Vilà, Gregori, Christopher M Meissner, Martin McKee, and David Stuckler. 2019. "The Economic Consequences of The 1953 London Debt Agreement." *European Review of Economic History* 23 (1): 1–29. https://doi.org/10.1093/ereh/hey010.

Ghosh, Jayati. 2021. "The Political Economy of Covid-19 Vaccines." *The India Forum*, March 3. https://www.theindiaforum.in/article/political-economy-covid-19-vaccines.

Ghosh, Jayati. 2023. "The Myth of Global Grain Shortages." *Project Syndicate*, August 11. https://www.project-syndicate.org/commentary/there-is-no-global-grain-shortage-by-jayati-ghosh-2023–08.

Global Preparedness Monitoring Board (GPMB). 2023. *A Fragile State of Preparedness: 2023 Report on the State of the World's Preparedness*. Geneva: World Health Organization. https://gpmb.org/reports/m/item/a-fragile-state-of-preparedness-2023-report-on-the-state-of-the-worlds-preparedness.

Gold, Shabtai. 2023. "How the Bridgetown Initiative Envisions Global Financial System Reform." *Devex*, July 13, 2023. https://www.devex.com/news/sponsored/how-the-bridgetown-initiative-envisions-global-financial-system-reform−105894.

Green, Andrew. 2024. "Devex CheckUp: Why the US Commitment to the Global Fund Has Cratered." *Devex*, March 14, 2024. https://www.devex.com/news/sponsored/devex-checkup-why-the-us-commitment-to-the-global-fund-has-cratered−107231.

High Level Advisory Board on Effective Multilateralism (HLAB). n.d. *A Breakthrough for People and Planet*. High Level Advisory Board on Effective Multilateralism (HLAB). Accessed December 24, 2024. https://highleveladvisoryboard.org/breakthrough/.

The Independent Panel for Pandemic Preparedness & Response. 2021. *COVID-19: Make it the Last Pandemic*. World Health Organization. https://theindependentpanel.org/wp-content/uploads/2021/05/COVID-19-Make-it-the-Last-Pandemic_final.pdf.

International Monetary Fund (IMF). 2023a. *Fiscal Monitor—Climate Crossroads: Fiscal Policies in a Warming World*. Edited by Fonds Monétaire International, October. Washington, DC: International Monetary Fund. https://www.imf.org/en/Publications/FM/Issues/2023/10/10/fiscal-monitor-october–2023.

International Monetary Fund (IMF). 2023b. *Fiscal Monitor—On the Path to Policy Normalization*, April. Washington, DC: International Monetary Fund. https://www.imf.org/en/Publications/FM/Issues/2023/04/03/fiscal-monitor-april–2023.

Iwunna, Obichukwu, Jonathan Kennedy, and Andrew Harmer. 2023. "Flexibly Funding WHO? An Analysis of Its Donors' Voluntary Contributions." *BMJ Global Health* 8 (4): e011232. https://doi.org/10.1136/bmjgh-2022–011232.

Kentikelenis, Alexandros, and Thomas Stubbs. 2023. *A Thousand Cuts: Social Protection in the Age of Austerity*, 1st ed. New York: Oxford University Press. https://doi.org/10.1093/oso/9780190637736.001.0001.

Martin, Matthew, and David Waddock. 2022. *A Nordic Initiative to Resolve the Debt Crisis*. Oslo: Norwegian Church Aid. https://www.kirkensnodhjelp.no/sites/default/files/2024–10/a-nordic-solution-to-the-new-debt-crisis-sep22.pdf.

Ortiz, Isabel, and Matthew Cummings. 2022. "End Austerity: A Global Report on Budget Cuts and Harmful Social Reforms in 2022–25." https://www.eurodad.org/end_austerity_a_global_report.

The Pandemic Fund. n.d. "Frequently Asked Questions of The Pandemic Fund." Accessed December 24, 2024. https://www.thepandemicfund.org/what-we-do/frequently-asked-questions.

Rodrik, Dani, and Ishac Diwan. 2023. "Bridging the Climate-Development Gap." *Project Syndicate*, September 26, 2023. https://www.project-syndicate.org/commentary/low-middle-income-countries-debt-development-climate-crisis-by-dani-rodrik-and-ishac-diwan-2023–09.

United Nations Trade and Development (UNCTAD). 2024a. *A Growing Burden to Global Prosperity. A World of Debt Report 2024*. Geneva: United Nations Global Crisis Response Group (UN GCRG). https://unctad.org/publication/world-of-debt.

United Nations Trade and Development (UNCTAD). 2024b. *Growth, Debt and Climate: Realigning the Global Financial Architecture. Trade and Development Report 2023*. Geneva: United Nations Publications. https://unctad.org/publication/trade-and-development-report–2023.

World Bank. 2022. *International Debt Report 2022: Updated International Debt Statistics*. Washington, DC: World Bank. https://doi.org/10.1596/978-1-4648-1902-5.

World Health Organization (WHO). 2023. *Health for All—Transforming Economies to Deliver What Matters*. Geneva: World Health Organization. https://www.who.int/publications/i/item/9789240080973.

World Health Organization (WHO). 2024a. *All for Health, Health for All: Investment Case 2025–2028*. Geneva: World Health Organization. https://www.who.int/publications/i/item/9789240095403.

World Health Organization (WHO). 2024b. "Pandemic Prevention, Preparedness and Response Accord." https://www.who.int/news-room/questions-and-answers/item/pandemic-prevention-preparedness-and-response-accord.

World Health Organization (WHO). n.d.-a. "Climate Change." Accessed December 24, 2024. https://www.who.int/health-topics/climate-change.

World Health Organization (WHO). n.d.-b. "Fast Facts on Climate and Health." Accessed December 24, 2024. https://cdn.who.int/media/docs/default-source/climate-change/fast-facts-on-climate-and-health.pdf?sfvrsn=157ecd81_5&download=true.

12 The New Economic Order

Do Market Mechanisms Deliver Better Growth?

Vera Songwe

12.1 Introduction

Raising resources for growth in an unprecedented crisis-prone environment remains the main challenge for low- and middle-income countries (LMICs) in today's world. Traditional public finance cannot meet these challenges; new tools are necessary and must be complemented by more efficient implementation of existing policies towards resource mobilisation.

The 2008 global financial crisis marked an important turning point in global resource mobilisation, as policymakers unlocked new tools to mobilise capital and to shore up the global economy. Special Drawing Rights (SDR), quantitative easing by central banks, accommodative macroprudential policies, debt forbearance, and fiscal stimulus packages were accompanied by a massive deployment of capital to LMICs. Between 2010 and 2020, total official development assistance (ODA) disbursements to LMICs grew from US$105 billion to US$153 billion.[1] However, this still failed to meet the demands of growing populations and massive infrastructure needs of LMICs.

As a result, LMICs diversified their sources of funding and expanded their toolkits, leading to new and often more onerous sources of finance. An unprecedented number of LMICs accessed market finance in the decade to 2020. Eurobond issuances in LMICs increased 151%, from US$101 billion in 2010 to US$253 billion in 2020.[2] The 'lower for longer' phenomena—interest rates staying down—led some economists, such as Blanchard (2019), to encourage debt accumulation as a means of growth, stressing that the low rates and high growth environment were conducive to debt accumulation.

That strategy has, however, created significant challenges. The rise in inflation—10.6% at its peak in the United States, which followed the COVID-19 pandemic and was the result of excessive stimulus and supply chain constraints—brought the period of low rates to an abrupt halt in early 2023. Currencies depreciated, debt service increased, fiscal space dried up, and capital markets shut down for many LMICs.

It is against this backdrop that developed and developing countries are working to raise resources to deliver prosperity, protect the planet, and ensure peace. Yet LMICs exist within a system over which they have limited influence and in which

DOI: 10.4324/9781003571384-12

they are almost always price takers. This chapter thus proposes policy changes that could deliver better, more transparent, and enforceable global governance systems for improved revenue mobilisation. Section 12.2 discusses the importance of global macroeconomic stability for LMICs and the role of private capital. Section 12.3 proposes ways of improving country debt burdens to allow for more capital to be raised. Section 12.4 looks at access to grant financing and SDR, while Section 12.5 discusses ways of improving prudential regulation and levies on emissions and remittances as additional ways to improve resource mobilisation. Section 12.6 concludes.

12.2 Global Macroeconomic Stability and Private Capital

It has been estimated that LMICs (excluding China) need over US$5 trillion of investments to meet the Sustainable Development Goals (SDGs). They (excluding China) require US$1 trillion in external financing for the climate challenge alone (G20 IEG, 2023). Growth in the next 2 decades and the efforts to limit the impact of climate change will be underpinned by decisions made in the next 3 years to improve access to and to crowd in associated finance. Private capital will continue to grow as the main source of development financing, but access to this capital remains challenging to access in a high-risk market environment where capital is discerning. Competition for that capital could grow further as developed economies introduce subsidies to support their energy transitions and to respond to climate change.

First, to increase private capital flows to LMICs, the macro balances of developed countries—countries that, faced with huge debt burdens and stubborn inflationary pressures, have turned inwards—must be improved. High interest rates at over 5% in LMICs means that there is a flight to safety and yield. For high-yield economies, the cost of finance is close to 10% (IMF, 2023), and no LMIC can raise capital at affordable rates under these circumstances. Moreover, to combat inflation, developed countries have enacted policies that are constraining and costly to the growth of LMICs. Closing the fiscal space has led to a drop in ODA; for example, US interest rate increases have resulted in a net exit of over US$27.0 billion from local currency non-resident governmental debt from 20 LMIC (excluding China) from January to November 2022, compared with US$25.6 billion of inflows in 2021 (IMF, 2023). Until inflationary pressures ease, LMICs will remain unattractive for private capital.

Improving credit ratings for LMIC debt is another important challenge, because real or perceived risks keep investors away and/or increase the cost of capital. LMICs generated 42% of global gross domestic product (GDP) in 2023, up from 39% 1 decade ago, but they only account for 5% of the total global private credit market (IMF, 2023).

To access more private capital and to improve ratings, LMICs must improve their overall macroeconomic management, financial ratios, debt and deficit levels, reserves, business climates, governance, and security. In the interim, private capital would be most efficient and secure when accompanied by public sector credit enhancements such as guarantees, subordination, reserve accounts, over-collaterisation, and foreign exchange covers. These blended finance instruments would shift non-market risk to public sector balance sheets. Indeed, adequately leveraged public finance could help crowd in US$600 billion–US$1 trillion in private finance in LMICs (Songwe, Stern, Bhattacharya, 2022).

Spreads fell to 386 basis points in February 2024—the narrowest since February 2022. As markets re-open for investors seeking to enter or to hold LMIC hard-currency debt, multilateral development bank (MDB) assistance can also help improve these spreads and increase the number of countries with market access. MDBs are the largest pool of blended finance available, which can help improve LMICs' sovereign and project risk. However, MDBs currently mobilise only US$0.60 in private capital for each US$1.00 that they lend (G20 IEG, 2023). They should aim to at least double this target, focussing on investments in human capital as well as transformational infrastructure projects that can help crowd in the private sector. MDB and grant resources spent on education or infrastructure projects that do not lead to job creation or crowd in more private investment are not an optimal use of resources.

In addition, MDBs could help crowd in local pension funds and development agency funds to provide cheaper capital and local currency capital to manage foreign exchange risk. Asset recycling by LMICs—part of the work done by Africa50,[3] for example—would free up domestic equity capital, which could be then co-invested into new projects. This capital could cover the construction phase of projects that are traditionally considered the riskiest. MDBs could also guarantee LMIC bond issuances, thereby raising ratings by more than a notch. Of course, this should only be done in cases where the International Monetary Fund (IMF) and MDBs agree that growth prospects are robust. In this regard, the recent release of the Global Emerging Markets Risk Database Consortium (GEMs) would also contribute to improving the risk assessment of countries and impact the cost of capital. Moreover, the Multilateral Investment Guarantee Agency (MIGA) is currently in the process of updating its guarantee tools, and the World Bank Group plans to create a one-stop guarantee shop with more straightforward, simplified processes to accelerate and to simplify the process but also to allow leverage guarantee use for all. In addition to this, MIGA guarantees could be extended to a subset of domestic investors with global reach.

Since the World Bank Group has discontinued the *Doing Business* reports, MDBs must continue to work to create more conducive business environments in LMICs. Improving governance frameworks and better country ownership of development projects in LMICs are a prerequisite for resource mobilisation.

12.3 Existing Country Debt

In 2024, LMICs are expected to pay about US$67.5 billion in debt service (Holland and Pazarbasioglu, 2024). Many of them (e.g. Kenya and Egypt) will not be able to service these debt obligations without support. Thus, liquidity and debt restructuring must be seen as a macro de-risking exercise, permitting these countries to regain entry into markets or to substantially reduce spreads.

For those countries unable to service debt as a result of fundamental macroeconomic imbalances, Diwan, Kessler, Songwe (2024) proposed a bridge solution—a Debt Service Suspension Initiative (DSSI)-type liquidity operation similar to what IMF and the World Bank did for Kenya to re-allow market access. The proposal offered a solution to the intertwined challenges of debt overhang, sustainable development, and climate action by addressing liquidity constraints for the more than 20 LMICs with US$1.7 trillion in GDP and US$600 billion in external debt. It complements the G20's Common Framework, with a second window dedicated to countries needing rescheduling but no deep debt treatment. It proposed to operationalise a tripartite deal under the following conditions:

(i) **MDBs agree to boost funding.** MDBs would increase funding for sustainable investments, particularly those aligned with climate objectives.
(ii) **Markets re-open, and creditors agree to reschedule debt claims.** These actions would alleviate immediate financial pressure on debtor nations. Private sector spreads would also compress to allow for renewed and sustainable market access.
(iii) **Countries commit to growth-enhancing reforms.** Debtor countries would commit to stabilising economies and implementing reform measures to promote a green recovery while protecting the poor.

Successful implementation would require a standardised framework featuring strong incentives for all stakeholders and dedicated logistical and financial coordination to facilitate collective action amongst debtors and creditors. First, the two largest private creditors or their representatives should be allowed to work with IMF in the development of a debt-structuring agreement, which underpins debt negotiations. Second, the definitions of comparability of treatment should be interpreted in relation to the level of the 'haircut' and not the tool used. Finally, debtor countries should be fully transparent in regard to all of their obligations. The negotiations should be time-bound, and relief to countries should be triggered early and sufficient to allow for a real reset.

For countries not constrained by debt ratios but still suffering from poor market access conditions, several tools can help. A vibrant, deep repo market for LMIC debt securities would address the liquidity premium imposed on sovereigns. Recent market tightening showed that access to liquidity is an important component of investor decisions, especially in an environment of tightening monetary policy. As such, the Liquidity and Sustainability Facility created a repo market vehicle for LMIC securities that could address challenges created by creditors pulling back from non-liquid assets.[4] The development of a more active swap arrangement would also be key to protecting LMICs from short-term liquidity needs. A full agenda of work is required to improve the strength of LMICs' currencies and to allow for a pooling of reserves to create hard currency-backed facilities, such as under the Chiang Mai Initiative. Intra-LMICs swap arrangements should be explored as well.

With private creditors now constituting over 60% of debt to LMICs, there is a need to review subordination structures. Here, MDBs can take steps to crowd in private capital at affordable rates and optimal maturities (Alfaro and Kanczuk, 2007).

12.4 Grant Financing and Special Drawing Rights

12.4.1 Rethinking the International Development Association

The absence of affordable and adequate resources, poor policy prescriptions, and weak governance compounded by multiple exogenous crises have undermined the development outcomes of many International Development Association (IDA) countries over the last 3 decades. Only 21% of the 81 countries that were part of IDA in 1996 have graduated to middle-income status (IDA, 2021). With the additional challenges of climate change, the COVID-19 pandemic, and slowing growth, a tripling of efforts and resources is needed to achieve the SDGs (Kahn, 2019).

IDA is possibly the most advanced development fund—it borrows against its equity to lend out greater volumes of finance than it takes in as donor contributions, which totaled US$3.50 in concessional lending for every US$1.00 from donors (Songwe and Aboneaaj, 2023). Since 2020, it has led other MDBs in annual commitments. IDA resources are unique for their leverage, concessionality, ability to finance regional projects, and focus on conflict-affected economies and climate—all under one umbrella. Its highly concessional rates allow countries to undertake long-term transformational infrastructure and social projects, whose rates of return pay out over longer periods (Kharas and Rivard, 2024). IDA countries have had the best growth run in decades, and, for many years, the fastest-growing economies were IDA countries. Yet this catching up still requires sustained and increasing financing, commensurate with demand. As the largest single source of development finance for the world's poorest countries, any pullback on IDA finances would dramatically impact development outcomes.

Despite IDA's strengths, donor contributions have been falling for 1 decade. Traditional donors, such as the United Kingdom, the United States, and Germany, registered drops in contribution of 50%, 15%, and 7%, respectively, between 2012 and 2023, when countries were consolidating growth following the 2008 global financial crisis. Only 0.10% of gross national income across IDA donors will deliver US$92.4 billion more resources by 2029; a more ambitious target of 0.15% would deliver over US$135.0 billion (Songwe and Aboneaaj, 2023).

To reach these goals, IDA needs a permanent and persistent global advocate. The G20 trio—including past, current, and future country chairs—could take ownership of IDA and support its replenishment process every 3 years by setting the standard for contributions as a percentage of gross national income and monitoring performance as part of their agendas. IDA could also work directly alongside countries to provide some credit enhancements for bond issuances, thereby lowering the cost of market access while optimising IDA works. Working with countries directly on bond issuance would allow IDA to support project implementation while accelerating access to long-term affordable capital for countries that qualify.

12.4.2 Recasting Special Drawing Rights

The issuance of SDR provides a least-cost option for developed and developing economies to generate resources to combat global commons such as climate change and pandemics, particularly at a time of tight fiscal space in the developed world. The US$250 billion issuance of SDR in 2008 played a catalytic role during the global financial crisis to help provide liquidity to economies to prevent the disorderly unwinding of contracts and to allow developed countries to pull LMICs back from the brink. Aside from IDA, the largest amount of grants over the last decade has come from SDR. With the release during the COVID-19 pandemic of a US$650 billion SDR equivalent, low-income, lower-middle-income, and upper-middle-income countries received $6 billion, $46 billion, and $95 billion, respectively. IDA countries—mostly comprised of low-income and lower-middle-income countries received less than 4.5% of the allocation, while all LMICs received less than a third (IMF, 2024a).

Yet these SDR served countries well. In Sub-Saharan Africa and Latin America and the Caribbean, many countries used their SDR to support their economies (91.1% and 62.5% uptake rates, respectively). Overall, 98 countries used SDR from the 2021 allocation during the following year, with low-income countries using about 93% of their aggregate SDR allocation and middle-income countries about 103% (Cashman, Arauz, Merling, 2022). However, with the climate emergency and a general lack of resources, the issuance of SDR to support global commons may be even more important today.

While it may take a long time to revise the quota system that allocates SDR and SDR issuance, an immediate off-the-top allocation to MDBs and IMF for climate action would be instrumental in accelerating the fight against climate change. Indeed, if a new SDR allocation of US$650 billion were issued, US$100 billion could be carved out immediately for climate support. A development injection of this magnitude into MDBs in addition to their usual allocations could accelerate the drive to net-zero emissions. Countries could also use their allocations to address their fiscal space issues, shore up their currencies where needed, and reignite growth.

On 10 May 2024, in a historic decision, the IMF Executive Board approved the use of SDR for the acquisition of hybrid capital instruments issued by prescribed holders. This new use of SDR, which adds to seven already authorised prescribed SDR operations, is subject to a cumulative limit of SDR15 billion to minimise liquidity risks (IMF, 2024b). This decision, which the African Development Bank and Inter-American Development Bank sponsored, has opened a new financing opportunity for regional development banks and can be used to support and to direct new SDR for climate in the future.

An off-the-top allocation of SDR to regional development banks will require discussion of—but not amendments to—any country's quota. The US$100 billion would be calculated as an allocation for climate as a global public good. It could be used to augment IMF's Resilience and Sustainability Trust; complement World Bank funding for Small Island Developing States, middle-income countries, and IDA countries; and amplify lending from the African Development Bank, Asian

Development Bank, and Inter-American Development Bank. SDR, as the African Development Bank has shown, will keep their reserve asset status but will allow regional development banks and the World Bank to hold and to use them to leverage additional private sector funding.

12.5 Leveling the Playing Field of Regulations, Taxes, and Levies

12.5.1 Regulating the Capital Market

The 2008 global financial crisis exposed many regulatory and prudential weaknesses in the financial and banking sectors and underscored the need for effective regulation and adequate capital buffers and liquidity in the system. Yet in a bid to preserve the soundness and stability of the financial sector, some of the regulations in Basel III[5] have proven detrimental to LMICs trying to raise resources, by driving up costs and slowing down capital deployment.

First, Basel III imposes larger liquidity coverage ratios on composite structures in response to asset securitisation, one of the primary triggers of the crisis. Blended finance guarantee instruments are considered a securitisation. This is counterintuitive, as blended finance tools are meant to improve the risk rating of the underlying asset. As a result, the regulation—intended for the private sector when engaging with itself in developed countries—leads to a punitive result when extended to LMICs.

Second, jurisdictional identity penalises LMICs under Basel III. For example, an energy project undertaken in an Organisation for Economic Co-Operation and Development (OECD) country requires less liquidity coverage than when undertaken in a non-OECD country. The system thus implicitly assigns higher risk to non-OECD jurisdictions; as a consequence, this increases the cost of projects and/or disincentivises investors. Other criteria can be used to assess the liquidity coverage ratio for non-OECD countries, such as previous experience investing in that sector or country, however. Many LMICs have undertaken projects in the energy and transport sectors; these are areas where the risk assessment should be lower, and fiduciary and prudential regulations need not be as onerous.

Third, current regulations under Basel III penalise long-term debt and investment instruments. Although aligning loan periods with project development timeframes is logical, these impose higher capital charges on a financial institution.

Market actors can take steps to (i) ensure consistent treatment of transactions across jurisdictions and (ii) recognise the risk-mitigation features of blended finance transactions and de-risking instruments. Prudential banking regulators should ensure conformity of capital treatment across jurisdictions in regulatory capital calculations for instruments, such as A/B loans that carry preferred creditor status and currency control privileges as well as concessional capital and de-risking instruments provided by MDBs, development finance institutions, export credit agencies, or insurance companies. Moreover, prudential regulations for insurance companies and pensions should be updated to reflect the actual versus perceived risk of investments in LMICs, working with credit-rating agencies to improve methodologies for risk assessment.

Capital allocation targets for banks, insurance companies, and pension and asset managers could be used to increase investments to LMICs. Financial institutions and banks could allocate a portion of their risk capital buffers for sustainable finance transactions in LMICs within applicable risk frameworks and capital adequacy requirements: (i) banks could allocate 0.5% of their Tier 1 capital by 2025 and 1.0% by 2030, (ii) insurance and pensions could allocate 0.5% of solvency capital by 2025 and 1.0% by 2030, and (iii) asset managers could allocate 1.0%–5.0% of their assets under management by 2025 and 3.0%–7.0% for these transactions. The top eight US banks, for example, have over US$155 billion set aside. A small share of this could be deployed towards LMIC green projects. These banks have a median CET1 regulatory capital ratio of 12.7%, which is well above the required level of 4.5%, a total of about US$45 billion more than double the capital requirement (Bloomberg, 2024).

In addition, rating agencies should update their methodology in consultation with regulators using newly released databases—such as the GEMs database—and should improve transparency to help countries focus on addressing areas of weakness and progress shown in their ratings (Bhattacharya et al., 2024). The recent Fitch 2023 report has begun to respond to this issue (Fitch Ratings, 2023). Taken together, these regulatory measures will help crowd in more and additional capital to LMICs.

12.5.2 Carbon Markets

Of the US$5.3 trillion needed yearly to advance the SDGs, 64%—over US$3.4 trillion—will come from domestic resources (G20 IEG, 2023). Thus, focusing on how to improve domestic resource mobilisation must also be an integral part of the development and investment thesis. Moreover, the growth environments faced by most LMICs mean that new forms of revenue mobilisation are needed. This means improving tax policies related to services, which account for over 40% of GDP in many LMICs—and over 50% in Africa—and identifying other revenue sources such a global tax on airlines and the maritime sector.

Carbon taxes are another critical area for potential revenue mobilisation. The value of the traded global markets for carbon permits reached a record US$900 billion in 2023 (Twidale, 2024). Yet the significant potential for carbon markets to deliver revenue for LMICs is held back by an illiquid and fragmented market that lacks a global governance framework.

In 2005, the European Union was the first region to introduce taxes on carbon specifically intended to dis-incentivise increasing emissions, via the Emissions Trading System (ETS). The London Stock Exchange Group (LSEG) estimated that in 2023, this was worth roughly €770 billion or 87% of the global total carbon taxes (Twidale, 2024). China's national ETS, the world's largest in terms of covered emissions, began operating in 2021. It is now estimated to cover around 5 billion tonnes of carbon dioxide, which accounts for over 40% of the country's emissions; it is worth about €2.3 billion (ICAP, 2022; Twidale, 2024). Compliance carbon markets have also delivered substantial resources to developed countries; in Finland and Sweden, for example, carbon taxes account for nearly 1% of their GDPs. In comparison, the value of voluntary carbon markets was only about US$90 billion in 2022. These huge discrepancies are a result of the market structure, pricing, integrity, governance, and level of compliance imposed.

The European Union is augmenting its carbon market emissions taxes, moving from a system that taxes domestic companies to one where it also taxes companies exporting to the EU area. The new carbon levy, the Carbon Border Adjustment Mechanism (CBAM), is the tool used to put a fair price on the carbon emitted during the production of carbon-intensive goods entering the European Union and to encourage cleaner industrial production in non-EU countries, helping reduce emissions by 45 million metric tonnes inside and outside of the European Union and decrease carbon leakage by 8.2% (EC, 2024). The United States is also considering CBAM-type legislation that would make domestic steel and aluminium more cost-competitive and help these producers capture an additional US$8.5 billion and US$6.0 billion of their respective markets by 2030 (Joint Economic Committee, 2024).

Very few LMICs—e.g. Argentina, Colombia, Mexico, and South Africa—have carbon tax mechanisms or ETSs in place. However, a CBAM's trade-dampening consequences are important for LMICs. In Egypt, for example, 3.76% of all its merchandise exports and nearly 10.00% of its exports to the European Union will be affected by the CBAM, accounting for 0.3% of its GDP (Mohieldin, 2023). Given such a challenge, four steps could serve the dual purpose of reducing emissions and mobilising revenues in LMICs.

First, reciprocity should be granted with a system of proportionality for developing countries and industry classes. As an example, millions of cars shipped to Africa and Asia from the United States, European Union, and Japan are 'polluting or unsafe' (UNEP, 2020). The average fuel consumption of these second-hand cars is over 1.5 times the regulated consumption for European cars 1 decade ago. LMICs are 2 decades behind developed markets in terms of vehicle tailpipe emissions levels, with cars in Africa emitting, on average, three times more pollutants (WEF, 2023). A CBAM focused on reducing emissions from carbon-intensive products globally would consider these effects, minimise distortions, encourage technology transfer and investment, and adopt a system of proportionality to ensure equity. A reverse CBAM tax on steel and used cars, for example, could provide the resources needed to help LMICs acquire the technology to transition to electric vehicles. Agreement on the reach, scope, and timeframe for the implementation of such an extended CBAM should be governed by a global mechanism acknowledging the global externalities of all polluting entities and hence a sharing agreement that also benefits LMICs. Resources could be managed by MDBs.

Second, LMICs should move towards the implementation of compliance carbon markets. Indeed, the political will amongst African countries to access carbon credit markets has been emphasised by recent political statements, including the Kigali Declaration at the conclusion of the 8th African Regional Forum on Sustainable Development (UNECA, 2022). African countries could accrue vast revenues, ranging from US$1 billion per year at US$10 per tonne of carbon dioxide to US$82 billion per year at US$120 per tonne; the International Energy Agency estimated current prices could be up to US$200 per tonne (UNECA, 2022). Voluntary carbon markets could serve as a bridge to compliance markets, and countries should focus on adopting the Core Carbon Principles developed by the Integrity Council for Voluntary Carbon Markets.[6] The African Carbon Markets Initiative is one such regional effort to develop Integrity Council for Voluntary Carbon Markets-compliant principles.

Third, LMICs must focus on reducing fossil subsidies to allocate these resources to more productive green growth investments. With African consumption of 4 million barrels of oil per day, a carbon tax could generate US$40 billion per year for African countries (McKinsey & Company, 2021).

Finally, an agreement should be reached on the classification of the CBAM as a green trade-enhancing tool rather than a levy (Groenenberg and De Coninck, 2008; Hojnik and Ruzzier, 2016; Battaglini and Harstad, 2020). The World Trade Organization could then work on an acceptable technology-sharing agreement and protocol in which compliant technology is agreed upon collectively and concessional resources are made available to LMICs to accelerate their transitions, similar to the aid for trade agreements.

12.5.3 Remittances

A 1% drop in remittance costs—that is, costs incurred to send and to receive transfers—could generate over US$7 billion in additional transfers to LMICs. Remittance flows to LMICs doubled from US$339 billion in 2010 to US$669 billion in 2023, exceeding both foreign direct investment and ODA (Ratha et al., 2024). They represent over 15% of GDP for 25 LMICs and 5%–10% of GDP for an additional 34 countries. While remittances are not a direct source of public sector revenue, they contribute to consumption and investment in the receiving country's economy and, hence, taxes. They are also a stabilising revenue source and a significant safety net for populations in times of crisis, proving resilient over time due to their diversified nature. The increase in remittances to low-income countries over the past few decades has contributed to higher reserves and helped stabilise currency fluctuations, thus mitigating rising debt vulnerabilities (Chuku et al., 2023).

Remittances are increasingly being added into market assessments of credit ratings. For Egypt, Ghana, and Pakistan, for example, a drop in remittances has impacted ratings assessments (Ratha et al., 2024). Yet future inflows of remittances can also be used as collateral to lower the costs of international borrowing for national banks in developing countries. Remittances can play an important role in improving a country's ability to repay debt due to their large size relative to other sources of foreign exchange, countercyclical nature, and indirect contribution to public finance.

The contribution of remittances to debt sustainability in low-income countries was recognised in the 2017 revision to the IMF/World Bank debt sustainability analysis framework.[7] This change was associated with significant improvement in the evaluation of debt sustainability in some countries with large remittance inflows. Similarly, econometric results showed that the inclusion of remittances in the denominator of the debt–export ratio in middle-income countries with large remittance receipts would improve the sovereign rating by one notch.

Moreover, in countries where remittances exceed the exports of goods and services, the debt–export ratio of goods and services would decrease significantly if remittances were included in the denominator (Ratha and Mohapatra, 2007). For Standard & Poor's ratings, a country rated B or below can reduce borrowing costs by 100 basis points or more, substantially lessening the cost of capital.

However, remittances transactions are costly. The SDG target for reducing remittance costs to 3% has not been yet met by any country. The remittance tax represents a regressive tax from developed countries to developing countries. In fact, the cost of sending money from G20 countries increased from 6.1% in the second quarter of 2022 to 6.4% in the second quarter of 2023. Costs within the G20 range from 13.9% in South Africa to 3.6% in South Korea (World Bank, 2023). Costs across many African corridors remain significantly high as well; Tanzania is the costliest African source country from which to send remittances to another country in the region.

Developing countries lacking access to international capital markets tend to depend on remittances as a major source of external financing; in 2022, countries rated B or below received significantly more remittances than foreign direct investment. The G20 could focus on reducing remittance costs at least as a priority to low-income single-B and below-rated economies whose access to foreign direct investment is smaller.

12.6 Conclusion

The vicious cycle of low revenue leading to high vulnerability and lack of access to capital could be turned into a virtuous cycle where good governance leads to crowding in of development capital and private finance at scale. LMICs need substantial additional resources to meet their growth ambitions while protecting the climate. This requires substantial effort to improve domestic resource mobilisation from LMICs as well as the international community.

This chapter provided several options for augmenting resource mobilisation, focusing on the importance of unlocking private capital flows; MDB opportunities; and changes to global governance systems that could improve resource mobilisation in LMICs such as the SDR issuances, carbon markets, and remittances. The increasing clamour of LMICs for a new global economic order is principally about rebalancing rules and sharing opportunity. There is an important role to be played by developed economies' private sectors in calling for a rebalancing as they shift investments to LMICs in search of returns and for climate action. Such a combination may provide a new window for success.

Notes

1 OECD. "OECD International Development Statistics." Accessed April 2024. https://www.oecd-ilibrary.org/development/data/oecd-international-development-statistics_dev-data-en
2 World Bank. "International Debt Statistics (IDS)." Accessed April 2024. https://www.worldbank.org/en/programs/debt-statistics/ids
3 Africa50. https://www.africa50.com/fr/

4 LSF. "Repo Business Model." https://lsfacility.org/repo-business-model/
5 BIS. "Basel III: International Regulatory Framework for Banks." https://www.bis.org/bcbs/basel3.htm
6 The Integrity Council for the Voluntary Carbon Market. "The Core Carbon Principles." https://icvcm.org/core-carbon-principles/
7 IMF. "IMF-World Bank Debt Sustainability Framework for Low-income Countries." https://www.imf.org/en/About/Factsheets/Sheets/2023/imf-world-bank-debt-sustainability-framework-for-low-income-countries

References

"Africa50." n.d. https://www.africa50.com/fr/.
Alfaro, Laura, and Fabio Kanczuk. 2007. *Debt Maturity: Is Long-Term Debt Optimal?*, w13119. Cambridge, MA: National Bureau of Economic Research. https://doi.org/10.3386/w13119.
Bank for International Settlements (BIS). 2017. "Basel III: International Regulatory Framework for Banks." https://www.bis.org/bcbs/basel3.htm.
Battaglini, Marco, and Bård Harstad. 2020. "The Political Economy of Weak Treaties." *Journal of Political Economy* 128 (2): 544–90. https://doi.org/10.1086/704610.
Bhattacharya, Amar, Vera Songwe, Eleonore Soubeyran, and Nicholas Stern. 2024. "Raising Ambition and Accelerating Delivery of Climate Finance." https://www.lse.ac.uk/granthaminstitute/publication/raising-ambition-and-accelerating-delivery-of-climate-finance/.
Blanchard, Olivier. 2019. "Public Debt and Low Interest Rates." *American Economic Review* 109 (4): 1197–229. https://doi.org/10.1257/aer.109.4.1197.
Bloomberg. 2024. "Basel III Endgame May Cut US Banks' Excess Capital." *Bloomberg Intelligence*, May 7, sec. Financial Services. https://www.bloomberg.com/professional/insights/financial-services/basel-iii-endgame-may-cut-us-banks-excess-capital/.
Cashman, Kevin, Andrés Arauz, and Lara Merling. 2022. *Special Drawing Rights: The Right Tool to Use to Respond to the Pandemic and Other Challenges*. Washington, DC: Center for Economic and Policy Research. https://cepr.net/report/special-drawing-rights-the-right-tool-to-use/.
Chuku, Chuku, Prateek Samal, Joyce Saito, Dalia Hakura, Marcos Chamon, Martin Cerisola, and Guillaume Chabert. 2023. *Are We Heading for Another Debt Crisis in Low-Income Countries? Debt Vulnerabilities: Today vs the Pre-HIPC Era. IMF Working Papers, 2023/079*. Washington, DC: International Monetary Fund. https://doi.org/10.5089/9798400236709.001.
Diwan, Ishac, Martin Kessler, and Vera Songwe. 2024. "A Bridge to Climate Action: A Tripartite Deal for Times of Illiquidity." In *FDL Policy Notes*, 2401. CEPREMAP. https://econpapers.repec.org/paper/cpmnotfdl/2401.htm.
European Commission (EC). 2024. "Carbon Border Adjustment Mechanism." Accessed December 30, 2024. https://taxation-customs.ec.europa.eu/carbon-border-adjustment-mechanism_en.
Fitch Ratings. 2023. "Sovereign Rating Criteria: Master Criteria." *Criteria Report. Fitch Ratings*. https://www.fitchratings.com/research/sovereigns/sovereign-rating-criteria-06-04-2023.
G20Independent Experts Group. 2023. "Strengthening Multilateral Development Banks: The Triple Agenda." *Indian G20 Presidency*. https://www.cgdev.org/publication/strengthening-multilateral-development-banks-triple-agenda.
Groenenberg, Heleen, and Heleen De Coninck. 2008. "Effective EU and Member State Policies for Stimulating CCS." *International Journal of Greenhouse Gas Control* 2 (4): 653–64. https://doi.org/10.1016/j.ijggc.2008.04.003.
Hojnik, Jana, and Mitja Ruzzier. 2016. "What Drives Eco-Innovation? A Review of an Emerging Literature." *Environmental Innovation and Societal Transitions* 19 (June): 31–41. https://doi.org/10.1016/j.eist.2015.09.006.

Holland, Allison, and Ceyla Pazarbasioglu. 2024. "How to Ease Rising External Debt-Service Pressures in Low-Income Countries." *IMF Blog (blog)*, January 24, 2024. https://www.imf.org/en/Blogs/Articles/2024/01/24/how-to-ease-rising-external-debt-service-pressures-in-low-income-countries.

Integrity Council for the Voluntary Carbon Market. n.d. "The Core Carbon Principles." *ICVCM (blog)*. Accessed December 30, 2024. https://icvcm.org/core-carbon-principles/.

International Carbon Action Partnership. 2022. "China National ETS." https://icapcarbonaction.com/system/files/ets_pdfs/icap-etsmap-factsheet–55.pdf.

International Development Association (IDA). 2021. *IDA19 Mid-Term Review: Graduation Prospects for IDA Countries*. Development Finance Corporate IDA and IBRD (DFCII). https://documents1.worldbank.org/curated/en/322641636576099049/pdf/IDA19-Mid-Term-Review-Graduation-Prospects-for-IDA-Countries.pdf.

International Monetary Fund (IMF), ed. 2023. *World Economic Outlook: Navigating Global Divergences*. World Economic Outlook/International Monetary Fund, October. Washington, DC: International Monetary Fund. https://www.imf.org/en/Publications/WEO/Issues/2023/10/10/world-economic-outlook-october–2023.

International Monetary Fund. 2024a. *Use of SDRs in the Acquisition of Hybrid Capital Instruments of the Prescribed Holders. Policy Papers*. Washington, DC: International Monetary Fund. https://doi.org/10.5089/9798400275876.007.

International Monetary Fund (IMF). 2024b. *Regional Economic Outlook, Sub-Saharan Africa, October 2024: Reforms amid Great Expectations*, October. Washington, DC: International Monetary Fund. https://www.imf.org/en/Publications/REO/SSA/Issues/2024/10/25/regional-economic-outlook-for-sub-saharan-africa-october–2024.

International Monetary Fund (IMF). n.d. *IMF-World Bank Debt Sustainability Framework for Low-Income Countries*. IMF. Accessed December 30, 2024. https://www.imf.org/en/About/Factsheets/Sheets/2023/imf-world-bank-debt-sustainability-framework-for-low-income-countries.

Joint Economic Committee. 2024. "What is a Carbon Border Adjustment Mechanism (Cbam) and What are Some Legislative Proposals to Make One?"February. https://www.jec.senate.gov/public/index.cfm/democrats/2024/2/what-is-a-carbon-border-adjustment-mechanism-cbam-and-what-are-some-legislative-proposals-to-make-one.

Kahn, Matthew E. 2019. *Long-Term Macroeconomic Effects of Climate Change. IMF Working Papers, 2019/215*. Washington, DC: International Monetary Fund. https://www.imf.org/en/Publications/WP/Issues/2019/10/11/Long-Term-Macroeconomic-Effects-of-Climate-Change-A-Cross-Country-Analysis–48691.

Kharas, Homi, and Charlotte Rivard. 2024. "Investing in Development Works." *Brookings (blog)*, April 2. https://www.brookings.edu/articles/investing-in-development-works/.

The Liquidity and Sustainability Facility. n.d. *Repo Business Model*. The Liquidity and Sustainability Facility. Accessed December 30, 2024. https://lsfacility.org/repo-business-model/.

McKinsey and Company. 2021. *Africa's Green Manufacturing Crossroads: Choices for a Low-Carbon Industrial Future*. London: McKinsey and Company. https://www.mckinsey.com/~/media/mckinsey/business%20functions/sustainability/our%20insights/africas%20green%20manufacturing%20crossroads/africas-green-manufacturing-crossroads-choices-for-a-low-carbon-industrial-future.pdf.

Mohieldin, Mahmoud. 2023. "The Carbon Border Adjustment Mechanism (EU CBAM)." In Unpublished. https://doi.org/10.13140/RG.2.2.32342.42565.

OECD. n.d. "OECD International Development Statistics." *OECD International Development Statistics*. https://doi.org/10.1787/24142689.

Ratha, Dilip, and Sanket Mohapatra. 2007. "Increasing the Macroeconomic Impact of Remittances on Development." *Development Prospects Group, World Bank*, November. https://www.dilipratha.com/index_files/G8Berlin.pdf.

Ratha, Dilip Kumar, Vandara Chandra, Eung Ju Kim, Sonia Plaza, and William Shaw. 2024. "Leveraging Diaspora Finances for Private Capital Mobilization." In *Brief, 193029. Migration and Development Brief; KNOMAD Trust Fund*. Washington, DC: World Bank.

https://documents.worldbank.org/en/publication/documents-reports/documentdetail/099740408142422676/IDU184dfd61b1e135142421a20213728b2e8fa86.

Songwe, Vera, and Rakan Aboneaaj. 2023. "An Ambitious IDA for a Decade of Crisis," July. https://www.cgdev.org/publication/ambitious-ida-decade-crisis.

Songwe, Vera, Nicholas Stern, and Amar Bhattacharya. 2022. *Finance for Climate Action: Scaling up Investment for Climate and Development*. Report of the Independent High-Level Expert Group on Climate Finance. London: Grantham Research Institute on Climate Change and the Environment; London School of Economics and Political Science. https://www.lse.ac.uk/granthaminstitute/wp-content/uploads/2022/11/IHLEG-Finance-for-Climate-Action−1.pdf.

Sustainability-Linked Sovereign Debt Hub. n.d. *Unlocking Private Capital to Emerging Markets and Developing Countries in a Time of Crisis*. Sustainability-Linked Sovereign Debt Hub. Accessed December 31, 2024. https://www.ssdh.net/advisors.

Twidale, Susanna. 2024. "Global Carbon Markets Value Hit Record $949 Bln Last Year—LSEG." *Reuters*, February 12, 2024, sec. Commodities. https://www.reuters.com/markets/commodities/global-carbon-markets-value-hit-record-949-bln-last-year-lseg-2024-02-12/.

United Nations Economic Commission for Africa (UNECA). 2022. "Eighth Session of the Africa Regional Forum on Sustainable Development." *Regional Forum, Kigali*, March 3. https://www.uneca.org/events/technology%2C-climate-change-and-natural-resource-management/eighth-session-of-the-africa.

United Nations Environment Programme. 2020. *Used Vehicles and the Environment: A Global Overview of Used Light Duty Vehicles—Flow, Scale, and Regulation*. Nairobi, Kenya: United Nations Environment Programme. https://www.unep.org/resources/report/global-trade-used-vehicles-report.

WEF. 2023. *How Used Car Exports to Africa Could Become the Development Opportunity of the Decade*. https://www.weforum.org/stories/2023/01/used-car-exports-to-africa-development-opportunity-davos-2023/.

World Bank. 2023. *Remittance Prices Worldwide Quarterly*. An Analysis of Trends in Cost of Remittance Services, issue no. 46. World Bank. https://remittanceprices.worldbank.org/sites/default/files/rpw_main_report_and_annex_q223.pdf.

World Bank. n.d. *International Debt Statistics (IDS). Text/HTML*. World Bank. Accessed December 31, 2024. https://www.worldbank.org/en/programs/debt-statistics/ids.

Index

Note: numbers in **bold** indicate a table. Numbers in *italics* indicate a figure on the corresponding page

FSC
www.fsc.org
MIX
Papier | Fördert gute Waldnutzung
FSC® C083411

Kolibri 360 GmbH
Ferdinand-Jühlke-Straße 7
99095 Erfurt, Deutschland
produktsicherheit@kolibri360.de